Transformative Professional Practice
Personal Construct Approaches to Education and Research

Transformative Professional Practice

Personal Construct Approaches to Education and Research

Pamela M Denicolo and Maureen L Pope

Department of Professional Education in Community Studies
University of Reading

W

WHURR PUBLISHERS
LONDON AND PHILADELPHIA

First published 2001 by
Whurr Publishers Ltd
19b Compton Terrace, London N1 2UN, England and
325 Chestnut Street, Philadelphia PA 1906, USA

British Library Cataloguing in Publication Data
A catalogue record for this book is available from the British Library.

ISBN: 1 86156 199 7

Printed and bound in the UK by Athenaeum Press Ltd, Gateshead, Tyne & Wear

Dedication

To Marie-Anne and Paul, Adrian and Kathlyn, who have been a constant source of constructive revitalization.

Contents

Foreword

I have had the pleasure of knowing and working with the authors for many years, particularly in relation to their work with students and colleagues in the professions. I also know that this book results from many and frequent exhortations from professionals in the public and private sector for a permanent record of their help and advice.

This is a scholarly work produced by renowned and respected experts which will be seminal in the field. It combines a detailed, well-referenced exposition of the underpinning philosophy and theory of Personal Construct Psychology with extensive practical guidance, derived from their many years of combined experience. This latter is beautifully illuminated by the presentation of examples of the theory applied in practice in many professional fields of endeavour. It is typical of the authors that they disseminate and give credit to the work of others for which they have provided the inspiration.

This book emulates the style and ethos of their lectures and workshops. The information and guidance is founded in intellectual rigour but pains have been taken in its presentation to make it always accessible and sometimes fun. Readers will be challenged but also encouraged to clarify and experiment with their own views and their application in practice as well as finding new ways of helping others to do so. They should enjoy the book and find it stimulating as it opens windows on alternative perspectives about the world. It will also be one on which they will draw for many years as a comprehensive resource for transforming professional practice.

Professor Judith Lathlean
Professor of Health Research
University of Southampton

Prologue

We have developed this book to meet the needs of professionals in a range of occupation sectors whose work involves them in developing their own knowledge and concepts and those of others. Our extensive experience of supporting a range of professionals to do this from within a framework of Personal Construct Psychology has encouraged us in this enterprise. We have drawn on this experience to produce a book which combines theory and practical guidance with suggestions and examples of applications of personal construct psychology in professional settings.

The concept of 'transformation' appears in the title, and throughout the book, to acknowledge that the development of an alternative way of looking at professional education and research can result in productive change which is intrinsic to the person instead of being imposed from without.

We argue that professionals and researchers have their own implicit theories of what constitutes effective education, training and practice. We begin the book by examining various educational ideologies, each of which embodies theories about the nature and development of the person. Any theory about teaching is inextricably linked to an underlying view or model of the nature of the learner. Each of these represent alternative views on education which may influence the lived experience of all those engaged in education and training, whatever their role in the process. As personal construct psychologists we suggest that Personal Construct Psychology, developed from George Kelly's seminal work on Personal Construct Theory, provides a fruitful framework within which to explore professional practice. In the book we share with you what we see are the implications of such an approach for education and training in the work context. We also suggest that the approach has ramifications for research in and on practice. We have endeavoured to describe in detail a range of instruments that have been productively employed within interventions in such practice. Inevitably we have discussed the repertory grid technique, perhaps the most well-known technique emanating from Kelly's original work. However, we have also suggested a range of alternative techniques which are innovative methods consistent with a constructivist approach. Towards the end of the book the reader will find examples of applications of these approaches and techniques for the transformation of knowledge and practice within the professions and in business and industry. We hope that these illustrative examples will stimulate readers to consider ways in which the approach and techniques may be implemented and adapted in their own professional contexts in order to address productively current problems and dilemmas relating to professional development.

This is our interpretation of Personal Construct Psychology. It is drawn from our experience and our reading of the work of others. We have learnt a great deal from our students and colleagues and they have influenced what we have become as a result of our experiments with life.

In the book we draw attention to the role of biography as a research tool and as a technique that can be used in teaching and learning. We think it is proper, at this stage, to share with you some of the connecting threads in our own biographies that have salience for our construing of education for and within the professions. Readers will find in Chapter 7 some clues about how we explored our own memories using a technique called 'snakes' or 'rivers of life' to lift out those incidents which have special significance for who we have become as professionals.

Pam Denicolo

Since there are some aspects of my school days in Scotland that still impinge on my life, I reminisce about them here, particularly the teacher who encouraged my love of literature, instilled a joy of writing and taught me punctuation (much to the chagrin of some of my later students!). There were, of course, less happy memories but ones nonetheless of significance here. I will never forget the physics teacher who would tell any of the three girls in the class who had the temerity to study physics and to ask searching questions of him – 'away and do your knitting, girl!'. He encouraged my stubborn and rebellious streak to such an extent that I made sure that my Physics, Chemistry, Biology and Maths Highers were as good as those in English, French and History!

Lacking any form of careers guidance (this was the olden days!), but encouraged to do something involving both science and people, I chose to embark on the first year of a medical/dentistry degree. It did not take me long to discover that I was not too keen on investigating people's bodies, besides which a handsome young Italian had come on the scene, so I married, withdrew from the course, and threw myself into domestication – and read every book in the local library. When the joy of growing up together with two lively toddlers began not to fill every corner of my mind, I discovered that the Open University was about to start up. Triggered back into academic action, I enrolled for a new degree and found myself proof-reading the courses as they came on stream. More out of habit than informed choice I started with the Science Foundation course but then moved to England. The obligatory second foundation course, in Social Sciences this time, coincided with my also studying for a teacher's certificate (I have never been able since to do anything other than pack my life with demands).

Of course, my children had started school by then and, thinking I might be bored during the day without them, volunteered myself to their teachers to help with science lessons. I recall the fun of it all – the bricks, the planks, water and oil, weights and string, crystals and bugs; the wonderful questions the children asked; how we explored the possibilities in our meagre resources to find the answers; the whole sense of 'let's find out together'. It never occurred to me to tell them the answers, nor did they expect me to – after all I wasn't a teacher, I was a Mum.

What happened next was to influence my views on teaching and learning significantly. I applied for and gained a teaching post at the local technical college. How the sights, sounds and smells differed from the last image. I became a professional teacher rather than an amateur, my jeans were replaced by a white coat, eager children by sullen adolescents, relevant and interesting/interested questions by pages of detailed notes. A sense of fear of being asked a question to which I did not know the answer replaced the sense of adventure, and an abiding concern was what would I do if these big lads refused to co-operate. I was trying to fulfil the role imposed on me by the context and expectations of colleagues. But my confidence grew, the jeans came back, the sullen students metamorphosed into interesting people, succinct handouts replaced note-taking and we experimented not just with chemistry but with small group work instead of lectures. I learned to smile enigmatically when colleagues queried what could possibly cause gales of laughter, and whoops of delight, to emanate from a science lab – from their perspective but not mine, precision and objectivity precluded mirth and wonderment.

Thus began my drift away from science and into exploring through psychology how people learned. The last vestiges of science as a subject are to be found in my PhD, an investigation into the use of metaphor in chemistry teaching and learning. My OU first-class honours degree helped me win an ESRC scholarship at Surrey University and I was able to indulge my abiding love of language and my growing passion for exploring people's ideas rather than their bodies. At Surrey I met Maureen, my supervisor, then mentor, and now dear friend and co-author. Our first official foray together set the pattern for the coming years. At a time when qualitative research was undervalued as an approach, we presented a paper on constructivist approaches at a conference of fellow psychologists – and were overwhelmed not by their cynicism but by their interest.

Before I finished my PhD, serendipity found me again and I was appointed to a post in the Education department at Surrey. Years fled swiftly by as Maureen and I cultivated and refined our work as teachers of professionals and staff developers, travelling the world together and returning from each trip with a fund of funny stories about our adventures as well as a wealth of learning about new perspectives. As time went by, I became leader of the course for developing the teaching skills of professionals, the Director of the Centre for Staff Development and the doctoral training course, eventually becoming the Director of the Professional Studies Unit. By that time Maureen had moved to Reading but we kept in contact through the PCP research interest group which I had established to help my brood of research students share ideas and support.

A group of others interested in PCP approaches began to meet in London to develop a pan-European network and from this the European Personal Construct Association (EPCA) was born. Since then I have been its Treasurer for six years, and its Convenor for four years while I joined Maureen in the International Study Association on Teachers and Teaching (ISATT), becoming the UK national representative and now being on its Executive Panel. The conferences and networks of both these groups, several of which we have organized, have been a continuous source of inspiration.

Another wave of serendipity found me taking up a post of Reader at Reading. My departmental work has a focus on developing research in professional education while I hold the faculty post of Director of Postgraduate Research. Maureen and I were able to conjoin our large entourages of doctoral students into one research group and they catalysed the development of the dynamic university research centre which is now our base for research and development activities.

Working across a department which includes community nursing, social work, youth and community, careers guidance and counselling within a Faculty of Education has enhanced my understanding of diverse professional perspectives, as has my long-standing work with the educational division of the Royal Pharmaceutical Society. I was delighted recently to be made an honorary member of that society in recognition of my contribution to the profession's education and practice, though I suspect that my gain as a learner from it far outweighs theirs.

As we work and write together, exploring sensitive and exciting ideas with our research students and study groups, Maureen and I are inclined to forgive some of the members of our Centre for occasionally mixing our names up. Though we do not look alike (we have been known to style ourselves as Hinge and Bracket when running workshops), from reading both biographies, remarkable coincidences in life patterns emerge. One of them is that both see ourselves as in the process of growing up with both our children to whom this book is dedicated. We have a girl and a boy each, one being a lawyer and the other being inclined towards the arts, performing and craft. So it is not too surprising that we have some common constructs and can share sociality with others. Thus we have enjoyed crafting this book together.

Maureen Pope

One of my first memories: I can still recollect many of my experiences at primary school and my favourite teacher. However, I shall begin with my experience in the sixth form which was probably one of the precursors of my interest in science education. I went to an all girls' school. Three of us wanted to do physics A-level alongside chemistry and biology. There was only one problem – physics was not on the syllabus at that school. In those days, in Northern Ireland, it was deemed improper for three young ladies to attend the local boys' school so we were bussed 13 miles to a neighbouring town where there was a co-educational establishment offering physics A-level. All three of us found this a liberating experience and we were taught by a teacher who respected our enquiring minds. How we looked forward to those weekly trips. Things took a different turn when I went to university armed with three good A-levels in physics, chemistry and biology. It seemed to everyone, myself included, that reading for a Pure Science degree was my destiny. In my first year the students were faced with the fact that the chemistry nomenclature was changing. When I asked why this was the case I was told, 'just learn it, you do not need to know why'. Disillusioned with this response I found myself drawn to psychology which was offered as a fourth, but incidental, subject. I soon was drawn to this subject and neglected my chemistry. I decided to withdraw. I had met my future husband, an Englishman, and we decided to move to England. We soon had two young additions to the family, our son Adrian and our daughter Kathlyn, who have given us great joy over the years. However I was keen to resume work and contribute to something beyond the home front.

After a period teaching in kindergarten I resumed university studies at Brunel University, this time studying – you guessed it – psychology. The

Psychology degree at Brunel was a four-year course and we had to spend up to six months working in an applied area of psychology. As I was interested in teaching I spent a term as a teaching assistant in a primary school. The conversations with the five year olds provided an insight into the stories they created to account for their experiences. My next post was as an assistant psychologist at a 'subnormality' hospital. I was appalled at the constraints such an institution placed upon the development of the human potential of those in care. I realized, early on, that working in such an environment was not for me. The final placement was as a research assistant at the National Foundation for Educational Research. Now I found an activity which was to continue as a passion throughout my life!

On graduation, I was lucky enough to be awarded an ESRC quota award to continue my studies for a higher degree.

As an undergraduate I was introduced to Personal Construct Psychology although it was not until I studied for my PhD under the supervision of Laurie Thomas of the Centre for the Study of Human Learning at Brunel University that the full implications of this approach and its influence on my thinking became clear. As Beail (1985) noted, the Centre was one of the main institutions applying Personal Construct Theory and grid techniques in education. Pioneering work on the development of interactive computer packages for elicitation of repertory grids was carried out at that Centre. After a period of time researching and teaching within the Psychology department, in which the Centre for the Study of Human Learning was located, I obtained a post at the University of Surrey's Institute for Educational Development. I can remember the concerned expressed by the Head of the Psychology department at that time that I, as a good psychologist, was 'leaving the fold' and moving into education as an applied discipline rather than remaining closely tied to a Psychology department. However, my move to Surrey was tinged with serendipity. Professor Lewis Elton, who led the Institute, had established regular courses on academic staff development. These were attended by lecturers from the UK and abroad. The constructivist approach to teaching and learning was welcomed at the Institute. I collaborated with John Gilbert researching teaching and learning in science education. We directed the personal construction of knowledge research group whose work had a considerable impact on science education internationally. Pam Denicolo, a member of the group and one of my first postgraduate students, was to become a colleague and friend. Pam and I have published a number of books and articles together. We have also had the privilege of conducting workshops on teaching and learning, research methods, and Personal Construct Psychology in a wide range of institutions at home and worldwide including South East Asia, Europe, Australia and America. We have shared many interesting adventures on these visits. In the early 1980s I became a founder member of the International Study Association on Teachers and Teaching (ISATT) and chaired the Association for some time. I am now a member of the Executive Panel. I have also acted as a convenor for the Guidance Panel of the European Personal Construct Association (EPCA). My work for these organizations has also had a profound impact on my research and thinking in the area of teaching and learning as conversations with many colleagues have inspired me to pursue new lines of enquiry.

Having spent 11 years at the University of Surrey it was time for change. I became Professor of Community Studies and Education and Head of the Department of Community Studies at the University of Reading. I was reunited once more with John Gilbert who had also become a professor at the University of Reading. John had established the Models in Science and Technology Research in Education (MISTRE) group. Although I retained an interest in science education and young people's conceptions in science, I had become more focused on teachers and teaching. The department I joined was engaged in the education of a wide range of professionals including community nurses, social workers, career guidance specialists, community and youth workers and counsellors. Inevitably this widened the scope of my teaching and research. Coming up to date, I have just completed a four-year term of office as Dean of the Faculty of Education and Community Studies. During this period of time I became acutely aware of the pressures facing teachers in schools. Many of my colleagues and students were wrestling with the differences between their implicit theories of teaching and the requirements and constraints being imposed by government policies. Pam and I continued our PCP collaboration, but at a distance. However, a few years ago I was delighted that she was able to join the Department of Professional Education in Community Studies. We have established the Personal Construct Psychology in Education Research Group which is a designated Centre of the University of Reading. There are a large number of doctoral students working in the Centre and the Group has some 50 members including academic staff at the University of Reading and other institutions within the UK and a wide range of practitioners who are applying personal construct psychology in their professional practice.

From this base, we hope to continue our explorations of alternative ways of construing and alternative ways of illuminating that construal.

Both

It can be seen from the above that our ideas are part of an enfolded implicate order (Fransella, 1983). We have provided references within the book to the ideas and the work of others where we are aware of drawing on specific learning from our past. We apologize to those who have contributed to our tacit learning (Polanyi, 1958) must go unreferenced but not unacknowledged. They are certainly not unappreciated. We can, though, direct readers to the papers, theses and books in the Fay Fransella Collection and our own Resource Base at the University of Reading, through which our travels through the literature can be emulated, or new journeys undertaken.

Within the book the reader will note that we have drawn attention to the importance of language and its relation to construing. We have been careful to retain in quotations the authenticity of authors' language. Although we have, ourselves, adopted non-sexist language in our writing we have not peppered quotations with the use of [sic] to draw attention to sexist language. We recognize that many of the authors we quote were living in an era when such political correctness was not part of the literary genre. We hope our book will be enjoyed and that our ideas will be both explored and challenged by those who engage with it. We can be contacted for debate and help at:

The Centre for Personal Construct Psychology in Education
The Faculty of Education and Community Studies
The University of Reading
Bulmershe Court
Earley
Reading RG6 1HY

Acknowledgements

We have already acknowledged, although not by name, the many colleagues and students past and present who have shared their ideas and been part of our personal journey. However, the writing of the book is a very specific journey and a number of people have helped us to realize this task. We would like to take this opportunity to thank our colleague Jon Roberts for his punctilious help with proof-reading early drafts and Pam Burnard and Hafdis Ingvarsdottir for their very helpful feedback at the draft stage. Brian Peters, who worked magic in helping us with the diagrams, deserves a special mention too. However, in particular, we must thank Amanda Harvey, our excellent secretary, who typed and retyped various drafts with good humour and the utmost of patience. Last but not least we want to thank our husbands Vince Denicolo and Michael Pope who had to forgo a great deal as the book increasingly impinged on the joys of family life.

Chapter 1
Alternative perspectives on education and training

O wad some Pow'r the giftie gie us
To see oursels as others see us!
It wad frae mony a blunder free us,
And foolish notion.
Robert Burns 1759–1796 (To a Louse)

Introduction: from inside the chrysalis

In common with many of our readers, our work context, education for the professions, is in a constant state of flux and we with it. Though we seem to have relative stability in a core of ideals and principles, it is the stability of running along a moving walkway – much about us and around us seems to change and develop moment by moment. As educators/researchers we work with other adults, some of whom are undertaking initial professional or registration courses, though most are seasoned professionals engaging in developing their practice through courses, programmes of study or research. All of us together are subject to a turbulent life whether we seek to maintain stability, to 'go with the flow' or to influence the course of events, to name but a few options.

It is difficult to identify any profession or occupation which is not heir to the knowledge explosion, or indeed to the obsolescence of some forms of knowledge within it, to the technological revolution and to modifications in both values and practices. For those whose profession involves the support and training of colleagues, keeping up to date is a double duty since not only our own but their work will depend on it. Although we might try 'just to get on with our jobs', a life composed of rapid and continual change makes it imperative for us to engage in learning, for mere survival if not for personal growth. Therefore we begin this book with a focus on education, but education in a very wide sense.

Because we are defining education in a broad way, to encompass the formal and informal, the implicit and explicit, the personal and the professional, we will in our general discussion use simple terms for participants in the process. Thus 'learner' and 'teacher' will be used generically to subsume those with whom the individual reader might identify: student, pupil, trainee, apprentice, mentee, lecturer, instructor, preceptor, trainer, mentor etc. Where we are referring to specific case studies or examples of practice, as well as when we cite informative or influential literature, we will try to honour the terminology used in that context. That context may be work in the public sector including education, health, social, support and charitable services, or in the private sector including business and industry.

Identifying potential participants in generally educative (or transformative) processes is an easier task than to define what we mean by 'transformative practice' or indeed what we intend to convey by the common word 'learning'. Transformative practice is something that we hope will be understood better as the message contained in the book unfolds. Meanwhile, the rest of this chapter will explore further a range of interpretations about learning so that we clarify our own view on this nebulous concept.

That view derives from our own lifelong learning (a concept we will return to later in the chapter), beginning with our experiences as children in formal and informal educational settings. That early learning was then built on and modified by our training as psychologists and later by our experiences as educators, staff developers and researchers. Much of our learning as adults has been influenced by the work of George Kelly and others who have espoused the Personal Construct Theory perspective and so it is those understandings which pervade this book.

This philosophical and theoretical perspective includes models of humankind and learning which fit comfortably with our own experiences. These models are proving more resilient to challenge than other models that we were exposed to, but held more tenuously, in the past. Each person has a 'philosophical style' encompassing an implicit model of the learning process which impacts on behaviour as a learner or a teacher. These models are intellectual tools or devices which give coherence to our experiences, thoughts, feelings, and actions, within the context we believe or know to exist. They also allow us to make predictions and to create experiences. Thus the models we adopt are exceedingly influential, as Eisner (1993: 5) noted:

> Humans do not simply have experience; they have a hand in its creation, and the quality of their creation depends on the way they employ their minds.

The next section discusses some of the more prevalent theories of education which have been adopted, in Western society, by people with an education or training remit. That remit may be formally acknowledged through a role title or may subtly pervade a differently focused role. For instance, many professions in the public sector have, as part of their duty of care to the client, a commitment to share information and develop good practice. They may be also expected, in common with those working in commerce and industry, to guide, support and encourage the professional development of more junior members of staff, whether or not the terms mentor or teacher are officially used. Frequently, just as senior members of the teaching profession are expected to take on managerial tasks without special training for them, it is assumed that other professionals will develop teaching skills by drawing on their own past experience as learners. In practice, that experience is diverse since what constitutes learning/teaching for each person depends on the model of education prevailing at a particular time and in a particular context, which is informed to a greater or lesser degree by familiarity with research on education.

The theories underlying the practice of educational research are also intimately linked to general educational ideologies. These educational ideologies embody theories on the nature and development of the person. As Bruner (1966) pointed out, instruction can be seen as an effort to assist or to shape growth, and any theory of instruction is in effect a theory of how growth and development are encouraged. Any theory about teaching is thus inextricably linked to an underlying view or model of the nature of the learner. A teacher may conceive of the nature of the learner as active or passive, meaning-seeking, impulse-driven, fixed or constantly developing. Whichever model is adopted will influence the teacher's strategy and aims.

Much of the current debate on education revolves around fundamental differences in the models of learning held by the individuals concerned. A major problem is that at any point in time educational issues tend to be dominated by one particular viewpoint or 'frame of reference' so that education becomes monolithic in structure (Joyce, 1972). Those involved in education often adopt rigidly opposing positions which militate against a more constructive and flexible approach. There is now a growing recognition that alternative models can co-exist and enrich, rather than detract from, development in education. Some educational researchers are seeking new approaches – recognizing that past educational research has been conducted on too narrow a base.

This chapter looks at some of the major themes inherent in differing educational ideologies and relates these to particular models of the nature of knowledge and psychological development. In Chapter 3 some of the current issues within the arena of professional education research are raised. It is suggested that alternative methodologies are needed if we are to adopt the perspective of the person in educational research. Aspects of personal construct psychology which seem to have a direct bearing on current concerns in professional education are introduced in Chapter 2. Rather than the imposition of a monolithic approach to educational issues, a Kellyan framework allows for diversity of viewpoints and constructive alternatives in transforming professional practice through research and education.

Philosophical approaches which underpin education in the professions

Inevitably, any attempt to categorize perspectives on education will do an injustice to the great diversity of viewpoints on education held by particular individuals. Nevertheless, the following categorization represents one possible way of construing the alternative themes presented *within* differing perspectives on education. It is suggested that there are at least five major schools of thought in the development of Western educational ideology, each exhibiting a coherence based upon particular assumptions of psychological development and philosophies of the nature of knowledge. These assumptions identify what is of importance and what is problematic in the field as well as what its goals and standards should be. Together with political and economic constraints, they therefore largely determine pedagogic practice in schools and colleges and provide a framework for continuing professional education and research. They also provide educators with schemas for developing and analysing practice. Some of the major theoretical issues underlying each approach will be indicated in this chapter, starting with an indication of their origins in compulsory education. The practical application of these theoretical stances within professional education and training will be interwoven as appropriate in the discussion. These schools of thought may be termed:

(a) cultural transmission/instrumentalism;
(b) romanticism;
(c) progressivism;
(d) de-schooling;
(e) humanistic approaches.

Since cultural transmission is rooted in the classical academic tradition of Western education and is experiencing a resurgence of interest, though in a modified form as instrumentalism, particularly in continuing and vocational education, we shall consider this first.

Cultural transmission/instrumentalism

Theorists of this persuasion would see the primary task of the educator as being the transmission of information, rules or values collected in the past. The educator's job is the direct instruction of information and rules. For example, Robert Maynard Hutchins (1936: 66) wrote:

> Education implies teaching. Teaching implies knowledge. Knowledge is truth. The truth is everywhere the same. Hence, education should be everywhere the same.

In the classical tradition it was thought that by studying the great works of literature, philosophy, science and history, learners imbibe the 'truths' of their cultural heritage. Much of the basis of modern educational technology and behavioural modification approaches to education and skills training can be seen as variants of this cultural transmission approach. Knowledge and values are seen as located in the culture and are internalized by children or novices imitating adult or expert behaviour models or through explicit instruction and the use of such training strategies as reward and punishment. The criterion of successful education and training for such theorists is the learner's ability to incorporate the responses which have been taught so to respond appropriately to the demand of the system. The major objectives in traditional school settings are literacy and mathematical skills which are seen as necessary for adjustment to an increasingly technological society. In the professions, the emphasis is on accurate performance of tasks to set standards within a given value system or framework.

This philosophical approach is based on the assumption that absolute truth can be accumulated bit by bit, subject by subject. Knowledge is objective and can be measured by culturally shared test procedures. This approach is exemplified by the 'Black Paper – Fight for Education', edited by Cox and Dyson (1969: 56). The learner is seen as naturally lazy and must be prodded into action by external incentives. Thus, they said:

> Exams make people work hard. Much opposition to them is based on the belief that people work better without reward and incentive, a naiveté which is against all knowledge of human nature.

The view of absolute truth accumulating in fragments corresponds to the basic principles of philosophic realism. In the Realist's view the world exists independently of man and is governed by laws over which we have little control. Most scientific realists deny the existence of free will and argue that individual behaviour is determined by the impact of the physical and social environment on genetic structure. John Locke assumed that the mind of the individual at birth was a *tabula rasa*. For Locke the intellect was essentially passive and acquired its content and structure through the impact of sensation through the senses. The world we perceive is not a world that we have recreated mentally but is the world as it is. The epistemological position of the Realist is that true knowledge is knowledge that corresponds to the world as it is; facts are independent of what we think about them. The task of the educator would seem to be the instruction of a body of knowledge whose truth had been repeatedly confirmed.

The Lockean tradition is central to psychological theories of development which stress the passivity of the human mind. This emphasis is found in all types of associationism, behaviourism, stimulus-response psychology, contingency theories, etc. One might suggest that the appropriate metaphor for the view of the person put forward by cultural transmission educational ideology, is that of a machine. The machine can be anything from the wax upon which the environment makes its mark (Locke) through to the computer. The environment is seen as 'input' whose information is more or less directly transmitted to and accumulated in the 'organism'. The resulting behaviour is the 'output'. Using this mechanistic metaphor, cognitive development can be seen as the result of guided learning and teaching, and behaviour is the result of an association between stimulus and response (Hull, 1943, Classical Learning Theory).

Skinner (1968) viewed teachers as architects and builders of learner behaviour. He defined learning as a change in the probability of response. He explained all human behaviour in terms of respondents and operant reinforcement. On the basis of his animal laboratory work he set out a detailed methodology for the timing and spacing of scheduled reinforcement. Through progressively changing the contingencies of reinforcement in the direction of the desired behaviour (as defined by the experimenter) learning is seen to occur. Education change is evaluated from performances, not from changes in thoughts or feelings. Thus Skinner (1971: 15) stated:

> We can follow the path taken by physics and biology by turning directly to the relation between behaviour and the environment and neglecting ... states of mind ... we do not need to discover what personalities, states of mind, feelings ... intentions – or other prerequisites of autonomous man really are in order to get on with a scientific analysis of behaviour.

This 'Black Box' or 'Empty Organism' approach with its emphasis on human behaviour being controlled by the environmental situation, flourished in the decades following the 1920s. Theorists holding to a cultural transmission or instrumentalist educational ideology find much support in the Realists' philosophy and the psychological theories put forward by the behaviourists, neo-behaviourists and contingency theorists. Although this dominant position has been challenged by three major contenders – the Romanticists, the Progressivists and the Humanistic school of thought

– remnants of it can be found in the contemporary move towards Instrumentalism in Western society.

It is asserted that an educated workforce is needed to respond to international competition. Competence-based courses in which particular behaviours indicate achievement of learning for assessment purposes illustrate the tenacity of this perspective. Armitage et al. (1999: 9) noted the paradox in that:

> competence-based training schemes are often couched in the empowering 'student-centred' language of progressive or humanistic education. But by emphasizing learning by doing, rather than becoming critical thinkers, competence-based programmes require students to be both intellectually passive and yet very busy.

Romanticism

The Romanticists stress that what comes from within the child is the most important aspect of development. Thus the pedagogical environment should be permissive enough to allow 'inner good' to unfold and 'inner bad' to come under control. The emphasis is on 'health' and 'growth' and working through aspects of emotional development which may not be allowed expression in the home. Rousseau's *Emile*, although written over 200 years ago, contains what many consider are the fundamental principles behind more humanistic modern educational ideas. Believing that people are born naturally good, Rousseau considered that by lifting social and pedagogical restraints, one would preserve natural goodness. Rousseau's 'Negative Education' was not to be an education of transmitted norms, but one based on the psychological principles of natural development of the child and a non-directive approach on behalf of the teacher. The writings of G. S. Stanley-Hall in the early twentieth century suggested that before we let pedagogy loose on children we would have to overcome the fetishes of the alphabet and of the multiplication tables and must reflect that but a few generations ago the ancestors of all of us were illiterate. He maintained that there were many who ought not to be educated and that these would be 'better in mind, body and morals if they knew no school'. The type of school which Stanley-Hall was critiquing was that in which the transmission of public knowledge was instilled without reference to the thoughts and feelings of children and the perceived relevance of such knowledge to them. This stress on emotions, thoughts and feelings can be seen to be part of a romantic philosophy which was prevalent in the nineteenth century and whose epistemology involved the discovery of the natural and inner self.

The Romanticists probably come closest to the Idealist school of philosophy which holds that ultimate reality is spiritual in nature rather than physical, mental rather than material. Although not denying the existence of things in the 'Real World', the idealists believe that these are part of a more fundamental incorporeal reality, although individual idealists, e.g. Plato and Kant, disagreed about the nature of the ultimate reality and the relation of the spiritual being to that reality.

Idealist educators instil a closer intimacy between the person and the spiritual elements of nature. However, within the idealist tradition, different philosophers have produced different theories of knowledge. Thus for Plato, since the material world is only a distorted copy of a more perfect reality, the impressions which come directly via the senses must be uncertain and incomplete. True knowledge for Plato was the result of the process of reasoning, since this process transcends the material world and can discern pure spiritual reality. More modern idealists in the Kantian tradition maintain that knowledge is the imposition of meaning and order on sense impressions. This latter view of knowledge is held by many Progressivists but the goals of the two philosophies are distinct. For Idealists their aim is communion with the ultimate reality, whilst the Progressivists, within the context of moral relativism, acknowledge no such ultimate goal.

Romantic ideology would seem to be supported by maturationist theories of psychological development, e.g. Freudian psychoanalytic theory and Gessellian maturational theory. While individual rates of development may be inborn, cognitive and emotional development is seen to depend on the unfolding of the biologically given although remaining vulnerable to fixation, as in the Freudian sense, or frustration by the environment.

Rousseau in *Emile* made a plea for recognition that 'Childhood had its own ways of seeing, thinking and feeling; nothing is more foolish than to try to substitute our ways'. Accordingly we must 'Hold childhood in reverence, watch him, study him constantly'. A similar idea was expressed by Freud (1913: 189) in *The Claims of Psycho-analysis to the Scientific Interest – the Educational Interest*, he said:

> Only someone who can feel his way into the minds of children can be capable of educating them and we grown up people cannot understand children because we no longer understand our childhood.

Although the tenets of this school of thought do seem to be most relevant to childhood education, the Romantic movement has left a legacy to those involved with post-compulsory education. In counterpoint to the mechanistic, 'personless' approach of the Cultural Transmission/Instrumentalist school, this perspective on learning and teaching emphasizes the imagination, emotions and their freely individualized expression which has had particular impact on the Arts. In addition, followers of the movement introduced the notion of using introspective autobiographical material as a means of gaining greater understanding of the other's perspective and advocated the development of a freely accepted 'contract' between learners and teachers.

Contract learning methods became very popular in the 1970s in recognition of the benefits of allowing learners to pursue their own specific interests and to take some responsibility for their own learning. Egan (1975) argued that, for adults to learn in an adult way with freedom granted to all participants, contracts or formal agreements about boundaries, expectations and commitments contributed to generating greater respect and valuing of each other. These ideas formed a basis from which the multiplicity of self-directed learning methods grew.

This philosophical approach has also contributed to interpretative forms of research by noting the rich resource provided by folklore, fairy tales, songs and legends for supplying insight into the perspectives of groups of people. Of particular note for constructivist approaches, the Romanticists are credited with drawing attention to the world view that is implicit in particular language use. We will refer to this important concept while describing techniques and methods in the chapters which follow and will include further detail in Chapter 6.

While the Progressivists and Romanticists are in agreement in their rejection of the cultural transmission approach, Progressivism is based on a different set of theoretical assumptions, both psychological and philosophical.

Progressivism

John Dewey is usually cited as the founder of the Progressive School Movement. Two of his most quoted books are *Schools of Tomorrow* (1915) and *Experience and Education* (1938). Progressivism holds that education should nourish the person's natural interaction with a developing society or environment. Unlike Romanticists, adherents of this approach do not assume that development is an unfolding of an innate pattern or that the educational aim is the creation of a conflict-free environment in order to foster healthy development. They see development as a progression through ordered sequential stages and their educational goal is the eventual attainment by the child of a higher level or stage of development in adulthood. In 1895 Dewey and McLellan said:

> Education is the work of supplying the condition, which will enable the

> Psychical functions as they successively arise to mature and pass into higher functions in the freest and fullest manner.

Thus the educational environment for the Progressivists should be one which actively stimulates development through the presentation of a milieu in which the organizing and developing force in the person's experience is the person's active thinking. Thinking is stimulated by cognitive conflict. Like the cultural transmission theorists, they emphasize knowledge as opposed to feelings and experience but they see the acquisition of knowledge as an act of change in the pattern of thinking brought about by experiential problem-solving situations. The Progressivists view morals, values and the nature of knowledge to be in constant change.

Progressivism in its pure form declares that education is always in the process of development. Education is not a preparation for living but it should be life itself. Like Rousseau, Dewey and his followers maintained that learning should be directly related to the interests of the person; motivation to learn should come from within the person rather than knowledge being externally imposed. The teacher is seen more as a guide or adviser in a process whereby the person reconstructs the subject matter in accordance with its perceived relevance to his own life. Learning should take place through problem-solving rather than the inculcating of subject matter. Knowledge itself is seen as 'a tool for managing experience'. For knowledge to be significant one has to do something with it and hence it must be linked to experience. For the Progressivists, education is not limited to a recollection of information obtained from the teacher or a textbook, it involves 'perpetual grappling' with the subject matter. In this sense, grappling is not only the physical handling of material, but it involves the critical thinking process of reconstruction of previous ideas and discovery.

The teaching method upheld by Progressivism encourages learner–learner interaction as well as learner–teacher interaction. Teachers are interested in learners developing their own criteria regarding the quality and relevance of ideas. Thus the teachers' role of arbiter of what is acceptable is minimized. Their aim is not the transmission of 'nuggets', but rather the facilitation of the process of 'learning how to learn'.

The particular philosophy aligned with Progressivism is that of Pragmatism. It is mainly a twentieth-century philosophy which has grown out of the British empiricist tradition which maintains that we know only what our senses experience. A basic principle of Pragmatism is that the world is neither dependent on nor independent of human ideas about it. Reality is the interaction of the human being with the environment; it is the sum total of what we experience. The emphasis is on active people reaching out to make sense of their universe by engaging in the reconstruction and interpretation of their own experiences. Pragmatists agree that knowledge is produced by transaction between people and their environment and that truth is a property of knowledge but they disagree about what can be defined as truth. William James maintained that an idea is true if it has a favourable consequence for the person who holds it. On the other hand, Dewey insisted that an idea was true only if it had a satisfactory consequence when objectively and, if possible, scientifically tested. As constructivists we suggest that the core of universal ideas is redefined and reorganized as the ideas' implications are played out in experience and as they are confronted by their opposites in argument.

Psychological theories which support these ideas are those which discard the dichotomy between maturation and environmental determinism in learning. For example, Piaget claims that mature thought emerges through a process of development that is neither direct biological maturation nor direct environmental pressure, but a reorganization of psychological structures resulting from organism–environment interactions. Cognitions are seen as internally organized wholes or systems of internal relations through which events in the person's experience are organized. For Piaget the processes of 'accommodation' and 'assimilation' are not passive processes which can result from a programme of reinforcement. Such a programme would only change the person's behaviour and cognitive structure if it was assimilated by the person in terms of his/her present mode of thinking. For Piaget the teacher's role is to facilitate movement to the next stage of development by exposure to the next higher level of thought and by conflict requiring active application of current thoughts to problematic situations.

Jerome Bruner (1966) also pointed to the necessity for learners to relate new material to relevant ideas already established in their cognitive structures, for them to apprehend in what ways it is similar to and different from related concepts and to translate it into a personal frame of reference, consonant with each person's idiosyncratic experience.

The 'symbolic interactionists' maintain that in a fundamental sense the 'self' is a product of a person's interaction with others. A person's self-concept develops in relation to reactions of other people to that person. They propose that we react to our 'selves' as we perceive others acting towards us (Cooley, 1964: 168–210). This view has been extended by G. H. Mead and role theorists who recognize that the self in a social structure is that which arises through communication. By anticipating the other's reaction to us and our reaction to the other's reaction, we are able to examine and evaluate several possible courses of action and choose a particular course which makes personal sense. A person's behaviour is seen to be influenced by such interactions, not based upon the action of the other per se but on the meaning which the person assigns to the other's acts. Thus individual action and development are seen to be constructed in relation to the other, rather than simply determined by outside forces or evoked by internal impulses.

Whether the psychological theories are emphasizing cognitive development, as in the case of Piaget, or social development, as in the case of role theorists, the emphasis is on interaction with the environment. These theories are in accordance with Progressivism which sees education as an interaction process rather than as a totally child-centred process as in the case of the Romanticists, or society-centred, promoting the discipline of social order, as seen by the Cultural Transmission theorists.

Although the originators of Progressivism couched their discussion in terms of children's learning, seeming to espouse a 'front end' conception of education, this is perhaps a reflection of the social mores in which they were working rather than an intellectual commitment per se. Certainly the roots of the approaches and methods which pervade late-twentieth-century post-compulsory education can be discerned in their work. Dewey (1916: 51) himself said:

> It is commonplace to say that education should not cease when one leaves school – The inclination to learn from life itself and to make the condition of life such that all will learn in the process of living is the finest product of schooling.

He went on to say:

> Since life means growth, a living creature lives as truly and positively at one stage as at another, with the same intrinsic fullness and the same absolute claims. Hence education means the enterprise of supplying the conditions which ensure growth, or adequacy of life, irrespective of age.

The contemporary concepts of lifelong learning, experiential learning and continuing professional development are echoes of this 'commonplace' saying which have taken almost a century to become an accepted and required part of education provision, although some people have benefited from the luxury of liberal adult education in the meantime.

De-schooling

The preceding three sets of philosophical and psychological assumptions and the one included in the section to follow humanistic approaches represent perhaps the main streams of development of Western educational ideology. However, for completeness it is necessary to mention another stream which emerged in the 1970s, namely de-schooling. Rousseau and Stanley-Hall both argued that the inculcation of knowledge could be harmful to the learner. Ivan Illich (1971), who is perhaps one of the best known de-schoolers, pointed out that, in his opinion, most of the really important and useful things learnt are learned outside the classroom, i.e. from friends or from interested others. These things are seldom learnt from certificated teachers or under the process of compulsion. He recommended abolishing the school as a unit and reorganizing learning by bringing together, within a given area, those who want to teach and those who want to learn. Some schemes modelled along the lines which Illich suggested were established for a time in both the USA and in Great Britain. They were known as the 'school without walls'. Staff made arrangements with pupils to meet for sessions in informal venues with the programme chosen by the group in a common desire to learn.

Illich was not alone in his attack on education as we know it today, although few would go so far as total demolition of schools. Charles E. Silberman in *Crisis in the Classroom* (1971) claimed that the school has been given too much credit as an agent of social change. Silberman proposed an educational process in which the rights of children are observed and learning methods are varied. Children would be expected to work on their own, at their own pace and at work of their own choosing. An institution might offer children advantages which their locality may lack. The leaving age would be open-ended, since this would be a school for the whole community where children and adults of all ages might come and go as they please. Some prototypes of this type of school were established in the private sector of British education. A. S. Neill's Summerhill and Dartington Hall are examples of schools based on revolutionary philosophies of education.

This accent on rejection of imposed structure can be found in Everett Reimer's *School is Dead*; John Holt's *How Children Fail*; Paul Goodman's *Compulsory Miseducation* and Neil Postman and Charles Weingartner's *Teaching as a Subversive Activity*. The majority of these theorists would acknowledge the attempts of Progressivists to initiate active enquiry on behalf of the learner but they felt that the pedagogy that has resulted still leaves a lot to be desired. Postman and Weingartner (1971: 59) made this point very forcibly in a chapter headed 'Pursuing Relevance' in their book *Teaching as a Subversive Activity*. Thus they wrote:

> There is no way to help a learner to be disciplined, active and thoroughly engaged unless he perceives a problem to be a problem, or whatever is to be learned to be worth learning. It is sterile and ridiculous to attempt to release the enquiry power of students by initiating studies that hold no interest for them.

Much of the thought expressed in the above mentioned works is reminiscent of existentialist philosophy. Existentialists reject the traditional view that philosophy should become detached. They say that philosophy should consist of reason informed by passion because it is in passion and in states of heightened feeling that ultimate realities are disclosed. They reject the notion of the 'natural development of man'. In his book *Existentialism* Jean-Paul Sartre (1947: 18) said:

> Not only is man what he conceives himself to be, but he is also what he wills himself to be after this thrust towards existence. Man is nothing other than what he makes himself.

For the existentialists, people have responsibility for their own being. What they become is of their own choosing and their freedom is in their potential for action. Every person must act according to their strongest feelings and be prepared to take the consequences which will result from their actions. Knowledge is essentially phenomenological – a person's knowledge depends on his/her understanding of reality.

For the existentialist it is not sufficient that a body of knowledge from a textbook or given out by the teacher is accepted unquestioningly by the learner. The learners must find their own truths for themselves. They must be able to incorporate these truths within their view of the world. In *Between Man and Man* Martin Buber (1965) wrote about what he believed to be the tyranny of impersonal knowledge. For him teaching should be a true dialogue in which the teacher is not simply a mediator between the learner and the subject matter. Rather than become a means for the transmission of knowledge, teachers should offer knowledge, i.e. they must familiarize themselves fully with the subjects they teach so that this subject becomes part of their own inner experience, which they can then present to the learners as something issuing from themselves. Each teacher and learner can then meet as whole human beings as the offered knowledge is not alienated from the teacher's real world of feeling. The learner must take responsibility for rejecting or accepting the teacher's interpretation of the subject matter. The aim of the teacher should be the establishment of an atmosphere of mutual trust in which the teacher sees the learner not as a category, a novice professional for instance, or in evaluative terms, e.g. as in 'bright' or 'dull', but as a person.

Many existentialists, Buber included, would maintain that as it now stands the school is a powerful reinforcer of alienation in modern society. Some psychologists share this concern with alienation and failure of real communication between people. In addition they regret the lack of emphasis on the person and individual 'views of the world' in some psychological theories of development – in particular those of the behaviourist and neo-behaviourist schools. They bring a Humanistic psychology approach to education which is particularly relevant to and has had much influence on contemporary education for adults. This approach will be discussed further in the next section but first let us summarize some points worth noting from the ideology of de-schooling.

First, its proponents varied in their aims – on one hand we have Illich, who advocated total demolition, and on the other Postman, who aimed for a revolution within the system, thus allowing for relevant education which would facilitate the growth of 'strategies for survival' and ability to cope with the ever-changing facets of our society. Secondly, there is the agreement that the cultural transmission approach is inappropriate to the needs of the person and modern society. Thirdly, there is the acceptance of many of the Romanticist and Progressivist principles put forward, for example by Rousseau and John Dewey. However, there is a rejection of the biological model found in much of the writings of the Romanticist. Although accepting the act of 'questioning' and 'learning by doing' approach of the Progressivist, two main criticisms are put forward by the de-schoolers. One is the disproportionate emphasis on the structure of cognitive processes rather than on the meaning content. The other is that despite innovations within the educational system, the power structure within professional hierarchies remains static. For the de-schooler 'relevant' education will only take place within a framework in which the power structure barriers are broken down between teachers and learners, within the professions and between the professions and the community at large.

The humanistic approach

Sullivan, Laing, Bateson and Carl Rogers have all been influential in raising the interpersonal encounter as an important topic within psychology. The writings of Laing and Rogers in particular lay great stress on personal experience as the origin of action. Their views on personality, psychological development and methodological issues in psychology also bear a great resemblance to the thinking of existential philosophers. R. D. Laing was quite specific in his connections with the works of Martin Heidegger, Jean-Paul Sartre, Maurice Merleau-Ponty, Friedrich Nietzsche and Søren Kierkegaard. Thus in his book *The Politics of Experience*, R. D. Laing (1967: 20) talked about personal experience:

> It is tempting and facile to regard 'persons' as only separate objects in space, who can be studied as other natural objects can be studied ... one will never find persons by studying persons as though they were only objects.

Carl Rogers in *On Becoming a Person* (1961), *Freedom to Learn* (1969) and *Freedom to Learn for the 80s* (1983) took up this perspective of the personal with specific reference to the learning situation. Rogers differentiated between two processes in learning: teacher-based (the traditional cultural transmission approach) and learner-based learning.

Learner-based learning is self-initiated, has a quality of personal involvement and is evaluated by learners in terms of whether or not it is meeting their needs. This significant learning is pervasive, i.e. it makes a difference in behaviour, attitudes and personality of the learner, and its essence is meaning. The knowledge/truth that evolves in self-discovered learning is 'private' knowledge – truth that has been personally appropriated and assimilated in experience. According to Rogers this 'personal' knowledge cannot be directly transmitted from the teacher to the learner. This is not to say that the 'public knowledge' or the facts, ideas, and so on that the teacher is trying to impart can never become personal knowledge. What Rogers contended is that the process is not one of direct impersonal association between the issues to be learnt (stimuli) and knowledge of them (response). If the public knowledge to be imparted is personally appropriated by learners and has significant influence on their behaviour and attitudes, then public knowledge becomes personal knowledge. While distinguishing between the two processes, Rogers made a value judgement that personal knowledge should be the aim of the educational process. For Rogers, personal knowledge is facilitated by a specific type of interpersonal encounter between the teacher and learner.

The encounter he advocated is similar to that found in the client-centred, non-directive therapeutic process that Rogers used in his psychotherapy. A main feature of this encounter is the quality of regard one for the other. The teacher needs to have regard for what the individual learner is, i.e. independent of her/his ability, interests, social class etc. Labels should be abandoned. Only within the context of unconditional acceptance may learners feel free to express their best and most creative aspects instead of merely regurgitating imposed knowledge. This type of interpersonal encounter does not necessitate sentimentality or laissez-faire attitudes within education, rather it encourages self-directed discipline with the learners setting limits rather than obeying imposed rules.

Reaction against the imposition of both rules and the dominant cultural perspective on knowledge and values pervades the writings of Paulo Freire, whose work based in literacy education in Brazil is now well known to adult educators. Like the Romanticists, he recognized that each language form contains a construction of reality so that the language of education used, in a didactic form, perpetuates a world view and subjugates the learner's self identity. He referred to this as 'education for domestication' (Freire, 1973: 79). In common with others taking a humanistic approach to education, he emphasized the need for an interactive dialogue between the teacher and the learner and, like the Progressivists, he advocated experiential learning in which reflection on experience is facilitated as a means of *empowering* the learner.

Donald Schon judged the power to make independent judgements and to exercise personal discretion and creativity in one's work to be at the heart of professional practice and this can be achieved best, he asserted (1987: 300), by teachers and learners in professional learning contexts articulating their reflections on practice:

> When inquiry into learning remains private, it is also likely to remain tacit. Free of the need to make our ideas explicit to someone else, we are less likely to make them explicit to ourselves.

Jack Mezirow's particular concern, too, is with emancipatory education and his work draws heavily on Habermas' theories of emancipatory learning. Mezirow (1990: xiv) defined emancipatory education as an organized effort to precipitate or to facilitate transformative learning in others, while he proposed that this involves *critical reflection*, that is, the assessment of the validity of the presuppositions of one's meaning perspectives and examination of their sources and consequences. From this latter definition and elsewhere in his writings (1981: 5) it is clear that challenging our presuppositions is essential if we are to be liberated 'from libidinal, institutional or environmental forces which limit our options and rational control over our lives but have been taken for granted as beyond human control'. (Some reverberations of the concerns of de-schoolers can be detected in this.)

For many, the beginning of a career marks release from the confinements, or prison, of school yet it does not, or should not, mean the end of an obligation to learn. Recently, in all walks of life, the importance of learning beyond school has been emphasized. Indeed, we noted at the beginning of this chapter that it has become a necessity in the world of work as changes and challenges confront us daily. In the next section we explore this further.

Lifelong learning and continuing professional development

From the foregoing historical review of schools of thought influencing education in general, it is clear that current knowledge which informs education has not been accumulated by building on incremental 'nuggets of truth' but has been contributed to by the interaction of different ideas and ideals, perspectives which sometimes have much in common and sometimes take radically different stances. Practice within particular sectors of education has, at different points in recent history, been influenced by particular ideologies, sometimes leaving practitioners open to censure when learning outcomes fail to meet expectations of competing interest groups within society. One example in the 1990s was the politically motivated denunciation of 'progressive teachers and teacher educators' (though whether they or the original Progressivists would recognize it as such is debatable) who were failing to produce a workforce with the skills required by the technological society.

Dogmatism, political or philosophical, can be a major block to development in education. Much non-productive argument in education is due to the adoption of opposing dogmatic viewpoints which determine that this method or theory is correct, therefore all others are wrong. G. Kelly's meta-theory (see Chapter 2) recognizes all theories as temporary constructions which should be abandoned when another theory leads to a better prediction of events. His theory acknowledges the importance of the personal theories which we all erect to explain events in our experience and to predict future happenings. This recognition allows one to break down barriers in education and to recognize that for different people with different purposes faced with different circumstances to predict, alternative constructions regarding the nature of education, teaching and learning will evolve. Thus dogmatic ideologies could give way to a more flexible approach to education which recognizes the viability of these alternative constructions.

Alternative constructions also pervade the literature on lifelong learning or lifelong education. Pucheu (1974: 375) suggested that it is an 'elastic concept' which means whatever the person using the term wants it to mean. Knapper and Cropley (1985: 16) proposed that the concept of lifelong learning is a rationalization of a number of existing trends in contemporary educational theory and practice, combining an espousal of principles related to the democratization of education, the elimination of inequality in education and the achievement of higher levels of self-actualization. At the same time it encompasses a strong rejection of authoritarianism (but not necessarily of authority) and the role of the conventional school as a dominant institution of learning. They also considered that the concept subsumes a dissatisfaction with the view that all necessary qualifications can be acquired prior to the commencement of working life, a dissatisfaction fuelled by the social and economic pressures, alluded to earlier in this chapter, which impinge on contemporary occupations and professions.

In a context of change it has become increasingly important that professionals continue to develop their practice. Not just to keep up to date, by adding new knowledge as it is generated or by developing new skills to deal with burgeoning technology. They need to challenge their conceptions about what constitutes good practice and what they understand by the knowledge that underpins it. Eraut (1992) identified three different kinds of knowledge that are essential in professional education, though each professional area might require them in different proportions. In short these are:

- propositional knowledge – discipline concepts, generalizations and practice principles;
- process knowledge – knowing how to implement the processes of practice;
- and personal knowledge through which experience is interpreted.

The last of the three poses a challenge to educators of professionals since, although influential on practice, the implicit assumptions embedded in it are not easily elicited or articulated for public scrutiny. It is not self-evident that all initial professional courses prepare people to become either lifelong learners or to scrutinize the personal knowledge which mediates their practice. This is an issue which Imogen Taylor (1997) explored in her book *Developing Learning in Professional Education* in which she quoted Usher and Bryant (1987: 211) as emphasizing the particular role required of initial preparation courses as a crucial contribution to lifelong learning:

> If we want practitioners to be reflective, critical and self directing in the world of practice then we must create conditions, through teaching, for them to be reflective, critical and self directing in the world of the classroom.

Taylor built a strong case that for effective continuing professional development all the stakeholders should be involved in a partnership to support and encourage it. These stakeholders include senior colleagues, employing agencies, professional educators and service users. Each should share some responsibility for the continued development and transformation of practice.

Learning as sharing and developing understanding of practice

In the rest of this book we will explore ways of creating appropriate conditions, as deemed necessary by Taylor, Usher and Bryant above, for professionals to learn both in formal educational settings and in the workplace in partnership with colleagues and clients. We will also describe ways in which professionals can choose to illuminate and develop their own understanding and gain insight into personal meaning, should they wish to do so, either alone or with others. We hold the view, like Schon (1987) quoted earlier, that we cannot comprehend our own misconceptions, or the limits on our understanding, unless we confront that understanding by first articulating it and then contemplating how it could be otherwise. Nor can we identify mismatches in understandings, whether they be knowledge or value based, without sharing those understandings or frames of reference with others and allowing them to share theirs with us. Without such identification, and without the means for each participant to become active, meaning-seeking individuals, attempts to dispel them will be frustrated. In a previous work (Denicolo and Pope, 1990) in which we reported on a technique used to help professionals gain from an exploration of their personal perspectives on their professional development, we referred to the words of Dilthey (as translated by Rickman, 1976) who observed:

> Understanding of other people and their expressions is developed on the basis of experience and self-understanding and the constant interaction between them ... it is not a matter of logical construction or psychological dissection but of an epistemological analysis.

Though these words were written at the turn of the last century, they have special relevance in this chapter written as a new millennium is upon us. We have explored the epistemological positions taken by educationalists and reviewed the implications that they saw them as having for practice in their day, and that we might view them as having for our current practice. Readers might like to contemplate at this point which, if any, of the schools of thought explicated here comes closest to their own position and also to the implicit or explicit philosophy which pervades the culture of their work context.

We have been privileged to participate in similar explorations by other professionals from many discipline fields, which we in turn will share in this book as examples and illustrations of the principles and methods in the vast field of Personal Construct Approaches to professional education and the development of practice. From these we have derived much learning, as we hope they have. This learning has not merely been about other worlds and professional contexts, the people in them and what they do, but has been about research itself as a process. As Candy (1990: 272–3) argued, knowledge of one's meaning perspective in itself is not sufficient to bring about a perspective transformation, the opportunity to experiment with alternatives is also required. Like others, including ourselves in our own pasts, Candy was disillusioned with much of traditional educational research which ‘put words into respondents’ mouths’, or acted like ‘conceptual straight jackets’ or in which others interpreted the participants’ (subjects’) meaning for them.

However, just as at beginning of this chapter we commented that any attempt to categorize perspectives in education would no doubt do injustice to the great diversity of viewpoints that do exist, it would be a gross generalization to suggest here that all previous educational research has been of the same genre. In educational research the issues to be raised and the methodologies adopted to pursue them have themselves undergone shifts in perspective which in many ways parallel the changes in viewpoints outlined in this chapter. Having established in the next chapter the value of a Personal Construct Psychology framework for understanding current issues in professional education, some of the problems with alternative research approaches are discussed in Chapter 3 as a prelude to introducing a research approach congruent with that theoretical framework.

Chapter 2
Personal Construct Psychology approaches in education

> The teacher of 1985 is a constructivist who continually builds, elaborates and tests his or her personal theory of the world ... we have begun to move away from those cybernetically elegant, internally consistent but mechanical metaphors that guided our earlier work. (Clark, 1986: 9)

> Personal Construct Theory has also been categorized by responsible scholars as an emotional theory, a learning theory, a psycho-analytic theory (Freudian, Adlerian, and Jungian – all three), a typically American theory, a Marxist theory, a Humanistic theory, a logical positivistic theory, Zen Buddhistic theory, a Thomistic theory, a Behaviouristic theory, an Apollonian theory, a pragmatistic theory, a reflective theory, and no theory at all. It has also been classified as nonsense which indeed, by its own admission, it will likely some day turn out to be. (Kelly, 1970a: 10)

When discussing personal construct theory, Kelly took great delight in raising the ambiguity of categorized systems which sought to place his viewpoint within one framework or another. The various categories of cultural transmission, romanticism, progressivism and de-schooling which we elaborated in the previous chapter represent alternative ways of looking at education. At different times these approaches and their underlying metaphors have had their heyday. We should not assume, however, that these categories have rigid boundaries nor indeed that there may not be alternative educational perspectives that will arise in due course.

In this chapter we seek not to categorize Kelly's work but, instead, *we will highlight areas we see as relevant to constructivist education*. This abstraction represents, of course, our own perspective and preoccupations. We do not intend to cover in detail Kelly's theory nor do we seek to encapsulate it in the proverbial nutshell. The reader is referred to the personal writings of George Kelly for a fuller appreciation of the implications of personal construct psychology. Consideration here will be given to aspects of Kelly's work which relate to the educational process in whichever context it takes place, in the traditional classroom environment or in the workplace.

Kelly was a true radical whose education and interest spanned a range of disciplines. He first studied physics and mathematics and intended to complete an engineering course after graduation. His interest in social issues led him instead to study educational psychology in which he obtained a MA at the University of Kansas in 1927. After a period of teaching, he obtained a B Ed at the University of Edinburgh and a PhD in Psychology at Iowa University. Thus Kelly engaged with a number of disciplines. It is not surprising then that he advocated a multi-disciplinary approach to education rather than rigid subject boundaries. Kelly rarely wrote specifically on education. However, while studying at the University of Edinburgh he wrote a paper which was eventually published in 1979, in a book edited by Stringer and Bannister. The paper was entitled 'Social Inheritance' and in a foreword to the paper, Bannister suggested that:

> the most significant aspect of this early essay is the argument running through it that education should be about personal meaning. (p. 3)

It is this emphasis on personal meaning that harmonizes Kelly's perspective, and that of those who have drawn on his seminal writings, in tune with contemporary approaches in education. In particular we will concern ourselves with issues such as the 'perspective of the personal', the focus on relevance and responsibility within the teaching and learning process and the epistemological issues surrounding relativity of knowledge. Underpinning all of these is Kelly's recognition and valuing of alternative perspectives.

Perspective of the personal

The current vogue for constructivism may mask Kelly's pioneering spirit which enthused many personal construct psychologists to take his lead and explore the implications of his work. Bruner (1990: 163), when discussing the 'cognitive revolution', noted that Kelly's two volumes *The Psychology of Personal Constructs* appeared in 1955, 'a year before the by-now-standard date for the "opening of the cognitive revolution"', and noted that when he reviewed the work, he 'hailed it as the first effort to construct a theory of personality from a theory of knowledge'. Bruner recognized that Kelly was in the forefront of those concerned with how people make sense of their worlds.

Britton (1976: 3) discussed his approach to teaching and drew heavily on Kelly's theory. For example in his discussion on the limitations of behaviour modification he said:

> there is in behaviour modification, that is to say, a method educators may use, ... no ethic for the educational process. For my part, therefore, I would go with George Kelly whose methods are themselves exponents of the philosophy that provide the ethic.

For many years writers on educational issues have argued that it is time that recognition be given to the perspectives of the people engaged in teaching/learning interactions. Blumer (1966: 542), writing on educational research, suggested that: 'Since action is forged by the actor out of what he perceives, interprets and judges, one would have to ... take the role of the actor and see his world from his standpoint'. We took this to heart in naming one module of a course we ran for professional practitioners 'Education as if people matter'.

This 'perspective of the personal' is central to the work of George Kelly. It is implicit in the title of his theory – personal construct theory – and explicit in his writings. e.g. 'We start with a person. Organisms, lower animals and societies can wait' (Kelly, 1970a: 9). The fundamental postulate of personal construct theory is that 'a person's processes are psychologically channelised by the ways in which he anticipates events' (Kelly, 1955: 46). For Kelly a person's behaviour is not driven by instinct (as in psychoanalytic theory) nor is it determined by the schedules of reinforcement and associations between stimulus and response (as in Skinnerian and Behaviourist theories). These were the dominant models within American psychology in the 1950s when Kelly wrote his two volumes.

There have been many metaphors used in psychology, for example man: the telephone exchange, man: the hydraulic system, and man: the computer. Man: the scientist was Kelly's metaphor. He suggested that people and scientists are both engaged in a process of observation, interpretation, prediction and control. According to Kelly, each person erects a representational model of the world which enables him or her to chart a course of behaviour in relation to it. This model is subject to change over time since constructions of reality are constantly tested out and modified to allow better predictions in the future. Thus for Kelly the questioning and exploring, revising and replacing in the light of predictive failure which is symptomatic of scientific theorizing, is precisely what people do when attempting to anticipate events. The person can be seen as a scientist constantly experimenting with a personal experience. For Kelly a person is 'a form of motion' – thus he denies the necessity of 'carrot and stick' or 'impulse driven' theories of motivation. People are inevitably and constantly attempting to make sense of their environment. A person's anticipation of future events, is 'both the push and pull of the psychology of Personal Constructs' (Kelly, 1955: 49). Kelly did not deny the importance of early experiences or present environmental circumstances, but he suggested that it was more important to know what and how people think about their present situation than to know what their early childhood experiences were or what environmental circumstances they now find themselves in. This stems from his fundamental postulate; central to this was the view that people are constantly engaged in testing their anticipation and their understanding of their worlds.

Clandinin (1986: 166) used the term 'image' in a similar way to our reading of personal constructs in her concern with the development of teachers:

> Images as components of personal practical knowledge, are the coalescence of a person's personal, private and professional experience. Image is a way of organizing and reorganizing past experience, within reflection and as the image finds expression in practice and as a perspective from which new experience is taken. Image is a personal, meta-level, organizing concept in personal practical knowledge that embodies a person's experience; finds expression in practice; and is the perspective from which new experiences is taken.

The Progressivist movement in education emphasized the activity of the person struggling to impose meaning on his or her experiences and rejects the notion of a passive receiver of knowledge. The following quotation from Berman and Roderick (1973: 3), writing about the school context but pertinent to a broader field, indicated some assumptions about curriculum which appear to us to be compatible with Kelly's viewpoint:

> Curriculum has long been thought of as that which is taught to somebody else ... The view of these writers is that curriculum must put the person at the centre of what is learned. Curriculum development and subsequent research on the curriculum will then see the person as the meaning maker and plan curricula experiences which enable the child to consider, contemplate, and expand his meanings. Critical to curriculum development, then is the ascertaining of what is happening to the individual child as he interacts with persons, materials, time and space within the context of the school and the classroom.

This emphasis on the person as the meaning-maker is central to Kelly's position. In order to understand a person's behaviour it is necessary to know how he or she construes his or her particular situation. Kelly argues that persons differ from each other in their construction of events (individuality corollary). The structural analysis of the education system which was prevalent in the late 1970s had limitations. A major assumption of this approach is that the structural variables of a school are directly related to aspects of its pupils' success. Research on the pros and cons of particular structural aspects of schools, e.g. streamed versus unstreamed, produced contradictory findings. A Kellyan viewpoint would reject social determinism – as Kelly said, 'Societies can wait'. Kelly would not presume that the members undergoing a similar education system or belonging to particular groups would *necessarily* share the same system of construing. However, he did admit the possibility of shared areas of personal meaning and this was made explicit in his commonality corollary.

> To the extent that one person employs a construction of experience which is similar to that employed by another, his processes are psychologically similar to those of the other person. (Kelly, 1970a: 20)

Nevertheless, while acknowledging that we might share some constructs with others, it is Kelly's stress on the personal nature of meaning and the elevation of the person to the central focus of enquiry that aligns him with much of contemporary theorizing on education.

Beattie (1995: 146) emphasized the importance of construction and reconstruction within an educational process and the personal nature of these events.

> In the telling and retelling of our stories we change, we learn, we grow, giving up the stories of ourselves that we hold when we can replace them with richer and more significant versions most suited to our current environment and to the environments and to the future we foresee.

Relevance and responsibility

In the section on De-schooling in Chapter 1, we drew attention to the viewpoints of theorists, such as Postman and Weingartner (1971) and Rogers (1969), who argued that it is important that we realize that significant learning will only take place if the learner perceives personal relevance in the matter being learned. Personal construct theorists, Thomas and Harri-Augstein (1985: xxiv) argued that:

> for learning to be an enriching experience the meanings that emerge must become personal and they must be significant or important in some part of the person's life. The viability of these meanings depends on how richly the individual incorporates them into personal experiences.

Berman and Roderick (1973: 8) held a similar viewpoint. In their discussion on curriculum development cited earlier, they made the distinction between public knowledge, i.e. that which exists in books, films, museums etc. and personal knowledge. They suggested that it is only, however, 'when knowledge has meaning for the person so that he or she can take an idea and turn it to see its many facets that real learning has taken place'.

Kelly recognized learning as a personal exploration and saw the teacher's role as helping to design and implement each child's own undertakings. 'To be a fully accredited participant in the experimental enterprise she must gain some sense of what is being seen through the child's eyes' (Kelly, 1970b: 262). Teachers of novices of any kind, adults learning their professions in the public or private sector, would do well to gain a sense of what is seen through their eyes.

What is relevant to the person is of importance and, for education to be a joint venture between the teacher and learner, it would be beneficial if each has some awareness of the other's personal constructs. Kelly's sociality corollary states: 'to the extent that one person construes the construction process of another he or she may play a role in a social process involving the other person'.

The perspective of the learner as well as that of the teacher is important, although traditionally learning has been defined mainly from the latter's perspective. For the existentialist the ultimate responsibility for learning rests with the learner – people have responsibility for their own being. The existentialist rejects the notion of unquestioning acceptance by the learner. The responsibility lies with learners to incorporate public knowledge within their own view of the world. Knowledge should be part of a person's inner experience and is therefore emotional as well as intellectual. This point was stressed by Kelly in that, for him, the distinction usually made between cognition and affect was inappropriate. He eschewed the dualism of body and mind and used the term *construing* by which he meant 'placing an interpretation which subsumes thoughts and emotion'(Kelly, 1955: 50).

Central to Kelly's theory is the notion that people may construe their environment in an infinite number of different ways depending on their imagination and the courageousness of their experimentation. People are not stimulus-bound but they may well be bound by their construal of the world.

Rose (1983) discussed the way we choose to engage with our experiences. We can either live our lives according to plans predetermined by others or we can construct our own and choose to tell and retell our stories. As Rose put it 'all living is a creative act of greater or lesser authenticity, hindered or helped by the fictions to which we submit ourselves' (Rose, 1983: 17).

'Man is nothing other than what he makes himself', is a tenet of existentialism which also applies to personal construct psychology. Kelly was perhaps somewhat reluctant to accept the label 'existentialist'. However, in his dislike of labels, his view of construing as having an emotional as well as cognitive base, his accent on freedom and responsibility of the individual and on the relevance of events to the individual, he highlights areas of concern which are also of importance to contemporary education.

Relativity of knowledge

Kelly described his epistemological position as that of Constructive Alternativism:

> Constructive Alternativism holds that man understands himself, his surroundings and his potentialities by devising constructions to place upon them and then testing the tentative utility of these constructions against such ad interim criteria as the successful prediction and control of events. (Kelly, 1966: 1)

Although Kelly did not deny the existence of reality, he maintained that it is presumptuous to claim that a person's constructions of reality are convergent with it:

> The fact that my only approach to reality is through offering some responsible construction of it does not discourage me from postulating that it is there. The open question for man is not whether reality exists or not but what he can make of it. (Kelly, 1969a: 25)

This echoes the philosophy of Pragmatism we discussed in Chapter 1.

For Kelly events are subject to 'as great a variety of constructions as our wits would enable us to contrive' (1970a: 1). He rejected an absolutist view of truth and contrasted his position with that of Accumulative Fragmentalism – the notion that knowledge is a growing collection of substantiated facts or 'nuggets of truth'. His philosophical position is opposed to that of the Realist. Even the most highly developed scientific knowledge can be seen to be subject to human reconstruction.

For Kelly the construction of reality is an active, creative, rational, emotional and pragmatic affair. 'Man the scientist' evolves a set of constructions which is put to the test and may ultimately be discarded in favour of a new set of constructions if the former fails to anticipate events adequately. Kelly pointed out that all theories are hypotheses devised by people which may fit all the known facts at any particular time but may eventually be found wanting in some unforeseeable respect and be eventually replaced by a 'better theory'. An example from physics is the reappraisal of Newton's theory by Einstein. However, Einstein's theory is unlikely to be the ultimate truth and Einstein himself regarded his theory as defective and spent much of his life trying to find a better one.

Bell and Gilbert (1996: 46) suggested that:

> Kelly's great contribution to constructivism is his assertion that there are no pre-determined limits on constructs in terms of the nature and range of their application. The limit to their creation is only set by the imagination of the individual concerned and by the constructs being continually tested, for their predictive and explanatory adequacy in physical and social contexts; those that prove successful will be retained used again and used in a wider range of contexts, whilst those that do not will be modified or abandoned.

In putting forward his theory, Kelly suggested that, as a theory, it would be subject to revision since it is itself an example of a human construct and so can be seen as an hypothesis waiting to be put to the test (Kelly, 1970a: 10). This view of theory, science and knowledge was echoed in the writings of Karl Popper (1963). He saw science and knowledge as progressing through a series of 'conjectures and refutations'. Kuhn (1970) analysed the progress of science and suggested that growth of knowledge occurs when the dominant paradigm of the day is challenged by the revolutionaries who step outside the limits of present theory and engage in what Kuhn calls 'extraordinary science'. Kuhn suggested that professional scientists are educated in the 'normal' scientific mode which involves solving problems within the limits of the theory the scientist has been taught. The theory itself is not questioned. If problems are not solved the theory is not invalidated, the scientist merely lacks ingenuity! Kelly would see this as a lack of courage in experimentation.

Popper (1970), in reply to Kuhn, suggested that normal science in Kuhn's sense does exist but it is the activity of the non-revolutionary, the none too critical professional, the learner who accepts the dogma of the day. In discussing Popper's philosophy of science, Magee argued that it could:

> scarcely be more undogmatic ... it holds that we never actually know – that our approach to any and every situation or problem needs to be always such as to accommodate not merely unforeseeable contributions but the permanent possibility of a radical transformation of the whole conceptual scheme. A great deal of disillusionment with science and reason which is so widespread in our age is based on precisely such mistaken notions of what science and reason are. (Magee, 1973: 68)

Kuhn and Popper, like Kelly, are both arguing for the relative nature of knowledge. In recent years this relativity of knowledge is acknowledged by constructivist educators, although it was recognized many years ago by Postman and Weingartner (1971: 100) who argued:

> We now know that each man creates his own unique world, that he, and he alone, generates whatever reality he can ever know ... the purposes and

> assumptions and therefore the perceptions of each man are uniquely his ... among other things, this means that no man can be absolutely certain of anything. The best anyone can ever do is say how something appears to him.

These words echo the view of knowledge put forward by Kelly and could be seen to be a re-statement of his fundamental postulate and individuality corollary.

Kelly recognized the subversive implications of his views. They pose a direct challenge, and possible threat, to teachers who see their role as passing on bodies of substantiated facts or 'absolute truths' without the necessity of presenting these as problematic or conjectural. The idea that all facts are subject to revision leaves the door open for the learner to question the knowledge presented by the teacher.

More recently views on the sociology of knowledge emphasize a person's active construction of experience and offer a clear challenge to the static, analytic conception of knowledge which has failed to empower individuals in their pursuit of personal meaning. Many have drawn on the social phenomenology of Schutz (1967). Schutz suggested that action is mediated by a complex interrelational process within the constituted biography of the individual. Reality is interpreted in terms of the provinces of meaning which make up the individual's 'stock of knowledge', which is his/her *Lebensfelt*. This stock of knowledge seems similar to Kelly's view of a construct system. It is continually changing through the processes of constitution and accommodation in the same way as validation and invalidation lead to elaboration and reorganization in a person's construct system. Schutz, however, emphasized that the individual's 'frame of reference' is a social product in that confirmation or disconfirmation of it is likely to come from his/her 'consociates' – those with whom the individual has most social contact – with whom he/she is jointly engaged in reality construction.

The writings of Schutz and also of Berger and Luckmann (1967) have had significant effect on assumptions regarding the sociology of education. As Esland (1971: 96) pointed out:

> if knowledge is dereified, it is, then, a much more negotiable commodity between teacher and pupil ... there is no reason to suppose that these will remain within the 'boundaries' of what are now heuristically labelled as 'subjects'. New configurations of knowledge are likely to emerge from the combinations of questions which arise in the learning situations ... the boundaries are only human constructs and can, therefore, be broken.

The similarities between this position and that of Kelly's is most apparent when we compare it with Kelly's view of the relativity of categorization –

'subjects' being a case in point – and his view of teaching and learning as a process of negotiation between the joint experimenters in the venture, i.e. the student and teacher.

The area of curriculum development has become a focus of attention in education. Issues such as the relativity of knowledge and the recognition of the importance of the learner's, as well as the teacher's, perspective have had a profound influence. Those advocating humanistic foundations of education suggest that we should recognize that learning is more than an intellectual exercise. Joyce proposed that the curriculum should become pluralistic and should represent many domains of possible development. Within the compulsory education sector attention should be paid to the creative and performing arts, education for greater interpersonal sensitivity and affairs of international concern. A goal of curriculum planning should be: 'To create environments which enable individuals to actualize themselves on their own terms – emotionally, intellectually, and socially' (Joyce, 1972: 169). Such goals are not incompatible with learning to be an effective professional practitioner. Constructivists have advocated such an approach.

Change is occurring so rapidly that we can no longer foresee the information that would be necessary for a learner to have in order to be successful in the future. It is for this reason that education curricula should include helping learners to deal with change – the teaching of strategies for survival. It is of vital importance that the teacher acts as a facilitator of discussion, a resource for finding information and a stimulator of problem-solving. As we said at the beginning of this book, we live in an increasingly complex and uncertain world marked by accelerating technological and social change. As constructivists we suggest that educational procedures developed during an era of relative stability and certainty are no longer able to provide learners with the skills they need to exist effectively in contemporary society. Jordon (1973: 87) commented:

> How to learn is in itself something that has to be learned, though is rarely 'taught' in traditional schools ... the development of learning competence enables the child to become an active determiner of his own destiny and gives him the fundamental power of extending and releasing all other potentialities.

Professionals whose school experience did not encourage learning to learn may need extra support in developing those skills at a later date.

Educationalists have often been slow to rise to this challenge. Many argue that external constraints posed by government agencies and examining bodies militate against such an approach. However, other educationalists do support a move from an analysis of the curriculum content and sequence as a main focus towards an attempt to understand the learner's current experiences of concepts in the classroom and how these might change. As Driver (1982: 75) suggested 'we may need to pay as much attention to the learner's current ideas and how they change as we do to the structure of knowledge taught'. Driver's work has been informed by personal construct psychology. Bell and Gilbert (1996: 156) warned us that there can be threats to the development of a constructivist approach in teaching and learning, particularly in the traditional school environment, though lecturers and trainers may see much in common with their own context. They noted that:

> for example, in the United Kingdom, the new curricula are couched in terms of content to be learnt and the amount of content is high. The teachers are required to 'deliver' that content, a term which implies a process of passing over something tangible. This trend is against the professional judgement of teachers, fails to recognize the active agency of students in their own learning, and is in favour of a commodity-production view of knowledge. Assessment policies ... are often in tension with constructivist views of learning.

This notion of agency is central to the work of Thomas and Harri-Augstein who have applied tenets of Personal Construct Psychology within the wider field of learning. They have encouraged learners, teachers and managers in industry to recognize their potential through being able to become self organized as learners. By self organization Thomas and Harri-Augstein refer to a process by which learners are encouraged to reflect on their own learning process, often with the help of a facilitator. They have pointed out the limitations inherent in previous versions of learning theory that were predicated on experiments in the laboratory. Thus they stated:

> Experimental psychologists constructing theories in their meaning-isolated laboratories have largely ignored the simple truth that it is the meaning attributed to each event, not the event itself, which influences a person's reactions to it. It is their personal meaning which becomes the personal cause. Actions and subsequent events represent the 'effects' of this meaning, as it plays out in a given situation. The construction of personal experience is prior. This process is essentially conversational. An awareness of this process demands an awareness of a meta-conversation about learning. (Thomas and Harri-Augstein, 1985: 27-28)

Their book shares with the reader the various technologies they have invented which can 'represent personal meaning in ways which enable reflection, review and effective transformation of the quality of human experience and performance'. Learning-to-learn becomes a central task for the learner and the facilitation of this meta-cognition, part of the role of the teacher.

Kelly's epistemological position and the role of a teacher

So far in this examination of Kelly's basic ideas regarding knowledge and its implications for constructivist education we have stressed the relativity of knowledge and its personal nature. Lest the reader assume that this indicates that Kelly took a solipsistic view of personal construing it is important to note that, while Kelly advocated the position that events are subject to interpretation limited only by our creativity, he did acknowledge the existence of an external reality we are striving to map effectively. This is evident in the following:

> We presume that the world is really existing and that man is gradually coming to understand it. (Kelly, 1955: 6)
>
> Some of the alternative ways of construing are better than others. (Kelly, 1955: 45)

Since we all approach 'reality' with our existing constructions our appreciation of the external world is always represented or constructed in the light of our current theorizing and could well be improved upon by further experimentation.

Nystedt and Magnusson (1982: 34) noted the contribution Kelly's theory makes to the 'mainstream of constructivism in psychology' and neatly summed up the tenets of constructivism which permeate Kelly's writing.

> It is fundamental to the constructivist's view that the environment can never be directly known but that conception determines perception. We know reality only by acting upon it. This means that knowledge is neither a copy nor a mirror of reality, but the forms and content of knowledge are constructed by the one who experiences it. The active interaction between the individual and the environment is mediated by the cognitive structures of the individual. What we learn in interaction with the environment is dependent upon our own structuring of those experiences. Thus according to this view, man does not merely respond to the environment, he construes it.

This epistemological position has implications for how the teacher helps the learner actively to construe experiences. In viewing our constructions of reality as potentially open to reconstruction, Kelly's stance as a therapist and as an educator was to encourage clients/learners to articulate their world views and to recognize these world views as current hypotheses potentially open to invalidation. In this way he hoped the clients/learners would put themselves in the position of opening their minds to potential alternatives which might serve his/her cause better. He saw his concern as 'finding better ways to help a person reconstrue his life so that he need not be the victim of his past' (Kelly, 1955: 23).

He noted that people may be very resistant to accepting invalidation of personal construction (*hostility*). They may be reticent to experiment with alternative models. Their constructions may have been designated the status of 'the world as it really is' and thus not be amenable to contradiction. The pursuit of conceptual change and liberation from personal 'prisons', though potentially possible, may lead to anxiety. The very recognition that our personal construct system does not have the 'range of convenience' to accommodate events with which one is confronted is Kelly's description of *anxiety*. This point is of importance for educationalists who are concerned with conceptual change and transformative practice.

Conceptual development and change

Against the backcloth of Kelly's epistemology his theory is elegantly developed in terms of a fundamental postulate and 11 corollaries.

We will now draw attention to some of these and suggest implications for education. To reiterate, the fundamental postulate states: 'A person's processes are psychologically channellized by ways in which he anticipates events.'

Kelly had taken as his root metaphor 'man – the scientist'. He invited us to entertain the possibility that looking at people *as if* they were scientists – i.e. to view their 'scientist-like aspect' – might illuminate human behaviour. Just as the experimental scientist may design his/her experiments round rival hypotheses, so each of us can be seen as designing our daily explorations of life around rival hypotheses which form part of our system of constructs or 'world view'. People can be seen as scientists, constantly experimenting with their definitions of existence. Kelly saw the scientist as engaged in the *anticipation* of events with the view to the prediction and control of events. The scientist imposes meaning on events in the hope that his/her predictions will be fruitful and useful. It is the invalidation of our anticipation that encourages reorganization of our psychological processes, i.e. conceptual development and change.

> Successive relevation of events invites the person to place new constructions upon them whenever something unexpected happens ...The constructions one places on events are working hypotheses which are about to be put to the test of experience. As one's anticipations are successively revised in the light of the unfolding sequence of events a construction system undergoes progressive evolution. (Kelly, 1955: 72)

For Kelly, the person with a capacity to anticipate events successfully has built a 'coherent' construct system and, if she/he keeps an open frame on the world, conceptual and personal growth is viable. Viable but not necessarily easy. Kelly's clients often demonstrated that it was a traumatic affair to try to change their construing/anticipation of events.

Kelly's fundamental postulate stated his belief that a person's behaviour in the present is determined by the way he/she is anticipating some future event. This anticipation necessitates the use of the person's constructs. Kelly likened the *personal construct* to an hypothesis which is erected to account for present experience and to forecast events (theory building) and also to assess the accuracy of previous forecasts after the events have occurred, thereby testing and validating or invalidating their predictive efficiency (theory testing).

Constructs do not exist in isolation but are hierarchically grouped; some having subordinate and others having superordinate positions within the system. This is the implication of Kelly's Organization Corollary which states that 'each person characteristically evolves, for his convenience in anticipating events, a construction system embracing ordinal relationships between constructs'. This corollary has profound implications for the development of one of Kelly's tools for investigating construing – the repertory grid (see Chapter 4). It also explains why some constructs are relatively amenable to change while others are clung to tightly.

Fundamental to Kelly's view was that motion is an inevitable aspect of human functioning and his use of the term *evolves* in his Organization Corollary was to stress his view that this organization is not a static entity but that constructs are potentially in a constant state of motion and therefore open to change, though some are more open than others.

A key assumption within Kelly's personal construct theory was his Individuality Corollary: 'Persons differ from each other in their construction of events.'

This central theme runs throughout his theory as he lays great stress on the uniqueness of each person's construct system. For Kelly, it is presumptuous to assume that another person will have the same idea as oneself or others who have ostensibly experienced the same set of events. Constructs can differ in their focus, range, permeability, their position within an ordinal hierarchical framework and the strength of their relationships with other parts of the system. These formal aspects of the nature of constructs will affect the content and structure of a person's system such that, seen as a whole, each one of us is likely to have a unique system. The essence of Kelly's clinical work was to help people to articulate at least a part of their individual constructions. He saw effective teaching as requiring a similar process.

This articulation is important on two counts:

1. It allows the clinician/teacher to have some understanding of the personal models the client/learner is currently using to impose meaning on the world.
2. The process of articulation may help the client/learner to clarify thoughts, recognize the significance of the power of these thoughts and reflect on potential avenues for change.

For Kelly the first was vital if the encounter was to be fully effective. In his Sociality Corollary he states: 'To the extent that one person construes the construction process of another they may play a role in a social process involving the other person' (Kelly, 1955).

What Kelly intended to convey by this corollary was that, unless we have some understanding of another person's set of personal constructs about the domain within which we wish to converse, and that person has some understanding of our constructs, the process of communication between us will be inadequate. What is important is not that we share the same constructs but that we have some empathy with regard to each other's point of view. As a direct consequence of his Sociality Corollary Kelly recognized that learning is a personal exploration and that the teacher must come to some understanding of the experiments, lines of enquiry and personal strategies used by the learner. He saw the teacher's role as helping:

> to design and implement each child's own undertakings, as well as to assist in interpreting the outcomes and in devising more cogent behavioural inquiries. But usually she has to begin, as any apprentice begins, by implementing what others have designed; in this case, what her children have initiated.

This can readily be translated into professional contexts by the substitution for 'child' of 'novice' or , indeed, 'client'.

Kelly's Sociality Corollary implies the need to come to some understanding of the current conceptualization of the learner. His Individuality and Organization Corollaries alert us to the need to assume that these conceptions are part of what will be an idiosyncratic construct system of personal meaning organized within a hierarchical network. In order that we address notions of conceptual change at least two more of Kelly's corollaries need to be introduced – namely Fragmentation and Modulation.

The nature of the relationship between constructs within a person conceptual system was seen by Kelly as one where incompatibilities and inconsistencies between constructs have been minimized while retaining maximum potential for elaboration of the system. That is, each of the clusters of constructs (and there are many) represent coherent domains of meaning that a person uses to explain and explore certain issues or experiences. He argued that the ways in which a person's systems can change are not random or ad hoc but are themselves part of a regulated system of change. Each system (or domain of meaning) is part of a person's overall system which not only binds the subsystems together, within overarching superordinate constructs, but which also regulates the processes of change within the domains. Whether or not a person will change his or her constructs depends on the *permeability* of constructs. The success or otherwise of predictions entailed by the constructs and the extent of change will depend on the nature of the inter-relationships between constructs and their position within the person's repertoire. Thus the Modulation and Fragmentation Corollaries are intimately linked to the Organization Corollary.

The Modulation Corollary states: 'The variation in a person's construction system is limited by the permeability of the constructs within whose range of convenience the variants lie.'

The construction system being referred to here is the whole-person system. Kelly has a particular meaning for the term *permeability*, namely a degree of openness to change the potential to countenance new features. He said: 'What is meant by permeability is not a construct's plasticity, or its amenability to change within itself, but its capacity to be used as a referent for novel events and to accept a new subordinate constructions within its range of convenience' (Kelly, 1970a: 19).

If some parts of a person's system are impermeable then those parts will be resistant to change since those constructs will 'reject elements on the basis of their newness'. Resistance to change can also be the result of what Kelly referred to as 'hostility'.

Kelly's notion of 'range of convenience' also bears comment. Both a construct and a system of constructs is seen as having a limited sphere of applicability. Certain features or events can be ruled out of consideration by a construct on the basis that, for them it is an inappropriate or inadequate way of being viewed. The system is neutral towards them – they lie outside its range of convenience.

Kelly saw conceptual development as an evolutionary process which involved the progressive differentiation of conceptual structures (groups of constructs) into independently organized substructures and the hierarchic integration of these substructures at progressively higher levels of abstraction. The functional differentiation of structures enhances the 'range of convenience' of an individual's construct system. However, hierarchic integration of these differing substructures is necessary for the integrity of a person's construct system. Having a meta-theory which provides a linkage between a number of mini-theories can allow the individual to make a wider range of cross references than is possible within a very differentiated system. Bruner (1977) saw this as an essential aspect of the development of intelligence.

The Fragmentation Corollary suggests that a person might use successive subsystems that are inconsistent. Thus, it says: 'A person may successively employ a variety of construction subsystems which are inferentially incompatible with each other.'

Clearly some individuals can tolerate a greater number of inconsistencies in their construct systems than can other people, though this tolerance is itself a function of the permeability of the overall, superordinate system. We both might view some people as 'good' though each of us might have different tolerances of aspects of their behaviour viewed as 'incompatible with good', for instance.

While adequate cognitive functioning requires integration through the deployment of superordinate constructs, differentiation, inconsistency or *fragmentation* can have its merits. Kelly (1955) suggested that one implication of his Fragmentation Corollary is that the constructive alternativist can test out new hypotheses without having just to discard the old hypotheses/constructs. Constructs are hypotheses and we can hold on to constructs which are incompatible – Kelly saw this as a feature of human thought which was especially noted in children:

> The nice thing about hypotheses is that you don't have to believe them. This, I think, is a key to the genius of scientific method. It permits you to be inconsistent with what you know long enough to see what will happen. Children do that. What is wonderful about the language of hypothesis is its refreshing ability to free the scientist from the entangling consistencies of adulthood. For a few precious moments he can think again like a child, and, like a child, learn from his experience. (Kelly, 1970b: 258)

Kelly clearly valued the child's, at times inconsistent, theorizing as scientific while the adult's tightly ordered constructs could limit their theorizing, thus stunting the development of new knowledge. However, he saw limits to incompatibility of constructs – we can tolerate some incompatibility but not too much. The amount that can be tolerated is determined by the permeability of superordinate constructs.

Fragmentation and Modulation corollaries give a picture of a person using a variety of differing subsystems to make sense of what is happening. These are distinctive, semi-independent and are subsumed at some point by a unifying thread, some superordinate construct.

In this section we have highlighted some fundamental tenets of Kelly's theory that would underlie a Personal Construct Psychologist's view of conceptual development and change. In the following sections, we will indicate how these fundamental notions have been applied in the particular area of science education, teacher thinking and staff development.

Science education as a discipline example

A Kellyan approach to teaching would suggest that, as a matter of policy, differences between the learner's personal meanings, those of the teacher and the formal concepts of the 'received view' of the subject should be dealt with within an open forum where the differences are valued for what they are, i.e. constructive alternative ways of seeing.

As teachers we may see ourselves as in the business of encouraging conceptual change, particularly as it may lead to transformative practice. In science education there has been a growth in what is being called 'conceptual change teaching' based upon the premise that the instructional act starts with the learner's 'naive' conceptions being articulated and then 'experiments' devised so that these can be challenged and (hopefully) the 'accepted' view of science will prevail, given the 'failure' of their personal models to hold up to the challenge of experimentation. *Up to a point* this may seem to be an implication of some of Kelly's notions *but* Kelly had much more cognisance of the location of a particular domain of sense making within the overall construct system. The particular domain under experimentation may be more or less linked with other domains, may be more or less permeable and its position with respect to core constructs may be more or less of vital importance to the person. The *perceived consequence* of change may engender anxiety, fear or feelings of threat. What is difficult for a teacher to gauge is the perceived consequence and the degree of stress that 'conceptual change instruction' of the type referred to above, will induce. This is not to suggest that we do not engage in the *encouragement* of conceptual change or of transformative practice. However, we should remember that the goggles through which others view their worlds may not be easily altered. There are some constructs, which Kelly referred to as 'core constructs', which are fundamental and central to the maintenance of a person's sense of self and are often life and death matters.

This notion that people have core constructs permeated Kelly's Fixed Role Therapy, which was a model of the process of encouraging conceptual change. We too must recognize that by encouraging learners to articulate their personal meanings they are portraying something of their *selves*. As such, the climate has to be one in which this disclosure is valued. In putting forward the 'accepted' view of a concept we need to stress the conjectural nature of this current view. Fixed Role Therapy begins with the client 'painting a portrait' of him/herself – either through a written or spoken 'self-characterization sketch' or the completion of a repertory grid. These techniques are discussed in later chapters. In Fixed Role Methods, once the person's view of self, or some domain of the world under scrutiny, is exposed a negotiation may take place between client/learner and clinician/teacher. The person is encouraged to see his/her point of view (range of constructs) as current hypotheses and as such potentially open to change.

It is recognized that the client would not be able to cope with a concurrent series of experiments with the negation of *all* his/her constructs and so one of the person's current hypotheses is selected. It is likely that, at first, this construct would not be a core construct that entailed a large number of other central tenets. The person is encouraged to construct an alternative hypothesis to the construct selected and then go away and *behave as if* this construct was one she/he believed in. In this way the person puts him/herself into a position where an alternative *may* be validated. However, as indicated earlier in this chapter, there could be prolonged resistance to change. The role of the clinician is to *support* the client during the unsettling period of experimentation with new ideas *and* at times to suggest alternative hypotheses for exploration. As Kelly (1969c) pointed out, this strategy had much in common with how he tutored his research students. We would suggest the process is one which sensitive teachers could use in schools or in other educational contexts.

The outcome of strategies such as Fixed Role Methods could be diverse. Some learners might hold on to their current hypotheses and temporarily adopt another perspective (fragmentation). Others may choose to see their model as being invalidated and replace it with one proffered by a peer or the 'accepted' view supplied by the teacher. Yet another course of action may be that the learners hold resolutely to their original models and reject others given (however, they may have a better *understanding* of the other perspectives). The process of interchange of personal models could also result in a person discarding his/her previous model, rejecting all of the other models put forward by members of the group and erecting an alternative model which goes beyond any of the models. The latter type of change is essential in scientific progress, and for the *development of transformative professional practice*.

Whatever the outcome, it will be determined by the personal construction of the individual. This is *not* to say that issues such as the social power of the originators of alternative models, pressure towards group conformity, feelings of personal worth held by the person etc. will not be factors linked to the outcome. These issues will be *construed* by the individual in relation to his/her analysis of the adequacy of the prediction of the model within the particular domain. The expediency of changing one's viewpoint will be gauged and the outcome will be an integration of a number of issues such as range of convenience, modulation and permeability and the avoidance of excessive fragmentation of structure. For Kelly construing is an emotional *and* cognitive event and the personal construct system is in toto an holistic entity. Change in any part will have greater or lesser implications for other parts of the total system.

However, unless the learner's views are articulated, the teacher cannot devise a strategy whereby the learner's model can be put to the test. Kelly noted that change in construing will only take place if the person experiments with his/her way of seeing things, construes the implications of these experiments and sees that it would be fruitful, i.e. result in an elaboration of his/her constructs system if he or she were to adopt an alternative way of seeing things. For a Kellyan, the teaching of any science should be scientific, i.e. it should be based upon a rigorous consideration of alternative theories – *those of the learners, the teacher* and *'received wisdom'*. The ethos of the social context within which such a consideration should take place would be one where the alternatives are treated in an equitable manner. There should be sufficient support for learners as they try to articulate their concepts of science so that they are encouraged to talk about their ideas. As Sutton (1981) pointed out, talking about your ideas is one of the most powerful provocations to sorting out what you understand. Talking about ideas and listening to the conflicting opinions of others and the putting of these ideas to the test would represent an approach to teaching which is consistent with Kelly's model of 'man-the-scientist'.

The following extract from Bell and Gilbert draws attention to the work of White who summarized the implications of constructivist research on teaching and learning in science. These writers support the view that in the teaching of science, the nature of learners' prior understanding of concepts (constructs) is important. Although focused on science teaching the following summary is a useful one in drawing out the implications of a constructivist approach for conceptual development in any discipline domain:

- people construct their own interpretations of communications and experiences;
- personal interpretation is determined largely by existing beliefs, which are prior constructions;
- interpretation is often influenced, although not necessarily determined, by the interpretations expressed by others – parents, teachers, peers, texts, and other media;
- students at all levels enter the classroom already holding beliefs relevant to the topic to be studied;
- the extent of beliefs and the intensity with which they are held varies from topic to topic;
- in any given class, there will be a range of beliefs among the students;

- students' beliefs about scientific principles and natural phenomena often differ from the scientists' established beliefs;
- where students' views differ from those of the scientists, they are less economical in interpreting or predicting outcomes of an extended range of events;
- a person can hold beliefs that contradict each other, applying one belief in one context, another belief in another context;
- people often interpret events in a manner that supports a belief, and so avoid confronting discomforting instances. That is, they see what they believe;
- people might alter their memory of an event that contradicts a belief so that their recollection is consistent with what they believe;
- beliefs resist change but students can exchange an alternative conception for the scientists' conception; changes of belief, or resolution of contradictions, are usually slow and require repeated experiences that favour the final accepted interpretations; and
- teaching that encourages resolution of (the contradiction between) alternative conceptions with the scientists' view will include elucidation of the students' beliefs, discussion of the beliefs and their implications, and the design and execution of events that test the accuracy of the beliefs. (Bell and Gilbert, 1996: 4)

The professional development of the teacher as constructivist

Mahoney (1988: 2), discussing constructivist theories, noted that three basic features exist in psychological constructivism – proactive cognition, morphogenic nuclear structure and self-organizing development. She maintained that:

> psychological constructivism refers to a family of theories that share the assertion that human knowledge and experience entail the (pro) active participation of the individual.

Morphogenic nuclear structure implies a form-generating, centre-based, structural organization – a deep structure or nuclear core of an individual system which influences peripheral aspects. This core is less accessible and amenable to change – as Kelly (1955: 82) noted, 'core constructs are those which govern a person's maintenance processes – that is, those by which he maintains his identity and existence'.

Professional development strategies which do not invite challenge of a person's implicit theories may be seen as comfortable but may not lead to any reappraisal of current theory or practice.

Within pre- and in-service professional development teachers are being encouraged to rethink the 'metaphors they live by' (Lakoff and Johnson, 1980). The reflective practitioner (Schon, 1983) needs to reflect critically on the meaning of his/her thoughts and actions as a route to the enhancement of professional practice. Constructive Alternativism is a view about knowledge and action which supports this recognition that, if practices are to change, the teachers need to examine some of ***their fundamental beliefs***. Teachers may find consideration of their current constructs threatening, especially if they deduce that change is needed. Threatening and revolutionary this may be but some teacher educators see this as empowering the teachers to make education a positive experience for learner and teacher.

Ben-Peretz (1984: 106) advocated participation in ***action research***, e.g. in curriculum planning as a ***process of teacher development***. In discussing the investigation of teacher thinking within the framework of personal construct theory, Ben-Peretz argued that assisting teachers to become aware of their construing patterns should be planned as part of a teacher's professional training and development.

Pope and Denicolo (1991) emphasized an emancipatory approach to staff development and suggest a number of assumptions which are shared by personal construct psychologists and those advocating action research as a form of staff development. These assumptions are discussed in detail in Chapter 3.

It has been assumed that learning and professional development are enhanced by reflection on and in practice. However, we reiterate that it does not follow that this process is easy. Kelly warned of the potential hostility and resistance to change of the individual whose core constructs might be threatened by the consideration of an alternative model which would require too much adaptation of the system. The teacher educator/action researcher needs to be aware of the extreme sensitivity of the reflective material which can be evoked using certain techniques. They must be prepared to give time and support during periods of deconstruction and reconstruction which may occur when an individual is confronted with an image or action which he/she wishes to change. This is a fundamental requirement within constructivist approaches to professional teacher education.

Clark (1995: 124) alluded to the fact that for many the phase 'professional development of teachers' contains:

> a great deal of negative baggage: it implies a process done to teachers; that teachers need to be forced into developing; that teachers have deficits in knowledge and skills that can be fixed by training; and that teachers are pretty much alike.

As personal constructivists we reject such an approach to professional development.

Diamond (1985) has used a staff development approach based on fixed role therapy and has conducted research on the constructs of pre- and in-service teachers regarding their role. He argued that teachers would give up a viewpoint, even if it were an integral part of them, providing that they had become aware of the more personally meaningful implications of an alternative. He gave examples of comments made by pre-service teachers who had taken part in the research using techniques based on repertory grids and commentary on outcome. One was from a student teacher, Mitzi, who wrote:

> Everyone was looking for something different and went about adjusting to their particular perceived environments in different ways. However, the grid seemed to help most of us. To compare the three 'snapshots' of my year in Dip Ed has been a much appreciated reflective experience for me. I came to terms with how, as a person, I felt about the prospect of teaching as a chosen career, what fears and anxieties I had in relation to teaching, as well as my perceptions of students. I came to see both what and how I saw. (Diamond, 1985: 34)

As Diamond (1985: 34) said, 'if teachers can be helped to "open their eyes", they can see how to choose and fashion their own version of reality'.

Olson (1992: 78) explained some of the potential difficulties of such a process:

> Changing practice isn't merely a technical process – it involves considering what the change signifies. That entailed dialogue – a conversation between the old and the new. Some of those who hold a technocentric view of change, say that such dialogue is futile because innovations involve technical matters that practitioners cannot understand. This is a fake idea.

We have had the privilege of working closely with practising teachers from many professional sectors. We explored Personal Construct Psychology together and they considered the utility of the ideas within their own personal and professional contexts. The following comments reflect how some of these teachers saw the implications of Personal Construct Psychology:

> An environment which is conducive to student inquiry and exploration requires a supportive accepting instructor who is willing to acknowledge his students' theories and at the same time make his theories known to them.

> I think PCP could have a great impact in this area as teachers examine their own constructs towards students who have disabilities. If the teacher's perceptions of the disabled child are negative, then the mainstream experience would be a negative one for the child.

> It is not an easy task this process of being a 'scientist' and the ways are very uncharted and oftimes uncertain. The process seems to require a great deal of emotional energy.
>
> Since my recent introduction to PCP, I am not sure I want to 'play the game' safely, and less sure that I want to 'play the game' at all.

The challenge of Personal Construct Psychology for educators

We hope that in Chapter 2 we have shared with you our construing of the significance of Personal Construct Psychology for education. At the end of an earlier book, Pope and Keen (1981: 163) it was suggested that:

> it is our belief that individuals and groups working in an educational setting will have evolved a particular construction of education within which they operate and that many different views on what education is and should be can and do co-exist. It seems to us that problems arise when an individual or group operates with one set of assumptions to others without any acknowledgement or understanding of an alternative framework or set of assumptions which the other values.

We would suggest that each of us must, from time to time, review how we are construing education and the extent to which we understand the position of others with whom we interact. This seems to us to be a central message of Kelly's work and one which we feel is relevant to those who wish for an effective and democratic educational process.

We will pursue these notions further in ensuing chapters.

We all need to recognize that we are continually construing our world through constructive goggles. From time to time we may need to visit an 'optician' or take steps to 'alter our own eyes' to paraphrase Diamond (1985). As teachers and researchers we need to examine our own goggles if we are to expect our learners to adopt such a stance in their conceptual development.

Concomitant with the awareness of the need to extend our approach to teaching and learning to incorporate the notion of relativity of knowledge and to provide a medium through which personal strategies can be evolved, there is a growing emphasis on the need to reappraise educational research methodology which we discuss in the next chapter.

Chapter 3
Alternative constructions of educational research

> There is a growing body of opinion that the technology of psychometrics is largely irrelevant to education; from the application of psychometric techniques of analysis to the construction of tests. (Biggs, 1976: 280)

Introduction

Professionals in the public and private sector have a duty to develop their own knowledge and practice and they frequently have a role in training and acting as mentor to others. In spite of Knowles (1978) indicating that adult learners are a neglected species, the foundation for much adult education has only superficially been enhanced in recent years by research that has focused on the adult learner. Nevertheless, Goodlad (1984: 9) did emphasize that education for the professions 'must involve some conscious attention not only to the technical component of the professional's service ... but also to the fundamentally moral issue of who is controlling what knowledge for whose benefit'.

On the following page he went on to question whether it was possible that professional education in the 1980s was beginning to shift from a focus on: *control* (by which institutions dominate individuals) to *facilitation* (in which individuals plan the form, pacing and detail of their learning, aided rather than constrained by institutions).

In this chapter we will argue that such a shift is congruent with that taking place in research in other domains of education research. While Knowles noted that it is misguided to assume that what is educationally relevant to the young is equally so for the mature, we suggest that it is inappropriate to transpose unquestioningly into educational environments the approaches and methods of research from other disciplines. To do so not only ignores contextual factors but neglects the complexity of the process.

Systematic versus teacher effectiveness research

Biggs (1976), in our opening quotation, agreed with Snow (1974) who had pinpointed the source of the problem as the fact that educational researchers have been obsessed for years by 'systematic' research designs borrowed from agricultural research. In the last analysis it is the people within a particular educational context who will determine the outcome of education within it.

Many researchers began to criticize previous educational research which focused solely on learner performance measured by test grades. In a complex of factors determining a learner's achievement, it must surely be recognized that the teacher's attitudes and expectations are of paramount importance.

There were numerous pen and paper tests of teachers' values and attitudes but these were criticized in that:

- They put the teacher in a test position which is at once a distorting influence. If people believe that they are being judged as good or bad on the basis of their responses it is easy for them to present a desirable picture of themselves.
- They tend to produce only global measures of such things as permissive teacher attitudes and may be limited indicators of actual classroom behaviour.

There was growing dissatisfaction with research into teaching which was based on inventories and attitude scales which use the experimenter's criteria, often without reference to the particular situation in which they are applied. This is a particular problem when research results and principles derived from the compulsory education contexts are applied in adult and professional learning situations. What is deemed effective in one context may be inappropriate in another.

Morrison and MacIntyre (1973) commented on the extensive diversity of criteria used to judge teacher effectiveness. Examples of such criteria are teachers' knowledge of educational psychology, teachers' knowledge of methods of curriculum construction, teachers' knowledge of subject matter, teachers' intelligence, teachers' values, and teachers' emotional and social adjustment. They suggested that research into teaching neglected the fascinating diversity of personal goals that teachers, learners and others within the education learning situation may hold. These criteria may be at odds with those of the experimenter who enters as a stranger in the situation, and who is often seen as an agent of a controlling authority. In the social memory of many work arenas the vision of the 'time and motion' expert, examining overt behaviour without regard to meaning, still persists.

Observation schedules

Hamilton and Delamont (1974) noted that systematic observation schedules such as Flanders Interaction Categories tend to focus on surface aspects of interaction and neglect underlying features which may have more meaning. The Flanders system was also criticized heavily by Adelman and Walker (1975: 220) who maintained:

> We do not consider that interaction analysis provides information appropriate or adequate for any but the most limited of educational ideologies. The system is virtually unusable in informal contexts.

In more recent years attempts have been made to devise observation schedules which attempt to capture a more naturalistic appraisal of events in the learning environments, so that attributed meaning to actions and individual difference in achieving the same aim can be explored further. For instance, there was a growing emphasis on developing new forms of interaction analysis and on micro-teaching sessions in which personal feedback on practice was given to the learner-teacher. This was welcomed by educationalists as an attempt to bring the locus of inquiry to where it can have most effect. Wragg (1974: 193) hoped that such techniques would accelerate the move towards self-directed learning, both for teachers and learners. But he warned:

> To expect that the introduction of micro-teaching, interaction analysis, role playing or simulation will of themselves vastly improve the quality of teaching both within the institution and of the students being trained, would be akin to hoping that birthday toys would make an unhappy child contented, irrespective of the relationships within his family.

As Wragg pointed out, the student teacher's perceptions of the original lesson and their interpretation of the credibility of sources of feedback will determine how they teach after a micro-teaching session. Similarly, feedback on practical skills in any profession will be filtered through the expectations and value systems of the novice. There is, then, a growing emphasis on the person – a particular teacher or a particular learner's opinions, attributes or decisions. These have become a prime focus of interest for those advocating professional education built on humanistic foundations.

Reidford (1972) raised the dilemma facing those wishing to adopt a humanist approach to educational research. The major preoccupation of educational researchers in the seventies was the testing of hypotheses which were highly likely to be confirmed. As Reidford pointed out, few educational research journals were interested in publishing studies whose results indicate that the hypothesis investigated has not been confirmed.

Predictive research

In education research the tendency was towards the adoption of research strategies in which prediction and control are paramount. The aim of such research has been to discover 'laws' which can be generalized to other populations. Bakan (1967: 46) discussed the need to reconstruct psychological investigation. He argued that mastery, via prediction and control and studied ignorance of the meanings of the subject's protocol language, meant that the mystery of the psyche is not entered. He commented that the 'mystery-mastery complex is the neurotic core of contemporary psychological research enterprise'.

If the aim of research is to discover laws, it assumes an unchanging nature in those who are to be controlled. The scientist–subject distinction endows the scientist with autonomy, rationality etc. while denying the same processes in the 'naive subject'. Such an approach inhibits understanding. In our opinion researchers should be more open-minded about the areas they investigate and the methodologies they use. Good research into the unknown cannot be well designed in the usual 'controlling' sense of the term.

Tight control of variables in traditional approaches to learning experiments resulted in a tendency to trivialize the nature of learning and this may not be of much help to the teacher who is dealing with more complex learning issues. Earlier approaches to the study of learning had limited horizons and we need now to consider complex human learning in more natural settings. This necessitates alternative research strategies.

The disruption of the scientist–subject distinction provides an alternative framework for research. In discussing his 'conversational model' Mair (1970: 182), a personal construct psychologist, suggested that:

> As psychologists we seem to have an alarming tendency to transform important human characteristics into problems, weakness and sources of error. This largely seems due to a continuing, if often blurred, adherence to a view of science quite inappropriate to the subject matter we seek to understand.

The perspective of the personal

Educational research has largely based itself on a notion that, if a sufficient number of relevant facts are assembled, the laws governing these facts will reveal themselves. Here we provide a summary of some of the views that have dominated educational research. Positivism is characterized as a striving for principles or generalizations, the production of a set of 'law-like' accounts that will enable prediction and control. In contrast, phenomenology is aimed at understanding a particular individual's perspective using methodologies that focus on the language and interaction of participants.

It is perhaps not surprising that the positivist paradigm has been the dominant mode of research in education since it is predicated on the cultural transmission view of education we discussed in Chapter 1, which has dominated Western educational thought. We indicated in that chapter that there are alternative views on education and these viewpoints may benefit from the invention of alternate research methodologies. The 'perspective of the personal' now adopted by many educators, raises issues and problems which cannot adequately be tackled by the traditional empirical mode of enquiry. The traditional approach has been questioned by teachers and this has been well documented by Stenhouse (1975), Deforges and McNamara (1979), Elliott and Whitehead (1980). Jones (1989: 51) was forceful in his criticism of research which adopted a positivist stance.

> Much research related to education had the cutting edge of a sponge; for long time I have questioned the honesty of much that I read about in some of the academic journals. Don't get me wrong, I'm not suggesting that their authors were anything but sincere and well intentioned. What I am trying to say is that their research did not speak the truth to me. These works seemed more concerned with statistics than sensitivities; rats rather than brats; research rather than the researched.

Jones, along with many other educators, recognized the potential of applying a personal construct approach to education and this has had a significant impact on educational research today. Biggs (1976) maintained that the honeymoon between psychology and education was over. We would suggest that the marriage between a psychology based on the idea of absolute truth and education is finished. However, we argue that psychology based on personal construct theory offers a positive relationship – one in which the views of those actually involved in the educational process are paramount and not subordinate to the elegance of experimental design.

George Kelly would have agreed with Biggs regarding the limitations of psychometric approaches. He contrasted his philosophical position with that of the psychometrican.

> There are two ways in which one can look at psychological measurement ... fix the position of the subject with respect to certain dimensions ... [or] concern himself with the subject's freedom of movement ... the resources which can be mobilized ... from the point of view of personal construct theory the latter represents the more enlightened approach. (Kelly, 1955: 203)

Olson, who has been influenced by Kelly's writings, suggested that if one is concerned to engage in a process of improvement of teaching then the focus cannot only be on the teacher's behaviour.

> Comprehension of what another person is doing cannot be had through mere examination of the particulars of their behaviour ... we have to understand their behaviour as pointers towards the purposes which they serve and in terms of these purposes. The meaning of what people do lies in the purposes served by these actions, which are not meaningful in themselves but indicators of the purposes they serve which give them meaning. In themselves they mean nothing. (Olson, 1992: 55)

We share Olson's view. Much of contemporary educational research is not so much striving for the disclosure of the 'effective teacher' but for an explanation and understanding of teaching processes and the teacher's subjective experience. It is the teacher's subjective related knowledge which has implications for what happens in the learning context. As Halkes and Olson (1984: 1) said, 'instead of reducing the complexities of the teaching/learning situations into a few manageable research variables, one tries to find out how teachers cope with these complexities'.

Emphasis has shifted to educational research being of a value to practitioners and to the participants within the research. This has necessitated a change of relationship between teachers and researchers. Clark (1986: 4) noted, the goal of research has become that of 'portraying and understanding good teaching in all of its irreducible complexity and difficulty. Quality portraiture maybe of more practical and inspirational value than reductionistic analysis and technical prescriptiveness'.

Methods of enquiry have developed beyond the technology of micro-teaching to include a wide range of approaches which try 'to make visible the formally hidden world of teaching' (Clark, 1995: 56). He suggested that these alternative methods of enquiry offer 'interesting possibilities ... if an important goal of continuing education is to equip teachers to be reflective, analytic and constructively critical of their own teaching' (Clark, 1995: 57).

The current focus is now on trying to understand and interpret the ways in which teachers make sense of, adjust to and create educational environments within their professional contexts. This shift in educational research thinking has not been easy. Eisner (1988: 18) noted 'the research language that has dominated educational enquiry has been one that has attempted to bifurcate the knower and the known'. This point was also emphasized by Elbaz (1990: 20–1), speaking of traditional education environments, who suggested that:

> teachers concerned come to be spoken of in a detached and a dispassionate way: coping with the lively business of the classroom becomes '*classroom management*'. Caring for the welfare and development of each child becomes 'individualised instruction' and virtually every aspect of teaching has been similarly subjected to some form of labelling that empties the teaching act of any personal significance.

With the emphasis on personal knowledge in emergent curricula, objectivist/positivist research methods are limited. Such research methodologies are congruent with principles inherent in reactive curricular frameworks. If one recognizes the role of the emerging objectives of the learner in relation to the curriculum, one must entertain studies that are predicated on a conceptual framework that suggests a carefully delineated in-depth study of what happens to individuals in terms of processes as they interact with the components of their environment. Rather than consider participants in learning environments as actors to be viewed from the perspective of an outside detached observer, what is needed is a methodology which allows the person to elaborate on his or her personal meaning of events.

These concerns were central to Kelly's views on research and led to the development of his repertory grid and self-characterization techniques. These techniques and a range of other approaches will be discussed in detail in later chapters. Kelly was quite clear in his antagonism towards a psychology which sees a person as reactive, a mere input–output system, rather than constructivist: 'A psychology that pins its anticipations on the repetitions of events it calls "stimuli", or on the concatenations of events it calls "reinforcements", can scarcely hope to survive as man's audacities multiply' (Kelly, 1969a: 31).

If one adopts a construct theory approach to research, one rejects the assumption that 'laws of nature' will eventually evolve after a collection of an enormous amount of data. As Bannister and Fransella (1971: 190) pointed out:

> Construct theory does not argue simply that it would be very difficult to fathom the nature of man in practice – most psychologists would admit that. It argues that it is a meaningless ideal, since the nature of individual men and of mankind is evolving and therefore can never finally be explained by any theory.

This clearly sets a personal construct theory approach to research in opposition to those who hold that, through large sample, i.e. nomothetic studies, one will determine the 'nature of the beast'. It does, however, lend itself to support the methodology of the individual case. Kelly's viewpoint is also clearly in line with arguments put forward by contemporary researchers who argue against a rigid subject/experimenter boundary. Kelly saw research as a co-operative enterprise.

Kelly acknowledged that many of his views were similar to those who put forward a plea for a humanistic approach to psychology. However he suggested that much of what passed for humanism was 'backward-wishing' rather than 'forward-seeking'. He suggested that it would be a mistake for those who wished to depart from the dehumanizing tradition of psychological research to abandon technology. He suggested that humanistic psychology should devise appropriate technologies to realize its objectives: 'humanistic psychology needs a technology through which to express its humane intentions' (Kelly, 1969b:135). This statement is, we feel, of great significance for research. There has been a tendency to divide psychology into 'hard' and 'soft' psychology, hard psychology implying rigid experimental procedures requiring rigorous statistics for the analysis of the data. Soft psychology, on the other hand, recognizing the individuality of the person, often adopts the extreme position of rejecting any systematic attempt to explore this individuality. Kelly's theory and methodology offers a bridge between these divisions which are in themselves arbitrary. Hudson (1968: 84) noted the attractiveness of work such as that of Kelly in this respect: 'It frees the experimenter from the rival hegemonies of the billiard ball and putty.'

A 'thoughtful' approach to teaching

In Chapter 1 we discussed the relationships between particular assumptions of psychological development and philosophies about the nature of knowledge and suggested that these assumptions play a part in determining teaching practice in the workplace, schools and in colleges. In addition, these assumptions provide a framework for various perspectives on educational research. Clark (1995: 48) advocates a 'thoughtful' approach to teaching and proposes that educational research can be seen as 'research in the service of teaching'. Although discussing the education of children, his words have salience for much education that takes place within a professional context. He suggested that:

> when we look at teaching from the child's point of view the buzzing confusion of researchers' claims and counter claims fall silent. Looking at the faces of particular flesh and blood children, in their need and vulnerability, in their optimism and eagerness, we begin to become humble. For these children, all children, are subjects, not objects. They are not empty vessels to be filled, not animals to be trained, not computers to be programmed, not barbarians to be subdued, disciplined and civilized. All these metaphors and more have been acted out with gravely demoralizing effects, on many generations of school children.

The work of George Kelly offers both a theory and a methodology based on an epistemological position which would place emphasis within education on personal relevance and endeavour, relativity of knowledge, expansion of the curriculum and the extension of the objectives of educational research, supporting Clark's call for 'thoughtful' teaching and research.

It is Kelly's philosophy of constructive alternativism that we feel is of greatest interest for the educationalist. If one adopts this philosophy one can provide an adaptive educational system which assumes many ways of succeeding and multiple goals from which to choose. In such an educational system individual learning styles are important while educational research is predicated on the individual's perspective. Constructive alternativism invites innovation and rejects dogma. As Allport (1955: 18) suggested: 'Dogmatism makes for scientific anaemia.' Rather than be bound by the 'tyranny of fact' and tradition, a personal construct approach to *education, research and transformative practice* would suggest a forward thrust towards recognition of constructive alternatives.

The philosophy and theory which underpins PCP is congruent with many current approaches in educational research, particularly in what is often labelled qualitative research, which has now 'come of age' (Taylor and Bogdan, 1998: vii).

Although we prefer the term 'interpretative' the term 'qualitative' has been used as an umbrella term for a variety of approaches sharing basic ontological, epistemological and methodological assumptions. We have argued elsewhere that the terms qualitative versus quantitative would be best kept for the type of data collected during the research rather than used as the label for the paradigms (Gilbert and Pope, 1984). Crotty (1998: 15) said that 'every beginner researcher learns at once that all research is divided into two parts – and these are "qualitative" and "quantitative", respectively'. He too suggested that this division is inappropriate. The division is one of epistemology. He noted that:

> what would seem to be problematic is any attempt to be at once objectivist and constructionist (or subjectivist). On the face of it, to say that there is objective meaning and in the same breath to say that there is no objective meaning certainly does appear contradictory.

We agree with Crotty's sentiments that we need to be consistently objectivist or consistently constructionist (or subjectivist). For our part we will try to be consistently constructivist. However, since qualitative research is a term still extensively used within educational research, we will continue to use it, though carefully, within this book. Qualitative-interpretative research is predicated on the principle that one engages with participants (not subjects). Our participants are active meaning-seeking individuals, whose views of the world are valued. This represents our ethic for research and our approach has been influenced by a range of constructivist perspectives, particularly that of Personal Construct Psychology (PCP).

There are many aspects of PCP that could be used in support of current educational research practice. The reader may have found others that he or she deemed to be important. Here we restrict ourselves to aspects that we feel have particular relevance for the contemporary push towards a constructivist underpinning of qualitative research.

Knowledge as construction of reality

Figure 3.1 represents an abridged version of a diagram which appeared in Pope and Denicolo (1986). In that paper we drew attention to the constellation of ideas or metaphysical commitments surrounding two opposing conceptions of research and the dilemmas faced at that time by researchers wishing to adopt a qualitative approach to educational research.

We argued that a fundamental difference between researchers was often the model of the person who was the focus of investigation in the study. The model in Figure 3.1 was juxtaposed with an alternative, the model of the *person as a machine* as a metaphor underpinning much of quantitative educational research with its emphasis on reductionism through control of variables and nomothetic large-scale studies. We will use the framework in Figure 3.1 to structure our discussions in this section of the chapter.

For this model we draw on Kelly's root metaphor *Man the Scientist* as a pivotal theme. Person-the-scientist and scientist-the-person are both engaged in the process of observation, interpretation, prediction and

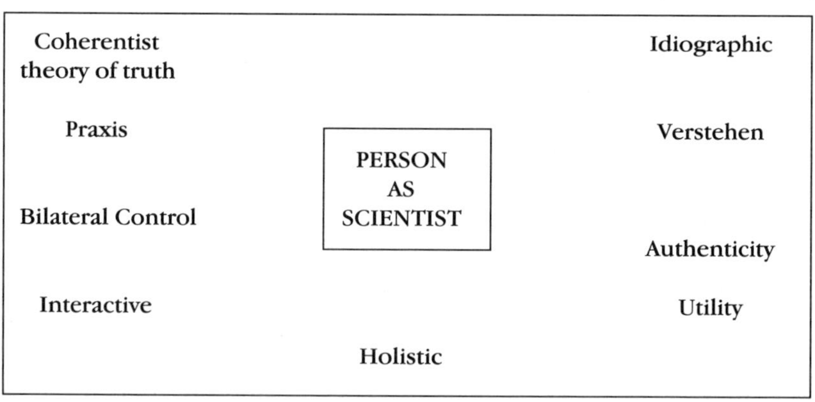

Figure 3.1 Knowledge as construction of reality.
Source: After Pope and Denicolo (1986)

control. For Kelly the questioning and exploring, revising and replacing in the light of predictive failure, which is symptomatic of scientific theorizing, is precisely what a person does in his/her attempts to anticipate events. Just as the experimental scientist may design his/her experiments around rival hypotheses, so each of us can be seen as designing our daily explorations of life around rival hypotheses which form part of our system of constructs or 'world view'. People can be seen as scientists constantly experimenting with their definitions of existence.

It is the 'world view' or personal constructs that qualitative researchers are seeking when they engage in research aimed at articulating the personal meanings of those who are participants in the research. It is recognized that differing actors in a situation may erect alternative perspectives and it is often the qualitative researcher's task to illuminate the rich diversity of meanings that participants have in relation to events or situations in their lives. *These alternative frameworks become the focus of research.*

Kelly's epistemological position was that *knowledge evolves as a construction of reality*. To reiterate what we said in the previous chapter, Kelly maintained that it was presumptuous to claim that a person's construction of reality is convergent with it:

> The fact that my only approach to reality is through offering some responsible construction of it does not discourage me from postulating that it is there. The open question for man is not whether reality exists or not but what he can make of it. (Kelly, 1969a: 29)

Since we all approach 'reality' with our existing constructions, our appreciation of the external world is always represented or constructed in the light of our current theorizing but that this may be subject to change can be a liberating thought. 'No-one needs to paint himself into a corner; no-one needs to be completely hemmed in by circumstances; no-one needs to be a victim of his biography' (Kelly, 1955: 15).

This is one of the ways Kelly wrote about his core metaphysical commitment. His notion of 'constructive alternativism' is fundamental to an appreciation of his theory. This epistemological position was a superordinate core construct of Kelly's construct system and, as such, permeates his writing. A major message is that our 'ways of seeing' reality can be likened to temporary goggles we wear to create a window on the world. Like goggles, they are subject to change. We can alter the clarity with which we inspect the world – however, in order to change our goggles we must recognize that we are wearing them!

Lakatos (1970: 104), in relation to this, noted an important demarcation between passivist and activist theories of knowledge:

> Passivists hold that true knowledge is nature's imprint on a perfectly inert mind: mental activity can only result in bias and distortion ... 'activists' hold that we cannot read the book of nature without mental activity, without interpreting it in the light of our expectations or theories. *Conservative 'activists'* hold that we are born with our basic expectations; with them we turn the world into 'our world' but must then live forever in the prison of our world ... but *revolutionary 'activists'* believe that conceptual frameworks can be developed and also replaced by new *better* ones; it is *we* who create our 'prisons' and we can also critically demolish them. [original emphasis]

Passivist views of knowledge were rejected by Kelly, which he labelled accumulative fragmentalism. He would also have rejected a conservative activist position such as that described by Lakatos, since it implies that the 'limiting cages' or 'goggles' of our constructions are permanent limitations. A Kellyan philosophy is akin to Lakatos' description of a revolutionary activist's views. Rather than see our constructions of reality as 'prisons', Kelly would see them as dynamic frames which could limit our creativity if we do not recognize the part we play in their construction.

There is much in Kelly's writing that is reminiscent of Goodman's (1984) philosophy. His constructivist philosophy is pluralistic and pragmatic. There are also shades of Von Glasersfeld's (1984:24) 'radical constructivism'. Von Glasersfeld used the term 'radical' to emphasise his vehement rejection of the concept of reality.

> It is radical because it breaks with convention and develops a theory of knowledge in which knowledge does not reflect on an 'objective' and logical reality, but exclusively an ordering and organization of a world constituted by our experience. The radical constructivist has relinquished 'metaphysical realism' once and for all.

Both Goodman's philosophy and that adopted by psychologist Von Glasersfeld have had a considerable influence in contemporary qualitative research. Such constructivist views can clearly be identified in research in mathematics and science education (for example see Novak, 1987; Driver and Oldham, 1986).

Authenticity

Lincoln and Guba (1985), in discussing the conduct of naturalistic enquiry, note similarities between the epistemological base of their approach and that of personal constructivism. It is interesting to note that Lincoln (1992: 381) now equates the constructivist and naturalist positions as models in scientific enquiry which are fundamentally different from positivist approaches in their epistemological underpinnings:

> For the constructivist or naturalist, knowledge is composed of those constructions about which there is some consensus (or at least some movement towards

> consensus) amongst those competent to deal with the substance of the construction. It is the most sophisticated and informed construction available, but it is construction subject to reconstruction, with the addition of new data input, new claims, new concerns, new issues, or new circumstances.

Compare this with the following quotation from Kelly (1955: 72):

> Successive revelations of events invite the person to place new constructions upon them, when ever something unexpected happens ... The constructions one places on events are *working hypotheses* which are about to be put to the test of experience. As one's anticipations are successively revised in the light of the unfolding sequence of events, a construction system undergoes progressive evolution. [our emphasis]

The researcher as personal constructivist recognizes the need to see the results of their enquiries as working hypotheses, potentially subject to reconstruction.

Lincoln and Guba (1985: 123) suggested that the classic idea of generalization be replaced by the notion of a working hypothesis – 'any generalization is a working hypothesis, not a conclusion'. In constructivist work it is important that caveats with respect to generalizability are given and readers are invited to assess the goodness of fit between the context described in the research and the particular circumstances they may inhabit.

Kelly suggested that in personal construing an individual will weigh up alternatives and choose a path which he/she thinks offers the best possibility for elaboration of his/her construct system (choice corollary). An important criterion was that of *utility* or usefulness of the outcome for the person's everyday exploration. This criterion of utility is also important for qualitative researchers. They are concerned to engage in research that will help individuals or groups to consider alternatives and, as a result of reflection, engender emancipatory *praxis*.

Kelly was critical of the over-reliance on psychometric methods in research. He emphasized that knowing that there was a correlational link between two variables did not help him to decide what approach should be taken with an individual client within the clinic. Kelly questioned the utility of such research in that such approaches did not lead to emancipatory praxis. Thus he suggested that there should be more emphasis on *idiographic* studies in research. This is a fundamental stance adopted by qualitative/interpretative education researchers today. Cohen and Manion (1989: 38) noted that 'the interpretative paradigm, in contrast to its normative counterpart, is characterized by *concerns for the individual*'.

Guba and Lincoln (1994) have begun to use the term 'constructivism' in a similar sense to naturalistic enquiry when they discuss essential aspects of interpretative or qualitative paradigms. Personal Construct Psychologists place a high premium on research which allows insight and understanding of the views of participants within the study. We highlighted this (Pope and Denicolo, 1986: 164) when we drew attention to the role of *Verstehen* in personal construct psychology research.

Schwandt (1994: 118) has similarly highlighted common points between constructivism and interpretativism as follows:

> Proponents of these persuasions share the goal of understanding the complex world of lived experience from the point of view of those who live it. This goal is variously spoken of as an abiding concern for the life world, for the emic point of view, for understanding meaning, for grasping the actor's definition of the situation, for ***verstehen***. [our emphasis]

Traditionally, educational researchers have concerned themselves with concepts of reliability and validity when judging instruments used and the significance or statistical credibility of research findings. With his belief that constructions are potentially open to change, concepts such as reliability were problematic for Kelly. He is quoted in Fransella and Bannister (1977: 8) as suggesting that reliability as a characteristic of a test is a measure of its insensitivity to change. Thus they say:

> the idea of a static mind is a contradiction in terms. We should look to the grid not to repeat the same results but to see, when it shows change, what is this signifying. In short, reliability is perhaps best seen as merely one aspect of validity.

Lincoln and Guba (1985: 222) also proposed that a demonstration of validity is often sufficient to establish reliability. These authors prefer to substitute other terms when considering naturalistic, or what they now term constructivist, research. The credibility or trustworthiness of data to those intimate with the situation/context is deemed to be important. Qualitative research has its own type of rigour. Aspects that are most important are the extent to which the researcher fully articulates the research protocol, gives copious verbatim evidence for interpretation and shows a concern for ***authenticity***. They have now extended their concept of authenticity to identify ***ontological authenticity*** which emphasizes the function of the personal constructions; ***educative authenticity*** which refers to the sociality in understanding the researcher obtains within the research; ***catalytic authenticity*** – the extent to which the research promotes action; and ***tactical authenticity*** where the research empowers action (Guba and Lincoln, 1989).

Concern for authenticity has implications for procedure in that it is helpful if an iterative stance is taken within the research and the researcher takes interpretations of data back to the participants for authentication. This is certainly an approach that we have advocated where the situation allows it. This necessitates an *interactive approach* where there is *bilateral control* of the process between both researcher and participant. It is an essential characteristic of action research which we will discuss later. What is clear is that the *qualitative educational researcher as constructivist will employ the art of the skilled conversationalist* (Pope and Denicolo, 1993).

In discussing his notion of a personal construct, Kelly argued that a construct had *both* intellectual and emotional aspects. He rejected the idea of splitting human functioning into intelligence, emotion, motivation etc. as was the norm in traditional psychology text books. He preferred a *holistic* stance. This holistic position is fundamental within qualitative research and is a guiding principle in the conversations held and the style of engagement to be pursued.

Collaborative participation

Reason and Rowan (1981) discussed the concept of collaborative enquiry as one of the 'new paradigm' research approaches within the social sciences. Unlike traditional research, in which the roles of the researcher and the subject are mutually exclusive, in cooperative enquiry there is bilateral initiative and control. For Reason and Rowan, ideally there should be full reciprocity; certainly there needs to be full consensus reached on all decisions, derived from free and informed debate, with respect to the research process. More recently, in discussing social constructions of reality, Guba and Lincoln (1994: 111) emphasized the hermeneutical and dialectical approach required if one adopts a methodological stance of constructivism:

> The variable and personal nature of social constructions suggests that individual constructions can be elicited and refined only through interaction between and among investigator and respondent. These varying constructions are interpreted using conventional hermeneutical techniques and are compared and contrasted through a dialectical interchange.

Personal Construct Psychology would support those in educational research who recognize the importance of incorporating, within their methodology, the views of all those involved in the particular educational issues with which they are concerned. Kelly (1969b: 132) made an explicit statement to this effect. He would tell his students that they

> should not overlook what their subjects have to contribute, for psychological research, as I see it, is a cooperative enterprise in which the subject joins the psychologist in making an enquiry. I am very sceptical of any piece of human research in which the subject's questions and contributions have not been elicited or have been ignored in the final analysis of results.

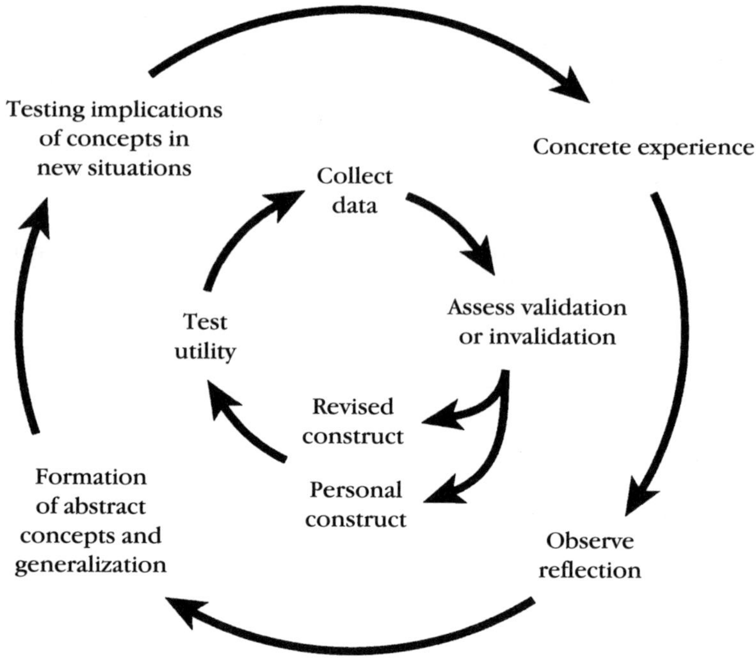

Figure 3.2 A comparison between Kelly's personal scientist model with Kolb et al's learning cycle (inner circle: Kelly, 1955; outer circle: Kolb and Fry, 1975).

Action research models particularly emphasize the participatory nature of research and the importance of researchers and participants engaging in a collaborative journey of enquiry (Carr and Kemmis, 1986; Whyte, 1991; Elliott, 1995; Fals-Borda and Rachman, 1991). Many of these authors have based some of their assumptions on the work of Jürgen Habermas (1971). Others have drawn inspiration from the work of Schon's (1983) model of the reflective practitioner, or Kolb and Fry's (1975) learning cycles. Figure 3.2 compares Kelly's personal scientist model with that of Kolb et al.'s learning cycle.

Figure 3.3 represents Kemmis and McTaggart's (1982) action research spiral. One purpose of action research is that the participants may come to a good understanding of their context and, in so doing, develop strategies for solving problems of their own identification. This highlights a parallel between Kelly, who saw the personal experiments of individuals as being a continuous process of forming a hypothesis (construct), testing it and reflecting on the outcome with a possible reformulation of the construct system, and Kemmis, who sees action research as critical education science with an ongoing process of problem identification, plans and

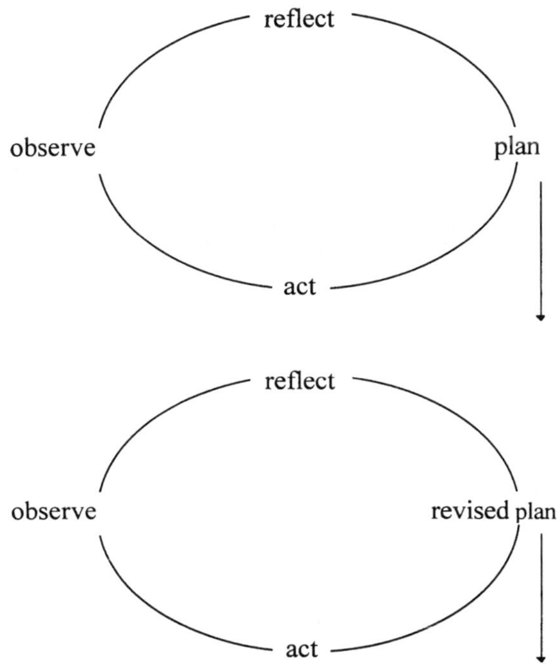

Figure 3.3 Kemmis and McTaggart's action research spiral.

strategies, reflection on outcome and redefinition of the problem.

In educational research, action research approaches encourage teachers to ground their analysis of educational issues in the evidence they generate from reflection on their own context rather than borrow from, or rely on, the 'grand' theories from psychology, sociology, philosophy etc., particularly those positivistic theories suggesting 'true' statements expressed as nomothetic context-free generalizations. Authentic contextual relevance and the empowering of participants both to contribute fully to such research and to apply the ongoing research in a practical way are of paramount importance, hence the emphasis on *praxis* (Figure 3.1).

In addition to the emphasis on collaborative participation, action researchers and personal construct psychologists share the following core assumptions:

- the person is a responsible agent;
- growth may occur through reflection on and in action;

- understanding another's perspective requires empathy and a 'conversational' approach;
- the participant's and the researcher's account of events may differ and need to be negotiated;
- participants and researchers are engaged in cooperative enquiry;
- human beings are active, meaning seeking, potentially open to change and lifelong development and are capable of self-direction.

Action research is but one method within the qualitative paradigm. It does, however, embody the values identified in Figure 3.1.

A coherentist theory of truth

We will now address the remaining notion within Figure 3.1, i.e. a coherentist theory of truth. This is inextricably linked with the view of knowledge as construction of reality. Educational researchers using a personal constructivist perspective would not be seeking to argue that their findings correspond to some absolute notion of truth. They would recognize the findings as having evolved from a rich interplay between participants and researchers and have reached a point where they feel that the findings best represent a coherent pattern within the data available. The results will often be presented with the caveat that readers should ascertain for themselves the extent to which their own context matches that which has been described in the research, with the entailed notion that results can be open to reconstruing. It is not unusual for a number of further questions to be raised at this point recognizing the heuristic value of the research in suggesting further constructive lines of enquiry.

The coherentist theory of truth, together with the other metaphysical commitments which follow from Kelly's root metaphor person-the-scientist, has been of considerable use in our own theorizing. More recently, alongside other personal construct psychologists, we have explored the implications of an alternative metaphor, that of person-as-storyteller. Howard (1988: 270) suggested that the model of *human as storytellers* may assist in the evolution of Personal Construct Psychology as a *living, viable, intellectual enterprises*. Mair's (1998: 130) article 'Psychology as Story Telling' is an important text which has influenced our current work. Mair advocated a psychology that shows more care for 'the stories we live and the stories we can tell'. We agree with Connelly and Clandinin (1990:2) who pointed out that 'the main claim for the use of narrative in educational research is that humans are storytelling organisms who, individually and socially, lead storied lives. Thus the study of narrative is the study of the ways humans experience the world.'

In our work we have noted an evolution in the techniques and metaphors that we have employed. In the next two chapters we will share the rich diversity of methods which we feel have been fruitful in our endeavour to allow authentic portrayal of the views of participants within our research. We will begin with the repertory grid since that is a technique most commonly associated with Kelly's Personal Construct theory. We will then move beyond the Grid to consider a range of biographical and autobiographical methods. The various techniques we will consider allow different stories to be told.

Both of us have engaged on research on teacher thinking. We recognize that much of teacher craft thinking is tacit – i.e. knowhow gained through experience and not carefully articulated. Constructivist tools endeavour to reveal something of this tacit knowledge. The telling of stories and reflection on information gleaned from repertory grids can make conscious for the teacher the images, core constructs and experiential metaphors that form part of the teachers' professional lore. It can be emancipatory in the sense that this telling of the story liberates an understanding of its power. By making, the tacit articulate it can be critically appraised. We invite you to consider the utility of the various techniques we offer within the book. Yours will be a personal choice. We hope we will have provided a range of alternative routes that you will be encouraged to explore.

Chapter 4
Practical considerations in the use of repertory grid techniques

> The purpose of grids is to inform us about the way in which our system of personal constructs is evolving and its limitations and possibilities. It is a way of standing in the shoes of others to see the world from their point of view, to understand their situation, their concerns. (Beail, 1985: 2)

Repertory grid techniques evolved from Kelly's personal construct theory (1955). Kelly's original technique was the role construct repertory test which he used to investigate the role relationships between patients and their families, friends etc. and for assessing the relationships between a patient's constructs about people. The repertory grid, however, is not a test but a methodology involving highly flexible techniques and variable application. Although in the past its main use has been to investigate constructs about people, denoted as elements in a grid, there is no theoretical reason why the elements of grids should not include inanimate objects or even abstract ideas. Indeed Bannister and Mair (1968) and Fransella and Bannister (1977) summarized many of the forms and applications of repertory grid techniques which have developed beyond Kelly's own approach. Examples in this book also bear witness to the variety of types of elements used in repertory grids at the present time.

The procedure has its theoretical roots in Kelly's definition of a construct: 'In its minimum context it is a way in which two elements are similar and contrast with the third' (Kelly, 1955: 61). The notion of contrast has been emphasized by Fransella and Bannister (1977: 5) who wrote:

> When we say that Bill Bloggs is honest, we are not saying that Bill Bloggs is honest, he is not a chrysanthemum or a battle-ship or the square root of minus one. We are saying that Bill Bloggs is honest, he is not a crook.

A construct is a dimension which may evolve when considering a particular set of elements (people, objects or events) but can usually be applied to a further range of elements. The dimensionality of a construct allows one to extract matrices of inter-relationships between constructs and between elements.

For Kelly, constructs do not exist in isolation. Indeed his organization corollary made explicit his view that constructs are linked with each other in a more or less coherent and hierarchical manner. The organization of constructs at any particular moment in time exerts a limit beyond which it is impossible for a person to perceive, and thus the organization of the constructs has a controlling influence on behaviour. Kelly noted the importance of eliciting more than one construct or dimension. Thus he wrote:

> An event seen only in terms of its placement on one dimension is scarcely more than mere datum. And about all you can do with a datum is just let it sit on its own continuum. But as an event finds its place in terms of many dimensions of consideration, it develops psychological character and uniqueness.(Kelly, 1969b: 118)

Many practitioners are now adopting the repertory grid as a means of entering the phenomenological world of an individual by exploring the nature and inter-relationships between various elements and constructs elicited by the method. However, since there is no such creature as 'The Grid', it is necessary to make certain methodological decisions vis-à-vis the format of a grid for any particular project. Five major considerations will be discussed at this point:

1. contract and purpose;
2. choice of elements;
3. construct elicitation;
4. going beyond the matrix;
5. methods of analysis and interpretation.

Contract and purpose

The repertory grid interview can be seen as a conversation (Thomas and Harri-Augstein, 1985). Although the form of data collection and analysis of the grids has systematic and scientific aspects, grid elicitation requires a sensitive approach exploiting the art of conversation. At the outset of such a conversation it is essential to negotiate a contract with the participant in any intervention. It is the investigator's ethical responsibility to convey to the participants the aims of the intervention and the commitment sought from the participant. The repertory grid can be a powerful instrument to tap an individual's view of self and his/her world. If the investigator/ researcher is not prepared to support a participant should he or she be distressed through the revelation of these personal viewpoints within the conversation, the onus is on the investigator not to probe too far. A distinction may need to be made between research and/or professional development on the one hand and therapy on the other. In constructivist research or in professional development contexts, therapy is not the prime raison d'être for the research or intervention. In negotiating the contract, the purpose of the specific repertory grid should be discussed between the participant grid-maker and the researcher or staff developer, combined hereafter as 'investigator' . The repertory grid is not intended to explore all aspects of a person's construct system but is rather focused on a particular topic.

The definition of purpose is important, since personal constructions on a topic cannot be gathered if the participants do not know what the researcher is interested in, or do not have a focus for the conversation. Defining the purpose helps identify a suitable element set and focus for construing within the grid conversation.

The 'purpose' of the grid is a most important preliminary consideration before the process of eliciting elements can begin. Purpose has at least two aspects:

1. What is the topic to be investigated?
2. What is the intended use of the grid information?

The negotiation of these issues is a crucial aspect of any grid conversation and requires more care than is usually recognized by the new user.

What is the topic to be investigated?

Since the elements in a grid should be representative of the problem area to be explored, it is essential that adequate time is given to a discussion of this aspect of purpose. Even in situations where elements and constructs are provided rather than elicited this is an important consideration. The elements in a provided grid should be representative of what Kelly referred to as the 'universe of discourse' which is central to the problem area, and similarly, provided constructs should be dimensions which are appropriate to the particular purpose. The repertory grid is a procedure used to help gain an understanding of how an aspect is perceived by a person. Each investigation will be on a particular topic and must be focused on an area which represents to participants an area they are able to construe.

Take for example an organization interested in collecting information on the personal constructs used in appraisal. One could say to the person who is to complete the grid, 'the purpose of the exercise is to explore your ideas about people'. However, a free exploration of the person's views of people *in general* may not be what is required. If the purpose is to obtain the person's views of subordinates and others which he or she may have to appraise in the course of work, then this must be clearly understood and an appropriate set of elements elicited/provided which contain such people and omits others who are outside this remit, such as spouse or partner, mother-in-law, friend from the golf club etc. Similarly, the constructs elicited could vary depending on the initial discussions of purpose. Once again, if the purpose is to allow the individual to express any of the constructs he might have about subordinates, this should be discussed. However, if the purpose is to explore the type of constructs the individuals bring to bear when they are appraising their subordinates from the *point of view of the adequacy of their performance in various activities at work*, then this more specific purpose should be conveyed. In this way constructs such as 'plays a good game of tennis/ lousy on the tennis court' may well be excluded – unless of course the person truly felt such a construct was relevant when appraising his or her subordinates' activities at work!

The art of conversational elicitation of elements and constructs is to help participants to focus their attention on those aspects of their thoughts and feelings which are relevant to the purpose, without hinting at, implying or suggesting what those ideas and feelings might be. A clear negotiation and definition of purpose is therefore a very necessary first step and one which has an effect on the types of elements and constructs chosen, an issue which we discuss later.

What is the intended use of the grid information?

This second aspect of purpose also has an impact on the format and procedure of grid elicitation. Examples of different uses of the grid, although not mutually exclusive, could be:

1. a conversation with one's self;
2. gathering of information about an individual's views on a particular topic;
3. a comparison of the viewpoints of two people in terms of either:
   (a) the degree of agreement between them; or
   (b) the degree to which either can gauge the other's point of view;
4. an exploration of the nature and sharing of construing within a group;
5. a monitoring of changes in perspectives.

Each of these purposes calls for a slightly different approach. If, for example, the purpose of the grid exercise was for an individual to explore his or her own views about a particular topic area and these views were not necessarily to be transmitted to any other individual, it may not be necessary to have anyone eliciting the grid from this individual. For example, the RepGrid 2 (Shaw, 1993) computer program allows an individual to sit down at a computer terminal and go through a grid elicitation privately. A similar exercise can be followed using a paper and pencil format. In these instances, the individual can choose how explicit he or she wishes to be in naming the poles of his or her constructs and also the label identification of the elements. Any codes used will have personal meaning.

Since the object of this exercise is that the process of grid elicitation allows the individual an opportunity to explore his or her views and thus raise self-awareness, the information contained in the grid is for him or herself alone.

If, on the other hand, the purpose of the grid elicitation is to gather information and come to some understanding of the views of another individual, an interactive and conversational approach is necessary. The person eliciting the grid must ensure that, as far as is possible, the intended meaning of a construct or an element has been understood. Although a person may from time to time have some difficulty in articulating a particular construct, the individual should be encouraged to articulate as clear a description as possible in order that a person reading/learning the construct can gain a degree of understanding or, as in the case of (3) above, another person could attempt to use the same construct. This is also important when the individual is required to use the same construct and elements on different occasions over a period of time, as in (5) above. Similarly, if one takes the case of (4) above, when one wishes to explore how different people within a group view the same set of elements, it is important that time is set aside for a negotiation and full discussion of the elements set so that each member of the group can identify with each one. If, for example, one is interested in exploring the similarity and differences amongst a group of teachers in terms of how they view a specific set of techniques, one should not automatically assume that the labels given to these techniques as the set of elements are fully understood by each member of the group. For instance, not everyone agrees with the number which constitutes 'small' in small group teaching.

Similarly, if the group generates the set of elements one should endeavour to select from a pool of possible elements, the set which the majority of the group feel represent items which they can construe. Without endeavouring to ensure this common base, any judgements about similarities and differences in the constructs which individuals in the group may bring to bear on the set of elements could be inaccurate if not nonsensical. The intended use of the grid information is thus an aspect of 'purpose' which imposes some constraints on the grid technique which will be implemented. One can construe uses of the grid which have as their prime focus awareness raising as representing the Reflective Mode, and those occasions where the focus is primarily gaining information about a person as the Extractive Mode of grid application.

Choice of elements

When considering the use of repertory grid techniques, one of the first questions often raised is whether one should provide the elements and constructs for an individual or whether these should be elicited from each individual on a personal basis. In its original use as a clinical technique, personal elicitation of elements and constructs was the method adopted. Indeed purists would argue that Kelly's theoretical base for repertory grid techniques emphasizes individuality and that, by definition, constructs are personal. However, there has been an increasing tendency of late to detach the technique from its theoretical base and so the use of a standard form of repertory grid in which both the elements and the constructs are provided for the person, rather than elicited from the individual concerned, is becoming more widespread. Our own approach is, where possible, to use free elicitation of elements and constructs, though the negotiation of elements relevant to purpose has been particularly useful in group or comparative situations.

Whether or not one provides or elicits elements and/or constructs may well depend on the initial purpose and mode of application. For example, if one is exploring the nature and sharing of construing within a group, it is often the case that a common set of elements is selected and provided for each individual – this could be followed by either provision or elicitation of constructs or a combination of both. It should be emphasized, however, that if one decides to provide elements/constructs then adequate groundwork should be done in order to obtain what one hopes are representative elements and constructs. This would entail a series of discussions with the type of people to whom the standard grid will be provided, so that the items selected for elements may represent a range of events which can be construed by such people, and that the nature of the provided constructs is in line with the sort of dimensions which would, in the main, be used by them when considering the elements chosen.

Kelly insisted that in order to be useful and meaningful, each item should be representative of an individual's life experiences. In some cases provided labels may be identical with those normally used by the person in practice, but on the other hand, they may be far removed or incomprehensible to particular person.

One should remember that whatever meanings words may have, they are assigned or ascribed to them by people. Thus when a person is provided with the investigator's labels on the construct poles, the meaning ascribed to those labels may not be isomorphic with the meaning the investigator assumes these labels hold. We will elaborate on this further in Chapter 6.

In summary, if one is forced through circumstances to use provided rather than elicited elements or constructs, one should be conscious of the need for extensive preliminary work to establish a reasonable selection of elements or constructs and the need for caution during the interpretation phase.

Whether elements are elicited or provided, it is important that they are representative of the area to be considered and that they span the range of items which are considered to be important in that area for the person or persons concerned.

A frequent question is 'how many elements should a repertory grid contain?' There is no fixed standard required. However, in practice, small numbers of elements may give rise to a grid which is devoid of sufficient detail or interest in terms of content, whereas construing large numbers of elements can be a very tedious exercise and thus should be avoided. In practice it has been the experience of the authors that between eight and 15 elements provide a useful basis for the elicitation of an interesting grid within a reasonable timeframe.

During conversational elicitation of the elements, the investigator may have to offer some guidance on the nature of the elements to be included in the grid. It is important at this stage that the investigators refrain from imposing their own views about what the precise items should be. However, some discussion may be needed, perhaps especially with regard to the level at which the element item is pitched. For example, one may find that the elements which are initially suggested by a person are very abstract and they may have some difficulty in eliciting constructs with respect to elements of this kind. Initial suggestions in response to a request for element items representative of aspects of for example teaching, might be Tolerance, Patience or Interpersonal Relationships. This type of element may be difficult to construe especially on the first occasion one is completing a grid. Specific teaching events, teaching materials or techniques are more easily conceptualized and thus may be more suitable for initial grids.

Having decided on a type of element, it is also important to ensure that all the elements are at the same level of specificity within the type. For example, if one is considering activities at work, one could include chairing meetings, conducting selection interviews, marking examination scripts, and sharpening pencils. The last one represents a different level of specificity from those it follows, since it could be included in each, and this can pose difficulties when comparing and contrasting elements.

The concreteness of elements is also important. In investigations aimed at eliciting constructs about effectiveness in teaching, one might have as elements ineffective teacher, effective teacher, adequate teacher, etc. However, it is important to ask the participant to think of an actual person that embodies such a role, rather than have them conjure up an abstract notion each time.

When considering the representativeness of the element set, it is important that it not only represents the universe of discourse under consideration, but also that it reflects a range of possibilities. For example, in considering teaching effectiveness, it would be important to have both effective and less effective teachers in the element set given the fact that the object is to compare and contrast in order to elicit constructs. All effective teachers would not easily lead to such comparisons. Kelly emphasized that we gain particular understanding from considering negative cases which illuminate particular aspects of positive cases.

It is generally suggested that the element set should be homogeneous. Lack of homogeneity can pose similar problems to a situation where there are different levels within the element set. Normally, the element set will consist of all people, all events, all situations etc. However, as we indicated earlier, there are no hard and fast rules regarding elements set selection. It has been our experience that, when considering significant others as an element set, one individual insisted on including the family cat! To the purist, this would not be seen as an homogeneous set. However, if a person is anthropomorphic about their cat, then this is an important aspect of their personal construing. Similarly, if the elements are all individually named family members except for one denoted 'the aunts', we would encourage differentiation, perhaps naming one but noting that, for this person, aunts are seen collectively. The essential issue must be that the person is able to construe the element set and finds it relevant.

Construct elicitation

Having defined a list of representative elements, the next step is a process of construct elicitation. In practice, it is often useful to have each element written out on a separate card. This allows individuals to physically sort through the elements and to consider them in groups of three or more, depending on the process of elicitation adopted by the investigator. Kelly (1955) describes six approaches to the elicitation of constructs. The Minimum Context Form or 'triadic method' is perhaps the most widely used, since it is closest to Kelly's theory about how constructs are actually formed. With the triadic method the participant is asked to consider first how two of the elements are alike and thereby different from the third.

When conversant with the procedure, participants may naturally move to the Full Context version whereby they can discern that there are two major groupings of the elements, one contrasting with the other.

As with element set selection, the investigator must decide whether to elicit or supply constructs. This issue has been debated widely in the literature (see for example Adams-Webber, 1970). We suggest that since it is the personal constructs one is interested in then, where possible, free elicitation of constructs should be adopted.

Depending on the purpose of the investigation, it is possible to consider that there may be at least four different types of constructs that may be central to the particular elicitation. These are sensory/perceptual, behavioural, inferential, and feelings/attitudinal. In a project aimed at identifying a professional's views of work effectiveness when appraising other colleagues then we would be more concerned with behavioural, inferential and feelings/attitudinal types of constructs than the sensory/perceptual. If the professional continued to offer constructs which are the sensory/perceptual kind, e.g. fat/thin, tall/short, swarthy complexion/pale complexion, the investigator is likely to encourage the grid maker to consider other types of constructs. This must be done with care, since these are obviously personal constructs of relevance to the individual. The fact that the individual offers such constructs is of interest to note and may be the starting point for further discussion.

The aim of the construct elicitation is to collect as many different constructs as the individual wishes to offer. Occasionally, the individual may repeat constructs when faced with different triads. These should be noted as part of the research record, but not included within the grid.

The investigator needs to be sensitive to situations where the participant needs help in 'splitting constructs'. In considering a group of three elements, the participant may, for example, offer that two of the elements are alike because two of them are *good company* and the other is *short-tempered*. On attempting to use these constructs for other people in the grid the person will have difficulty if some of the elements are deemed to be both *good company* and *short-tempered*. The person may realize this construct actually represents two dimensions and therefore can be encouraged to suggest two constructs, e.g. *good company* versus *boring* and *short-tempered* versus *even disposition*. The investigator needs to provide a facilitating climate in which this entailing of constructs can be fostered.

He/she needs to listen carefully to what the participant is offering by way of constructs. If the participants are not writing the constructs down themselves, and the investigator is transcribing what is said, it is important to retain the language utilized by each participant. The investigator needs to look carefully for signs indicating that the participant is struggling while completing the grid. In addition to the need to split, some other difficulties can arise; these are discussed next.

The individual may have no difficulty in naming the way in which a pair is similar (emergent pole) but may have difficulty in articulating the contrast or implicit pole. A climate needs to be created in which the participant is not threatened by pressure to complete the naming of the implicit pole, although through conversation they may eventually be able to find a form of words that encapsulates their thoughts/feelings. As with all forms of interviewing, grid elicitors must refrain from offering a suitable pole name! They may need to be content with a simple 'not' (the emergent description).

The triadic method can result in some of the elements not being able to be considered within a particular construct dimension. In this situation, the participant should be allowed to put a 'not applicable' in the relevant cell. This situation arises when the element is outside the range of convenience of the construct concerned. It is important that the participant does not feel compelled to fill in each cell with a rank or rating, if that procedure is used once a construct is identified.

The investigator needs to recognize that, as the grid conversation proceeds and the person fills in a number of constructs, there may be times when the person will want to change the labels given to the constructs as their ideas become clearer to themselves. They may then want to change the ratings given, having changed to a more focused or specific construct. Opportunities to change both the pole names and the ratings along constructs are important considerations. It is important to convey the freedom to make these changes. Participants may well be used to researchers/therapists using tests with assumptions of right or wrong answers. The participants may not wish to admit that they are having difficulty. The investigator in the contexts we are considering must provide a facilitating climate within which these opportunities are addressed.

Another aspect of the repertory grid that can pose a problem for some participants is the use of numbers within the grid. Kelly's original grids were done with ticks or crosses in which the person said whether an element could be best described by the tick end (emergent pole) or the cross end (implicit pole) of the dimension (see Figure 4.1).

The advent of computer programs and the desire for more sophisticated interpretation of the richness of a person's construing has led to the use of rating or ranked grids. Pope and Keen (1981: 45–7) discussed the pros and cons of the tick-cross (dichotomous) approach and the rating and ranking scaling methods.

One important consideration when deciding to use dichotomous, ranking or rating forms of the grid is the population who will be asked to

√	Mother	Father	Aunt Jane	Sara	Mr Grundy	Mrs Peabody	x
Good company	√	x	x	√	x	√	Boring
Happy disposition	√	x	√	x	x	√	Bad tempered
Etc.							

Figure 4.1 Example of repertory grid with ticks and crosses.

complete the grids. We prefer to use rating as opposed to ranked scales since, in practice, some individuals find the ranking form somewhat tedious, especially if there are a large number of elements to be ranked – they find it difficult to rank order large numbers and may be confused if tied ranks are allowed.

The advantage of rating elements between poles of a construct, as opposed to allocating them to one pole or another via the tick/cross method, lies in the detail of information shared. Participants are able to indicate the comparative degree to which elements match the description contained in each pole so that the poles represent boundaries on a continuum or spectrum (see Figure 4.2).

Three issues derive from this. The first relates to the nature of the boundaries, the identification of the poles. These should encompass the spread of descriptions that the participant would naturally use for that

	Mother	Father	Aunt Jane	Sara	Mr Grundy	Mrs Peabody	
Good company	1	4	5	2	5	3	Boring
Happy disposition	1	4	2	4	5	1	Bad tempered
Etc.							

Figure 4.2 Example of repertory grid with numbers.

construct within the universe of discourse so that each element fits comfortably at or between the poles in relation to the other elements. (For those readers with a statistical frame, this is to ensure ordinal correctness of the data.)

The next issue concerns the rating scale itself. A frequently used scale is 1–5, where 1 represents the closest match to the elicited pole and 5 the closest match to the contrast pole. This scale provides more detail than the dichotomous approach, and allows for a midpoint score. (For those without computer help, a grid, using this scale with approximately nine elements and ten constructs, is just about within the realm of human practice to 'hand' analyse using least sum of differences methods – see Pope and Keen, 1981: 67–70.) Obviously a scale of 1–7 provides more differentiation but as the scale increases so does the time and effort to rate each construct, so a balance must be struck between the value of detail accrued for each construct and the stamina of the participants.

Finally, the use of a numerical scale as a form of measurement requires some elaboration. Many researchers have been attracted to such forms of repertory grids because they have an air of both precision and research 'respectability' – the data seems to accrue the advantages of both qualitative and quantitative approaches to understanding human beings.

A note of caution is warranted here. A rating scale produces only ordinal information since the process contains no mechanism for ensuring that the intervals between, for example, ratings of (1 and 2) and (3 and 4) are the same within a construct dimension or between construct dimensions. Indeed, it is likely that the introduction of such a mechanism would be counter productive to the quality of the elicitation – compare the issues (i)–(vi) below. A simple example may illustrate this. In the universe of discourse of 'fruit I have eaten', and the construct 'soft-hard', strawberry may be rated 1, banana 2, pear 4, apple 5, but the difference in perceived texture between strawberry/banana and pear/apple may not be exactly the same, although they are in the right order. The numbers are, therefore, 'soft' and this imposes limits on the kinds of statistical operations which can be applied to them. Readers should be aware that not all software packages recognize this limitation and so apply operations only appropriate to 'harder' data. Other aspects of this issue will be addressed in the section on analysis and interpretation later in the chapter.

One is often asked the question 'How many constructs should be elicited within a repertory grid?'. There is no magic answer to this question, although there are some limits and issues to consider:

(i) The prime prerequisite is that the constructs elicited cover the range of constructs which the individual feels are important to the area under consideration. Construct elicitation should continue until the individual indicates that his/her repertoire of constructs for that particular range of elements is exhausted.

(ii) The elicitation of constructs can be tiring for both the person completing the grid and the other person engaged in the grid conversation, the investigator. One should recognize this and not extend the grid interview beyond the limits of tiredness for both parties.

(iii) In many circumstances there may be time limit constraints on behalf of either the participant or the investigator which may well impose a limitation on the number of constructs which are elicited at any one session.

(iv) For those who wish to make use of the various computer program facilities available for analysis of grids it is important to be aware of the limitations with respect to numbers of constructs which any individual program might impose.

(v) Some investigators may feel it is desirable to consider every possible permutation of triads when eliciting constructs by triadic elicitation, and may be concerned about the large numbers of constructs that might evolve if such a procedure were adopted. It is, of course, desirable that the elements are considered in various groupings but, in practice, the participant will often tend to repeat constructs and will have exhausted his/her sub system of constructs for the particular universe of discourse long before all possible permutations have been considered.

(vi) It is important to remember that the aim is not to encapsulate the whole of an individual's construct system but only that part of it which is relevant to the defined purpose.

The number of constructs which are included in the final grid will, therefore, be a result of some or all of the limits which have been mentioned above.

Figure 4.3 provides a flow diagram which may help the reader to capture the essence of the ebb and flow that may occur during the grid elicitation. It is provided as a guide only and should not be seen as a rigid formula.

Beyond the matrix

So far we have considered element and construct selection and issues that may occur when asking the person to describe the elements along the construct dimension. Constructivist investigators adopt an hermeneutic approach and the art of the repertory grid elicitation should encourage

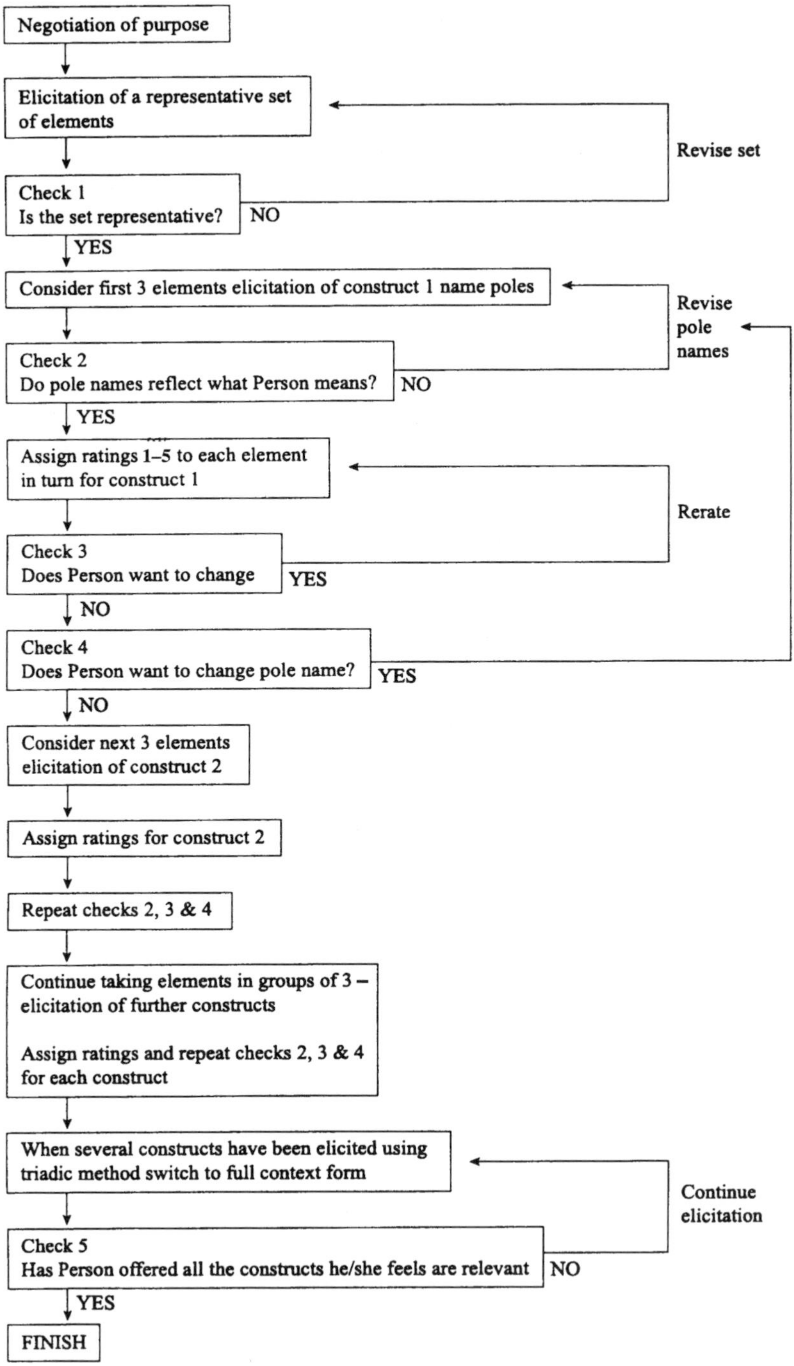

Figure 4.3 Flow diagram for grid elicitation.

such exploration. One way in which individual constructions are refined is through iterative interactions with the constructs listed. One example is through the use of laddering. Laddering can either be used as a grid is being elicited, when it is completed, or after is has been analysed. During completion, laddering is used when the investigator or participant feels it would be helpful to push the level of construing to a different plane. For example, in considering effectiveness in teaching, the participant may offer a construct *punctual* v. *does not turn up to class on time*. It may be informative to ask the participant which is more important, being punctual or not turning up on time, and '*why*'. The participant may then offer *It is important to be punctual because the teacher demonstrates commitment to the students versus uncommitted to students*. Continuing to ask to ladder up with the question 'why?' may result in superordinate constructs which identify critical dimensions of the person's value system regarding effective teaching.

The opposite process of laddering down (sometimes called pyramiding in other texts) can also be useful. Consider the overarching construct *effective* v. *ineffective*. When asked to say *what* it is about the effective teacher that is important, the individual may ladder down through such constructs as *commitment to students*, and *aspects of punctuality*. This gives information about how effectiveness can be recognized.

In reviewing a completed grid, the participant or investigator may wish to ladder one or more of the resultant constructs. When the grids are analysed for similarities between elements and similarities between constructs, it may be possible to ascertain further superordinate constructs by asking the person to comment on the connections that seem to be indicated. This going beyond the grid to encourage the participant to act as a co-participant in the enquiry process is an essential part of constructivist procedures. As Lincoln (1992: 381) notes, 'the aim of constructivism ... is deep understanding that is directed towards reconstructions of previously held constructions'. The participants' commentary on their grids provides a fruitful vehicle for such deep understanding. The joint exploration and discussion of grid data is, in our opinion, extremely important. The investigator should not reply on his/her interpretations alone. We will return to this issue later on.

Two further suggestions are relevant at this stage. The assigning of elements to one or other of the construct poles in no way, of itself, indicates which pole of the construct the individual prefers. The investigator may wish to collect such information by having the participant mark the grid form in such a way that this is indicated, by a rank order of preference for example. Likewise, one cannot automatically infer which of the constructs the person finds the most important for the purpose under consideration. One can ask the person to rank order the constructs in terms of importance by, for example, picking out the five most important constructs from the grid and rank ordering them. These are but two examples of where it is important to extend the discussion around the grid in order to maximize its potential.

So far, we have discussed issues that may arise when eliciting a grid on a one to one basis. However, a number of studies using repertory grids have used group grid elicitation. This often arises when the investigator wishes to or has to collect a large number of grids from a group of participants on one occasion. We have already identified the fact that it is important to elicit elements that can be personally construed. If the aims of the intervention are such that it is necessary to have the same element set in order to facilitate comparison between grids, then it is important to allow sufficient time for the negotiation of the element set among the group of participants. For example, if one was interested in teachers' thinking regarding appropriate methods for teaching, it would be important to recognize that not all teachers in the group may share the same wide range of teaching techniques that they can construe. There may need to be some negotiation of the final set that goes in the grid or the investigator would have to have a dual approach where there is the negotiated set plus a personal set. Denicolo in Kalekin-Fishman and Walker (1996) provided some useful examples of these techniques in practice.

Of equal importance is the recognition that, on a one-to-one basis, one gains the opportunity to have a full conversation with the individual regarding the meanings of the constructs and can tape-record this discussion. This material provides valuable contextual information that can be lost in group work. Another difficulty with group elicitation is that it is difficult to help each individual grid-maker to split constructs or to cope with a situation where 'not applicable' may be most relevant. The investigator may need to discuss these while circulating amongst the group while the grids are being completed. Of course, these conversations with individuals may be overheard and therefore there is a potential danger of people writing down constructs that they overhear rather than focusing on their own. If such circulation among the group does not take place, one can often find oneself in the position of collecting incomplete grid data, say with empty cells, and therefore it is extremely difficult to utilize these within an intervention. (Practical hint: one method of handling the empty cells would be to give these a rating of '3' if one was using a five point scale. However, this does not truly reflect what the person was actually thinking at the time of construction.)

It is possible to collect data from grids through a postal survey technique. However, very explicit instructions regarding filling in the grid should be given and, once again, one loses much of the richness of the grid conversation if one uses such an approach. Such grids may give some indication of the views of individuals but a conversational approach will provide a much richer data base and a firmer ground for interpretation, so again the intended use of the grid information should be taken into consideration when making methodological choices.

The grid technique provides a flexible methodology and used with sensitivity can provide illuminating material regarding professional thinking. As indicated above, there could be a variety of data collection methods and it is part of the investigator's craft to decide which is appropriate for the problem under review.

The next section will consider analysis and interpretation of grid material.

Analysis and interpretation

Once elements and constructs have been elicited, and perhaps assigned ratings, the result is a matrix which is open to several different types of analyses. One possibility is a content analysis of the types of constructs offered which is based upon assumptions about the similarities of meaning of the constructs, as indicated by the verbal labels used. A visual inspection of the similarities of pattern between rows and between columns of ratings will give some indication of possible relationships between constructs and between elements in the grid.

The type of analysis chosen will depend on the purpose of the study and the practical feasibility of implementing particular analyses. At this stage we would like to offer some initial comments.

Although there is much to be gained by considering the raw data of a grid and visually or manually extracting relationships from it, the advent of computer program packages for the analysis of grids allows for the ready extraction of the simple formal structural relationships between elements, or between constructs, which may be obscured by the detailed raw data matrix.

Traditional methods of grid analysis have been factor analysis and principal component analysis (Slater, 1977). These analyses are based on two matrices of similarity measures – an element matrix which includes the measure of similarity of every element with every other element, and the construct matrix which shows the measures of similarity between all pairs of constructs. These measures of similarity are viewed as distances in space or dimensions. As these matrices get larger one may have difficulty conceptualizing the geometry of a n-I dimensional space which might maximally require n-I dimensions. Factor analysis extracts the major dimensions or factors and then proceeds to describe each item by defining its position along each dimension, thus yielding factor loadings. Most matrices can thus be expressed as a series of factor loadings which are significantly less in number than the similarity measures in the original matrix. The usual procedure is to consider this 'simplified' expression of the raw data and place a label on the major factors.

Although this method is widely used it has some drawbacks. First, the different forms of mathematical 'pushing and shoving' can isolate different dimensions or factors. Secondly, we feel it is presumptuous for the investigator to name the factors; we consider it best to allow the participant to be involved in this process. Thirdly, it would seem that some people find it difficult to conceptualize or experience their construct system as a series of co-ordinate reference points along a limited set of axes. They find it difficult to conceptualize what has been done to their original data in order to arrive at this reductionist mapping of their system.

Cluster analysis also works with the two similarity matrices but instead of extracting the major factors, groups or clusters of similar items are extracted and the patterning of the original data can be exhibited. FOCUS, see Shaw (1993), is based on a type of non-inclusive two-way cluster analysis. This program produces a linear re-ordering of the elements to highlight similarities in the way in which they are construed and also re-orders the constructs in a similar fashion. Analysis of grids, whether one uses manual or computer methods, will give a structure to the original responses which can be the basis for valuable further discussion with the individuals concerned.

The reader can obtain more detail on FOCUS and principal components in Pope and Keen (1981), on a variety of computer programs in Shaw (1980), on principal components and *INGRID* in Slater (1977) and in Fransella and Bannister (1977). Stewart and Stewart (1981: 65) gave a useful table which indicates seven of the differences between cluster analysis and principal component analysis. Three of these are worth summarizing here:

1. *Cluster analysis* Throws away no detail of the relationships between elements/ constructs in its visual presentation of the data. *Principal component analysis*: Throws away some details of the relationships between elements/constructs in its visual presentation of the data.
2. *Cluster analysis* Uses non-parametric statistics on the data, that is, treats 4 as more than 2 and less than 5, but makes no assumptions about the absolute size of the differences. *Principal component analysis*: Uses parametric statistics on the data, that is, assumes that the distance between 5 and 4, and 4 and 3 are equal, and that a score of 4 on a construct indicates twice a score of 2. This is seldom likely to be the case.

3. *Cluster analysis* Relatively easy to demonstrate what the computer has done to get from the Grid to the map. *Principal component analysis*: Rather more difficult to demonstrate what the computer has done to get from the Grid to the map.

We prefer the use of cluster analysis, particularly because of the three points given above. Here we will show a variety of analyses using data from our research on teachers' views of teaching effectiveness.

The level of the analysis which one conducts with the grid data depends on the purpose of the intervention. In our research on teachers' views of teaching effectiveness, at one level we were able to identify, through content analysis, a range of recurrent themes amongst the teachers we studied. Themes emerged such as time management, listening skills, integrity, ability to cooperate within a team, administrative skills, pastoral care skills, instructional skills, and a variety of 'personality' characteristics, e.g. *adaptable* versus *rigid*, and *approachable* versus *stand-offish*.

Although, in our research we have often collected full grids, including ratings, at other times we have conducted studies using the triadic method without ratings in order to elicit constructs and then used content analysis to identify the themes that teachers within particular groups have deemed to be important for the issue under consideration.

However, if one does use full rating, the grid throws up a wealth of data and there can be a danger of being overwhelmed by it. The computer helps to structure the information, but the investigator still is left with the task of interpreting the outcome. We have already indicated above that we prefer to use cluster analysis to analyse the data from our rated grids. In one of our studies our purpose was to encourage student teachers to articulate their views regarding effectiveness in teaching and then to explore the extent to which they see themselves as similar to or different from their current constructions of 'an expert teacher'. For staff development purposes, while one can utilize the whole of the grid, it was particularly instructive for each of the students to consider a part of the grid where they could compare themselves with both the expert teacher and the worst teacher they knew.

Figure 4.4 shows a portion of L–'s grid, in which one can see that she sees herself as more like the expert teacher than the worst teacher she could remember. However, there are some areas where she sees herself as different from the expert teacher; particularly in terms of her oral presentation skills, she sees herself more towards *mumbles to the blackboard*, and also she is still not possessing sufficient *reflective skills* or *time management skills* and still needs *more experimentation with a variety of teaching methods*. One can also note that, for example, she sees herself

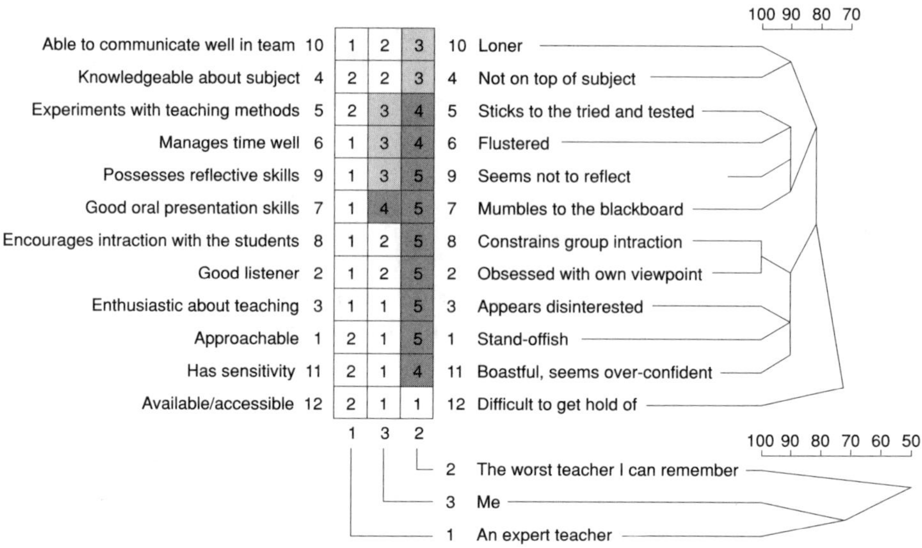

Figure 4.4 Portion of student teacher L–'s grid.

as more ***available/accessible*** as a student teacher than the expert teacher. She indicated in conversation around the grid that she recognized that there may be a limit to accessibility and availability and that teachers need to accept this, and this would link with their ability to manage time more effectively.

Most grid studies, however, utilize the full grid. Figure 4.5 shows the complete grid for the student teacher L– and one is able to see the fact that, at the moment, she is somewhat isolated from the rest of the elements in the grid – see element number 10 in the dendogram attached to the grid at the top. She does, however, veer towards the 'good or expert' teacher group. The poorer teachers are in a separate cluster. One can clearly see from inspecting the actual pattern within the grid where these poor versus expert teachers fall in her construing. The constructs also give a good indication of her current values regarding effectiveness in teaching. You will note some of the themes we alluded to earlier. One can see certain connections within her constructs, e.g. teachers she rates as being good listeners are also rated as encouraging interaction with the students. The construct ***stand-offish*** versus ***approachable*** is an isolated 'personality characteristic' not particularly linked with any skills aspect of teaching. The cluster 'possesses reflective skills, good listener, encourages interaction with students, and enthusiastic about teaching' was seen by L– as being those aspects which she felt were particularly connected with effectiveness in teaching.

One of the reasons why we prefer the FOCUS program, is that it allows the initial data to be retained and the patterns explored.

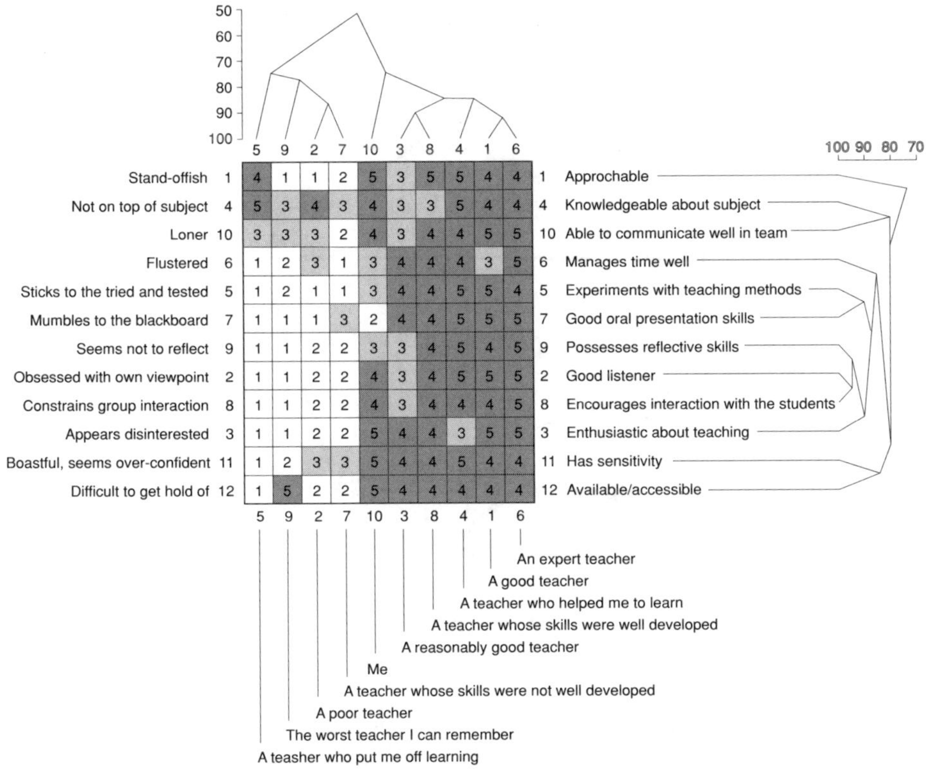

Figure 4.5 Student teacher L–'s complete grid.

In our own research we have been particularly interested in Action Research with student teachers intending to work in a variety of professional contexts and, as part of our work, we have often encouraged such students to compare theirs with others' grids and see the significance of the similarities and differences between their grids. Having the full FOCUS grids available for discussions in pairs and within groups leads to further rich data that can be utilized for research purposes.

The SOCIOGRID analysis allows the researcher to compare grids and identify some of the structural similarities between grids of various participants within the group. The similarity is based on how the participants have rated the elements on each of their constructs. (Shaw, 1980) Figure 4.6 – demonstrates this, this socionet indicating that two students, CC and SPe, were isolates. The content of their grid and the way they saw effectiveness was atypical of the rest of the group. The arrows between individuals show the degree of overlap and sharing between grids. HL particularly links with GP, JS and MC. These four form a sub-cluster. MC also links with SF and JM, and, although not complete isolates, RB and DW only link with JM's grid.

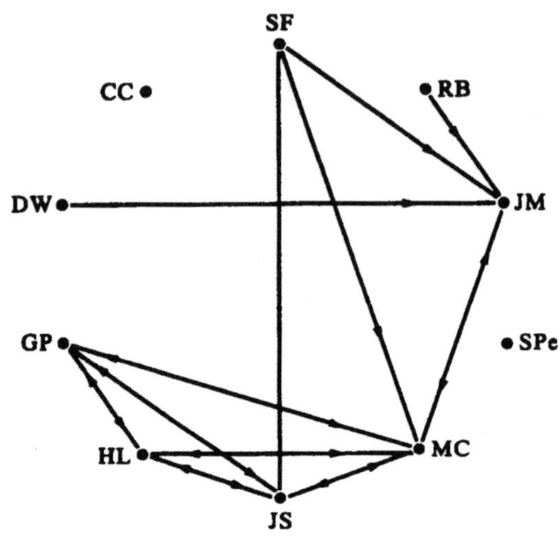

Figure 4.6 Socionet for two students (CC and SPe).

Analysis of the individual grids is particularly illuminative while the SOCIOGRID analysis produces useful socionets which give an initial basis for comparing and contrasting and sharing within a group.

We hope that we have, through the use of a worked example, given some insight into how one might begin to interpret grid data. We do find the grid a useful tool. It is a flexible methodology which allows personal meaning to be explored in detail with a public record that is easily compiled. What is more, it is an excellent catalyst towards further conversation. The focused grid can be discussed and participants can be encouraged to interpret their own grids. Figure 4.7 is a schematic outline of a focused grid.

Figure 4.7 is a diagrammatic representation of a printout of a grid with 12 elements and five constructs. The elements have been reordered so that the element 'tree' (a) shows the clustering or grouping of elements. In the figure elements 4 and 5 are matched at the 100% level (b). This means that these elements have identical ratings on all constructs. There is a group (c) made up of elements 9, 8 and 12 that are separated from the other nine elements. Element number 1 is least like all the other elements (d). As one 'ascends' the tree the degree of relationship between the elements decreases. The construct 'tree' (f) can be explored in a similar manner and the ensuing conversation often produces further very relevant information about the person's thoughts and feelings. During feedback one should encourage the individual to:

- note high relationships between pairs or groups;
- consider personal reasons why pairs or groups of elements or constructs within the total set may be alike or dissimilar;
- consider the clusters formed in order to ascertain possible superordinate constructs.

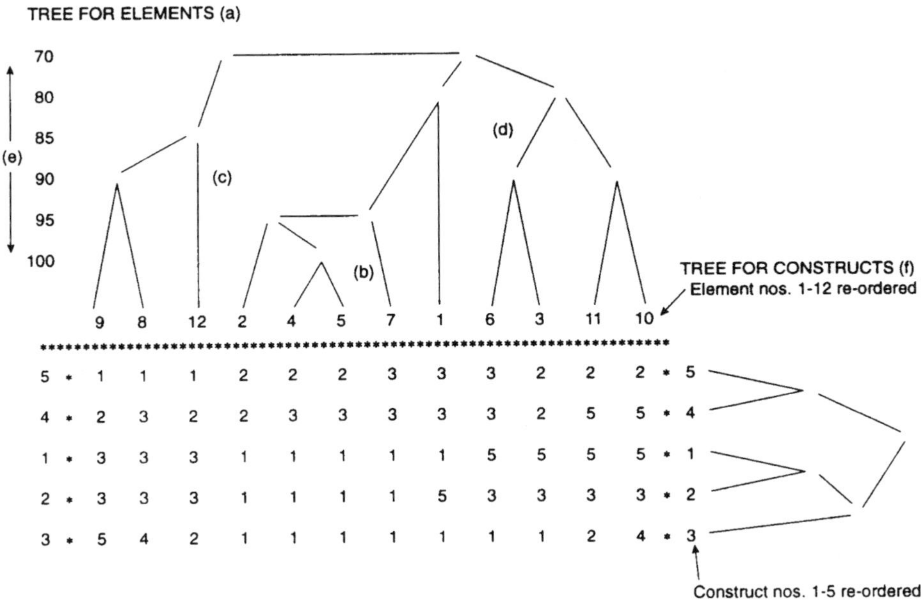

Figure 4.7 A focus grid.

However, one should be aware that, for some people, grid methodology may not be the best method of approach for certain purposes. For example, some report that they find assigning ticks or crosses, or numbers, too formal and structured an approach and thus this constraint interferes with the 'raising of awareness' which can be a major purpose when considering the use of grid techniques. For such individuals a freer discussion may be a more useful method. We elaborate on a range of possibilities in the next chapter, though at this point we note that a grid-like conversation without the formal compilation of a matrix may be one substitute.

If any form of repertory grid technique is used, and especially if feedback sessions are aimed at getting the individuals to think more deeply about their constructs, it is important to be aware of the need for some system of ongoing support for the individual. There are times when appraising one's construing of people or events can be very disturbing and thus some ongoing empathetic support is needed throughout this period. This is an important ethical consideration and we will return to it in Chapter 6.

Before concluding this chapter it is necessary to point out some other subtle dangers. For many, numerical analysis seems to be equated with absolute truth. The existence of numbers in repertory grids, and the ensuing development of computer programs for analysis, must be treated with caution, and considered in the context of the epistemological framework of the investigator.

The repertory grid, with its heavy reliance on numerical analysis, has been used by some investigators as a definitive measure of the persons concerned. This is totally unjustified on both statistical and philosophical grounds. The grid is perhaps best seen as a catalyst within a conversation between investigator and the individual. It can allow insight into some of the ways in which the individual construes the particular aspects of his or her world which is being investigated. It is certainly not a psychological test which accurately pigeon-holes the individual into a neat category system. It provides only a partial record because much process is still in the mind of the individual. We are reminded, at this point, of a comment made by Don Bannister in his foreword to Beail (1985: xii):

> At least two fair statements can be made about the development, to date, of grid method. First the grid has powerfully the attention of psychologists to the central importance of persons' interpretation of their worlds and thereby forced them to take heed of the central tenets of Personal Construct theory. Secondly, grid method is a Frankenstein's monster which has rushed away on a statistical and experimental rampage of its own, leaving construct theory neglected, stranded high and dry, far behind.

We would urge readers to avoid such a rampage. In Chapters 2 and 3 we drew attention to the central tenets of Personal Construct Psychology. We firmly believe that the grid must be underpinned by a sensitivity to these tenets.

It is important to recognize that the grid only provides information and a basis for structural/content analysis – it does *not* provide *solutions* to *problems*. Furthermore, the grid throws up a wealth of data and there can be a danger of feeling overwhelmed. This is where the computer can help. However, being familiar with the technique and having suitable analysis software should not be seen as a panacea for all constructivist research agendas nor for every staff development problem.

The process of grid elicitation is very time consuming, for instance each grid may take between one and three hours to complete, and this often places an unacceptable burden on the 'investigator' as well as on the 'participant'. Additionally a high level of skill is required to 'sense' the progress of the elicitation and to give 'prompts' and assistance when required, while not becoming over-directive in the approach. This kind of skill comes from practice and really cannot be learnt from books! The reader who is about to embark on such a data-collecting exercise will, therefore, find it essential to have some 'dry runs' eliciting grids to develop this sensitivity to what is actually happening during an elicitation session. It cannot be stressed too strongly that the grid is a powerful instrument and should not be used indiscriminately by folk who are not adequately prepared to use it.

Friends and colleagues can be encouraged to participate in practice sessions and will often give useful feedback about when they are confused about requirements or feel constrained or forced along a particular track by your comments. Listening to tape recordings of such practice grid interviews can be a salutary experience!

In our view the most efficient way of learning to elicit a repertory grid is firstly to sit in on an elicitation session with an experienced investigator and secondly to elicit some grid data oneself in the presence of a guide and mentor. We run seminars and training sessions for interested potential users. We would welcome any reader who has no '*struggling other*' who can help to contact us at the Centre for Personal Construct Psychology in Education, University of Reading. We would be delighted to be of service.

However, in the majority of our work, we feel it is important to exploit the use of a variety of methods, but still within the framework of constructivist research.

The next chapter elaborates these constructive alternatives.

Chapter 5
Beyond the grid

> We pass the word around; we ponder how the case is put by different people; we read the poetry; we meditate over the literature; we play the music; we change our minds; we reach an understanding.
>
> (Lewis Thomas, *The Medusa and the Snail*)

Introduction: in true spirit

> to the constructive alternativist the next step is to see if he can improve his hypothesis, perhaps by formulating his questions in new ways or by pursuing the implications of some fresh assumption that occurred to him when he was writing up the conclusions of the last experiment. (Kelly, 1969b: 126)

For us this quotation embodies the spirit of Kelly's writing and the challenge that is presented to all users of a Personal Construct approach to education and research. Kelly put forward his theory, his methodological argument and descriptions of tools or instruments as tentative hypotheses. Central to his epistemology was the 'invitational mood' – the presentation of ideas *as if* they might be a useful way of looking at things. He encouraged us to look at his theory in this light and to modify and discard aspects of it which do not prove useful to us in our endeavours. Thus we are specifically invited to engage in theoretical extension, elaboration and, indeed, reformation to inform our practice by extending our horizons.

In Chapter 4 we explored the use of grid methodology as one means of extending our horizons having first identified which ones we were bound by. We also raised some caveats about uninformed or uncritical use of this family of methods, recognizing that different tools may be required in different contexts, for different tasks, and certainly to suit the needs and skills of different people. In this chapter we respond to Kelly's invitation to extend method as well as theory. We will discuss alternative methods which we have discovered, invented, borrowed and amended, learnt from colleagues and students, or selected and adapted from other theoretical frameworks. As have other Personal Construct psychologists, we have recognized common themata and consonant practice in, for example, ethnomethodological approaches (Garfinkel, 1967; Patton, 1990); symbolic interactionism (Mead, 1934; Blumer, 1978) heuristic inquiry (Douglas and Moustakas, 1984) and Rogerian humanistic psychology (Rogers, 1965). All of these provide a variety of lenses with which to view the perspective of the personal so that a Kellian framework can be seen to fit within the tradition of a *Verstehen* approach, one which seeks to come to an understanding of the view of the world held by the actors in any particular situation.

Novak (1983) suggested that other approaches, those which use a 'personless' framework for studying and working with humans, negating their perceptual worlds, missed the essence of personhood and lacked respect for the integrity of people. He recognized in PCT the potential for justice to be done to the uniqueness and complexity of the perceived world of the person. We do, of course, recognize that *potential* deserves to be realized in *action* but such action may not be easy to undertake; coming to understand our own worlds is challenge enough while attempting to enter the world of others is an awe-inspiring task. Not everyone has the ability, inclination or time and technology to embark on grid elicitation for themselves or with their colleagues/ students/ clients while each of these latter may present challenges to the endeavour in being, for instance, limited in language skills (see Chapter 6) or alienated by approaches which require formally structured interventions. Equally significant in the choice of technique to explore personal worlds is the purpose of the exploration. Earlier we emphasized the need to be clear about purpose with participants when using a grid, but there will be times when the purpose itself precludes the use of a grid and demands exploration by other techniques.

Nevertheless, whether we are engaged in exploring our own or the worlds of others through research or evaluation, or whether we are helping others to understand and expand their own worlds through education, guidance or therapy, we should heed the words of Kelly (see Salmon and Bannister 1979), referred to in Chapter 3, when he urged his students that they 'should not overlook what their subjects have to contribute'. What we need are processes and tools which encompass 'helping a person to build for himself a viable system of ideas, on the basis of which he can find meaning in his own life, discover new aspects of reality for himself and help to enrich the ever-growing heritage of human experience' (Salmon and Bannister, 1974: 26). The problem is to find suitable ways to help people to access and represent their ideas or constructs of reality.

For Eisner (1993:6) representation is the 'process of transforming the contents of consciousness into a public form so that they can be stabilized, inspected, edited and shared with others'. While we recognize that any form of representation is only partial, that the nature of each form will inevitably filter, organize and transform the contents of consciousness, we suggest that each technique described in this chapter has the potential to contribute a small tile to the mosaic which displays personal meaning. The realization of that potential depends on the skill of the individual in selecting an appropriate form of representation, implementing it and interpreting the outcomes. The following sections provide some ideas, a little guidance and a few caveats. Let us preface these with a general warning: we can only present a summary here of the techniques and how they might be used. Each one deserves a manual in its own right and certainly each will require further exploration and practice. We have provided references to the work of others which we have found useful as a stimulus to resource building for others. (At the end of the previous chapter we referred to our Centre for PCP in Education. As part of this we have a Resource Base which includes the literature referred to here and to which we allow access to interested others.)

The techniques described and illustrated in the following sections allow us to explore further our own worlds and are conduits through which other individuals can illuminate for us their construing of themselves and the worlds they inhabit. As a prelude we present the words of Connelly and Clandinin (1990: 5):

> Data can be in the form of fieldnotes of the shared experience, journal records, interview transcripts, others' observations, story telling, letter writing, autobiographical writing, documents such as class plans and newsletters, and writing such as rules, principles, metaphors and personal philosophies ... The sense of the whole is built from a rich data source with a focus on the concrete particularities of life that create powerful narrative tellings.

Narrative techniques for exploring constructs

It is not our intention here to provide a detailed examination of the nature and role of narrative techniques in education, research and professional practice, nor to debate the semantics of 'story', 'discourse' etc. Others have done that ably before us and readers are referred to the compendium compiled by McEwan and Egan (1995) which addresses the theories which underpin the use of narrative in those contexts and abounds with examples of both its use and the work of others who have made it a special study. A useful text to read in contrast to the latter is Goodson's (1996) chapter in which he urges caution, while nevertheless valuing the antidote that narrative based methods provide to the misrepresentation or oversimplistic representation of reductionists' methods We should not, he contended, reify narrative techniques such that they become a new orthodoxy. In particular, he warned that stories should not just be narrated but also located:

> Stories and narratives are not an unquestioned good: it all depends. And above all it depends on how they relate to history, and to social context. (p. 215)

He went on to remind us that consciousness is constructed rather than produced completely autonomously by the individual so that, if narrative is divorced from the social context, we are in danger of perpetuating ideological pressures which influence thought and behaviour. Kompf (1999) also recognized as a major issue the limitations of selected disclosure in narrative methods of research. He made a particular point that what is experienced, and thereafter revealed, by the participant has its own character and tensions. He provided a summary (see Figure 5.1) of contrasts between the researcher and participant about what engages them at different stages of the research process. These provide subtle but nutritive food for thought for anyone choosing a 'storytelling' approach.

We will return to these authors' concerns in the last section of this chapter, having served our purpose here, which is to describe and illustrate a range of techniques which we and others have found to be productive alternatives to grid methods for elucidating personal constructs. However, to set the context and to provide our rationale for grouping certain techniques within this sub-heading, let us loosely define 'narrative' techniques as those: giving a connected order to a series of events in a verbal form; an organized text.

We contrast this with the techniques portrayed in the next section which owe much of their power to pictures or diagrams. In those the verbal accompaniment is usually spoken rather than written, as it is in those described in this first section. All of these, though, could be termed 'stories', and are derived from human experience. Perhaps we can be forgiven for repeating just a few of McEwan's and Egan's (1995: viii) words here:

> A narrative, and that particular form of narrative we call a story, deals not just in facts or ideas or theories, or even dreams, fears, and hopes but in facts, theories, and dreams from the perspective of someone's life and in the context of someone's emotions. It is helpful to remember that all the knowledge we have has been gained in the context of someone's life, as a product of someone's hopes, fears , and dreams.

If this is not constructivist enough, then we can do no better than to turn to Mair (1989: 2) who argues that all our psychological reporting is storytelling, although often of 'very limited, stilted, impoverished kinds'. He

	Participant	Researcher
Pre-activity (Anticipation)		
Pre contact	N/A	Issue and focus Development of methods
Initial contact	Thinking about being chosen	Thinking about choice
	Thinking about what to say and how to be	Impression formation
Inter-activity (Reflection-in-Action)		
Interview	Anxiety to provide desired information	Focus on issues and questions
	Demarcation of areas of disclosure	Methods and accuracy
Journal: Private	Stream of consciousness	N/A
Public (e.g. coursework, therapy)	Self-report	Assigned activity
	Marked domain of comfort with occasional stretching of boundaries	Pre-analysis of text, context and subtext
	Development of self-as-learning partner	Formation of classifications
	Enhanced ability to represent self	Increased richness of data
	Ability to discriminate more finely between and among experiences	
Post-activity (Reflection-on-Action)		
Deconstruction	How did I represent myself?	Analysis of text
Incorporation	What do my words mean to me? What does it mean to the researcher?	Determining classification
Interpretation	What did we learn? What did I learn?	Co-constructing meaning
Transformation	How am I different?	Distillation of content
Reconstruction	How do discovered differences in Self affect my life?	Analysis of findings
Anticipation	Where do I go from here?	Who's next?
Disengagement		
Residual from process	Effects of 'being studied' main point in reflective life psychological motion	Additional data

Figure 5.1 Participant and researcher reflections on the narrative process.
Source: After Kompf 1999

contends that PCP is particularly *story-valuing* and invites us to consider rewording the Fundamental Postulate and the Corollaries in playful recognition of this, thus:

> Persons' processes are psychologically channelized by the *stories that they live* and the *stories that they tell*.
>
> Individuals differ in the stories they live and the stories they tell.
>
> A story is convenient for the anticipation of a finite range of events only.
>
> A person's story varies as he successively construes the replication of events.
>
> A person may successively employ a variety of stories that are inferentially incompatible with each other.
>
> To the extent that one person construes the stories of another, he may play a role in a social process involving the other person. (Mair, 1989: 5; original emphasis)

With this in mind, let us now review some of the alternative ways in which other lives might be storied.

Seeking constructs in text and non-text documents

There are many textbooks devoted to research methods which provide detailed descriptions of the diverse forms of content, discourse or narrative analysis so it would not be appropriate to reiterate them here. (Our students have found Mason (1996) a useful basic introduction, Patton (1990) a comprehensive and comprehensible guide and Denzin and Lincoln (1994) a detailed encyclopaedic resource.) Instead we want to alert readers to the wealth of constructs to be found in written documents of all kinds: recourse to specific and special methods for eliciting constructs is not always necessary. Constructs, like the colour green, can be seen all around us once we have been alerted to them. The more obvious ones can be seen in descriptive words, adjectives and adverbs, which of course tell us about how the authors of documents, or the people whose words are portrayed in the document, see their worlds. We can find in interview transcripts and official documents, such as government papers, organizational procedures etc., similar evidence of world views.

We may only find the emergent pole of a particular construct within any one document – but this is still a clue! Sometimes the contrast pole can be found elsewhere but caution has to be exercised in linking the two without checking with the person whose construct it is.

Less obvious, but still worth looking at, is the way in which words are used. We will note in Chapter 6 that great care must be observed in interpreting language use, because words do not always mean to the user what they mean to us so that an exploration of *how* they are used in documents is as important as noting which actual words are used. Patton (1990: 394) provided an illustration of this when discussing the examination and analysis of interview data. He had found that a group of teachers all categorized the students who skipped class as either 'chronics' or 'borderlines' but individual teachers used different criteria to distinguish them. It was not so much that one teacher's *chronic* was another's *borderline*, for each teacher would categorize the same students under each heading, but that each had their own defining characteristic for the terms. Earlier Patton had noticed that no matter what the variation in ingredients or method of preparation, most people recognize a hamburger.

Further, there is usually a consensus on what fits the hamburger category and what are cheeseburgers. He suggested that what people say about them enables the analyst to discern how they experience them. We would suggest in addition that constructs can also be observed in action – so that a record of a screwed up face or a contented smile in observation notes can add to our evidence about the apparent constructs of others – or even ourselves (have you ever suddenly become aware of a silly grin or a frown on your face which made you realize what an incident meant to you – a construct creeping up behind your mask?)!

They say a picture paints a thousand words. Although in the second part of this chapter we will probe the deliberate use of pictures as aids to elicit constructs, while we are investigating the constructs inherent in public record documents, it is relevant to note that these texts often contain diagrams, pictures and other non-text material. These have been chosen by the authors or compilers of the document to illustrate points and they, too, contain evidence of what is considered important by them and of what they think their audience might find useful, or might not understand readily without this form of support. To build on the hamburger example above, consider what the public relations officials of a chain of fast-food outlets are attempting to convey by their illustrations on menus, posters etc. What significant features of the food are emphasized, and what does this say about the view of public requirements held by the purveyors? Another example comes from the work of one of our students who was investigating recruitment and retention in the profession of nursing. She surveyed the recruitment literature over a period of years and was surprised to find that although the rhetoric conveyed a developing professional image, and was couched in non-sexist language, the photographs of nurses used in illustration were predominantly of women, in poses by the bedside which reflected a more historic public view of the role. This led her to consider further how nursing is generally conveyed by the media, resulting in an overview of television programmes over the last thirty years which portray the profession in different ways. She argued that these both reflect and influence its public image. (Pope and Denicolo, 1997)

When describing roles, events (past or prospective), activities or experiences, people frequently compare or contrast them to other things with which they are familiar, or those they think others might relate to. You might think of how you would explain your job to a young, inexperienced person, or how you would describe a foreign holiday venue to someone who has never been there. To provide an image of the job or venue, you select aspects which are significant to you and try to capture the essence of them. What you choose and the way in which you present that essence is informed by your own constructs of both the job/venue and of what the other's comparable experience might be. Of course, there will be some influence too from what impression you wish to convey by your description – think of choosing postcards on holiday to send to different people. Why do you choose different cards for different people and select different views to convey how you see the context while rejecting others? How would you describe your job to a new recruit, to your child who wishes to follow your footsteps, to someone who wants you to change your job, to your boss who wants to add to it? All of these provide different kinds of evidence about your own constructs and need to be considered in relation to the context in which, and purpose *for* which, you are forming the description.

At different periods in our previous research, we have been interested in the metaphors which people use, either deliberately or inadvertently, in discussing aspects of their world. (Here we are using 'metaphor' to stand for any figurative language form – similes, analogies etc.) For an in-depth and fascinating treatment of this topic, see Lakoff and Johnson (1980). In this book, ***Metaphors We Live By***, they contend that metaphors, far from being just the province of poets and those who like to use rhetorical flourish in their speech and writing, are pervasive in everyday life, governing as well as describing our experience and actions. They invite us, for example, to consider the metaphorical concept of time is money. They present examples of the kinds of phrases used commonly in Western contexts:

> You're wasting my time ...
>
> This gadget will save you hours ...
>
> How do you spend your time these days ...
>
> I've invested a lot of time in her ...
>
> You need to budget your time ...
>
> Is it worth your while? ...
>
> He's living on borrowed time.

Later in that discussion they suggest that this concept of time 'as a valuable resource' is culturally specific, but where it exists and pervades language use it also structures how we act and conceive of time. Others too have found it instructive to become aware of the metaphors which permeate descriptions, and to consider how they represent and influence world views. (See Martin Cortazzi's (1993) excellent book *Narrative Analysis*.) In teacher training and professional development courses we have devised activities based on the work of Dennis Fox (1983). In summary, he asked teachers to describe their role and the process of teaching/learning, and what methods they use for different aspects of their role, for instance in lessons, in assessment etc. From the data, he identified four prevalent theories:

- the *transfer* theory, in which words like convey, impart, transmit information were used in conjunction with lecture-type methods and assessment of received knowledge;
- the *shaping* theory, in which words like mould, model, demonstrate, prepare were used in conjunction with exemplar and case study activities with assessment of practice;
- the *travelling* theory, in which words like lead, point the way, guide, help were used in conjunction with exploratory activities and descriptive/ discursive essay assignments;
- and the *growing* theory, in which words like cultivate, nurture, foster, enable were used in conjunction with student centred, experiential activities and assessment.

Although he found that the more novice teachers tended to subscribe to either or both of the first two theories, he noted that experienced teachers were able to apply all the theories flexibly, at different times, and appropriately, according to the needs of the students and the subject content – much as we urge you to apply judiciously the techniques discussed in this chapter. His work does demonstrate that constructs are discernible in the way in which people describe aspects of their worlds. The activities we have devised based on it follow this through. For instance, we have encouraged students early in a course to write such descriptions, to store these away and then to compare them with similar descriptions they write having completed the course or a particular experiential aspect of it and their chosen occupation. They can then discern for themselves whether or not they have changed their orientation towards their activity, what they understand by it and how they implement procedures. In addition, by noting the kinds of words used, categorizing them in terms of coherent themes and discerning the metaphors that underpin their use, we can gain some access to the shape and texture of their worlds (or the taste and smell of them, if you prefer that metaphor!).

Of course, a specially designed activity can provide a focus for exploring particular issues in which you and your fellow participants are interested. On the other hand, you may now be alert that data collected previously, perhaps in the form of interview transcripts or observation/ behaviour records, can contain information on constructs through the words used and images conveyed. Do remember, though, that the questions you chose to use in the interview, the language in which you couched them, and the observations recorded say much about your own constructs of the situation and may have influenced those who were the intended focus of attention. Psychology text books dealing with the limitations of eye witness evidence provide examples of this. One that sticks in our mind is the variation in speeds attributed to cars when the question changes from 'how fast was the car travelling when it hit the other car?' to 'how fast was the car travelling when it smashed into the other car?' The wording of your interview questions or the categories of behaviour you note may have a similar biasing effect which you need to be conscious of. This effect may be reduced when participants have a more general remit to respond to, as in the sources of data described below.

Accounts, logs and process descriptions

In education and training, the purpose is to help others examine their own ideas and practice in order to identify those which are useful and those which could bear some critical review or, indeed, those which are detrimental and need to be discarded. In research, the purpose may be to review such things either with or on behalf of others.

Whatever the purpose, the exercise should not be undertaken lightly because, to be effective, some considerable reflection on and in practice is required of participants and this process is seldom easy or free from potential hostility or resistance to change, as we have noted earlier. Tools are required to aid this reflection, especially reflection on deeply held core assumptions, and these tools need to be managed with sensitivity. Consciousness can seldom be raised without having implications for support and guidance, something to be expected perhaps in an education/training context but also something to be aware of in a research setting. Although as constructivist researchers we do not expect to take the traditional 'fly on the wall' stance, and do expect that our presence will affect the system we explore, we should nevertheless not leave our participants in a worse state than that we found them.

Thus, we introduce first the least 'invasive' of techniques for helping people to reflect on their ideas and practice.

Encouraging or requesting people to provide an account of their practice, or to compile a log of activities or to describe the process they engage in may at first appear to be a relatively easy task for them to undertake and may not seem particularly indicative of their construing. Possibly only trying this for yourself can convey the complexity of the task, and the load it imposes either on memory or on simultaneous recording and acting. Perhaps you might like to try now to provide an account of what you did on your most recent day at work, or imagine how you might cope with logging each of your various activities as they occur, or with describing the process of your work – teaching, nursing, managing etc. You, like us and those we work with, might find it helpful to concentrate on a particular occasion or to focus on a particular subset of the activity.... to make it more concrete, as we advised in relation to element selection for grids, and to limit the 'universe of discourse' to a manageable entity. On the other hand, you might be interested in the very complexity of a life activity, and its manageability. Again, purpose should determine choice although the time allocated to the task will have a considerable bearing on results! Respondents will, though, report what they deem to be significant to the declared purpose within the bounds of what they perceive as salient. One of us had a notice pinned to the office wall which said – 'I used to complain about all the interruptions to my work, until I realized that the interruptions were my work!' Such consciousness raising has its place in many spheres of activity, be it classified as ongoing work, research or teaching/learning.

We have long had a policy of encouraging research students to keep a fieldwork log or research diary. This has not been a prescriptive activity and the forms that these have taken have been as various as the students concerned. One common factor, though, has been that each has perceived the activity as valuable in some way: for documenting how their ideas and skills have developed; for illustrating the opportunities and constraints they have encountered; for providing information about the tone and tenor of situations they have been in. Perhaps most relevant to the discussion here is that they have provided them with salutary reminders of their own constructs, the spectacles through which they have perceived their fieldwork and all the participants in it, how these have changed over time and how these might limit their interpretations.

Others have used learning logs (Greene and Gibbons, 1991) and personal development journals (Pedler et al., 1986) as bridges between classroom and workplace learning. They involve the tracking of personal development through the writing up of what are considered to be influential learning experiences drawn from everyday incidents. This provides both a structured way of reflecting on practice for some people who are rather more inclined towards activity and alerts others to the learning potential inherent in what were previously viewed as mundane activities.

Participants often ask if certain activities 'count' – for instance, passing conversations in the corridor or cogitations during the journey to a venue.

A constructivist response would be that it counts if it is considered important or salient by the person conversing or cogitating. Thus, the categories of what might be logged might be better elicited from the person whose log it is, rather than imposed by those seeking the information. This is just as we advised for constructs in a grid, bearing in mind that some negotiation might preserve the focus of interest. That negotiation itself, though, forms part of the data. Similarly, negotiation might be relevant in relation to the level and detail in a process description. It might be more productive to ask for a general description of a process and then to elaborate the detail by further probing of how and why particular aspects were undertaken, in the form of laddering described in relation to grids.

Although they can be very informative in their own right, accounts, logs and process descriptions can usefully be used as a basis for deeper exploration in interview with individuals. In contrast, they can provide a means of exploring situations with a large group of people who compile them individually in their own time and then share the results. This sharing can be direct, perhaps by pairs exchanging products and then by 'snowballing', perhaps at that point only noting main similarities and differences. An alternative is that one person, the researcher, investigator or teacher perhaps, analyses the main points for group discussion. Our colleague Jon Roberts (personal communication) has used logs in his teaching of Masters students:

> I offered an MA group a foreign language learning plus logging course. They reviewed their logs and selected insights which they wrote on cards for the 'reflection on action' activity. They presented, explained and discussed these, and then arranged all their cards into thematic sets on table tops. It worked really well, producing categories of insight/issue and contrasts.

We reported one version of the latter process in a text about developing active learning in Higher Education (Denicolo et al., 1992). In a workshop, we asked lecturers to think of some specific situations in which they had been learners, both ones in which they had felt actively engaged and ones in which they had felt inhibited from learning actively. We then asked each of them to describe those situations, paying particular attention to factors which seemed to enhance the active learning process and those which detracted from it. From these individual descriptions we produced lists of 'positive' and 'negative' factors and shared these with the group. The lecturers were interested to find some factors in each list that they shared in common, some that individuals saw as significant whereas others perceived them as trivial, some that individuals had experienced frequently and others seldom or never, and some that they disagreed about in terms of which list they should be in! 'Getting negative feedback on efforts' and 'feeling on the edge of security' appeared in both aggregated columns, for instance. The group involved went on to discuss avidly and in great depth the individuality of learning and how to create learning environments which provide a variety of stimuli to suit a range of needs. Over the course of many such workshops, we were able to collect numerous such lists and review them for recurring themes. For interest, these are listed below. Note that they are not in any order of priority for it will be different for each person, depending on experience, context and personal constructs about learning.

Groups of factors influencing degree of active learning

- perceived salience of subject matter;
- the communication skills of the teacher;
- the degree of expected participation of the students;
- the structure of the learning experience;
- the social perception skills of the teacher;
- the subject expertise of the teacher;
- temporal and environmental factors;
- degree of security felt by the student;
- the amount of content of the session;
- the amount of excitement/interest generated;
- the personal style of the teacher.

You might like to consider the order of priority which you would allocate to these in a traditional course setting, and then think whether the priority might change if you were having a practical flying lesson. In the latter case, personal safety might perhaps become a higher priority.

Diaries and journals

Personal safety, or at least firm assurance of confidentiality, becomes a significant factor when asking people to share with you their diaries or journals whether it be for their own personal development or to inform research. Few people would be willing to share personal diaries compiled for their own purposes, though they may be prepared to share 'edited highlights'. Many professional registration courses, especially in the health and caring services, currently encourage students to keep a reflective journal so to encourage reflection on practice and to provide assessable evidence of their ability to engage in such a process. Obviously it is important and good practice that students are alerted in advance about which parts, or how much of such a journal, will be required to be shared with the tutor and others and about how such information will be confidentially treated. We would urge such good practice whenever asking others to share such personal reflections.(See section on Ethics in Chapter 6.)

As with other techniques and tools described in this chapter, diaries and journals provide examples of what is considered significant in a person's life, even if only through what is included as being of note, and what opinions are brought to bear on recorded events. However, it would be less than sensible to expect that everyone is equally adept at recording events, or has the same amount of time or commitment to such an activity. Since different people have different previous experience of keeping diaries or journals and differing purposes for doing so, then clarity about what is being requested in such an activity is paramount. Some people use diaries to record appointments only, others may include a list of most activities to be undertaken. Others see diaries as reflections on what is past rather than to aid future planning. Each form is informative about a person's lifestyle and experiences but each serves a different aim and set of expectations.

Anecdotes, life histories and autobiographies

We have combined these three: anecdote, life history and autobiography, under one heading to emphasize some important aspects that they have in common. Whether written by the person at their centre or transcribed verbatim from oral accounts, they provide a rich text from which to discern constructs. They include what is considered to be of importance from a complex stream of events. As Dilthey noted (see also Snakes, rivers and connecting threads, below, pp. 113–117), much of what we do or experience is lost in the complicated and intricate, if not perplexing, rush of survival in the present. Only specific examples from our past are selected out for special attention. Others may be stored in memory but it takes special stimuli to bring them to consciousness. Even when they are retrieved, they may be re-interpreted unconsciously by the individual concerned to make better sense in the current context or to suit the purposes of recollection and the audience with whom they are shared. They may be elaborated or played down in their telling, but nevertheless that telling has a subtext which allows the discerning listener/reader to identify constructs, perhaps for further exploration.

To elaborate on some of those points, it might seem that an autobiography provides a supreme example of the way a person views his/her life and of the constructs which orientate it. However, given the size of the task, it is clear that some selection must take place and that selection is likely to be determined by a particular perspective. Each of us could write a range of autobiographies, depending on whether we intend to write a best selling book or an historical account (though one may not exclude the other necessarily), whether we intend to inform or entertain, with the same caveat, and depending on which life role perspective is in focus at the time. Different emphases, examples and, yes, anecdotes would seem salient to us if we were writing our autobiographies as academics, as women academics, or simply, but not merely, as women. Just as a CV might have some things in common whatever the purpose (for different jobs or for a job as opposed to for an adoption agency), so too an autobiography, life history or anecdote is tailored to fit purpose, context and audience. It is important when interpreting such information to find out what these distinguishing factors are.

Ely et al. (1997) provide illuminating and sometimes touching examples of these 'multiple selves' that determine autobiographical work. They also describe the 'nuggets of meaning' embodied in and represented by anecdotes. The choice of outstanding event which is used to make a point or illustrate a perspective, what is emphasized and what is ignored in its telling and the language used, all contribute to the formation and sharing of meaning.

Some researchers are less attracted to autobiography being concerned that, in the confines of a research project, limited time to build rapport, seek out reflections and reminiscences etc. necessarily also limits the insight it can offer to any of the parties involved. Some researchers, and we would include ourselves when supervising higher degree students, consider that a brief autobiography which demonstrates the developing interest in a project of a researcher, the concerns and prejudices which are brought to bear, is helpful in providing readers with a frame of reference and some clues about the lenses through which the problem is viewed. It is also worth considering, even in relatively formal written presentations, whether brief anecdotes might encapsulate for the reader the tone or ambience of a research context.

Self-characterization sketches

Kelly (1955: 239–67, Vol. 1) wrote a whole chapter on this technique which we cannot better here, so we will only present the main points as an appetizer. We have already alluded to the notion that some requests for information about self produce rather self-conscious, sanitized responses. Kelly's well-honed version of the self-characterization sketch, originally for clinical interventions, has much to commend it for research and staff development activities, especially in cases in which a role relationship is sought in which the other person's personal outlook is valued as part of the interaction. He suggested asking the person to write a character sketch of him/herself from the perspective of a friend who knows him/her very *intimately*, perhaps better than anyone really could, and is *sympathetic*. It should be written in the third person, beginning something like – 'name of person' (e.g. Jo/Joanne) is ...'.

The phrasing of this request:

- permits people some latitude to use their own constructions of self;
- emphasizes that it is structure rather than detail that is important;
- allows them to make themselves plausible from an outsider perspective;
- indicates that something more than a superficial description of appearance is required;
- frees them from feeling threatened into providing either an incriminating description or a litany of what they 'ought' to be like.

We will provide in the chapters which follow some examples from practice of this technique. These will illustrate how replete with constructs, the emergent poles at least, such sketches can be, not only about how people view themselves but how they perceive the worlds that they inhabit. While these can then be explored further in a subsequent discussion, perhaps using laddering techniques, analysis of the sequence and linking of ideas, the organization of them, shifts in emphasis, the emergence of themes and the repetition of them, all provide evidence of personal viewpoints.

When we wrote earlier of autobiography we recognized that each of us is capable of providing several versions of our own, depending among other things on the role perspective from which we re-create it. This is also true of self characterization sketches. This is addressed by Millar Mair (1977) who posited that each of us sees ourselves as a community of several people – our family roles interacting with our professional and social roles – so that a self-characterization sketch might be drawn up for each of these, for the combination (very difficult to do though) or only one of them, depending on the purpose of the exercise.

Some of our fellow researchers have sometimes been concerned with one particular aspect of human frailty, asking 'but what if people lie, or exaggerate or miss out really obvious things about themselves?' Kelly did consider this, but invites us to consider a credulous stance. For the contexts in which we recommend the use of this technique, we are not in the business of scoring the sketches for accuracy – that is, our version of accuracy – we are concerned rather with how the individual seeks to project him/herself. We might wonder why anyone would go to the trouble of 'lying' or whether their 'truth' might be different to ours. We might also consider if another technique might be more helpful in stimulating a particular person to express his/her experience of the world.

Reflection on practice activities using pictorial artefacts

So far in this chapter we have concentrated on analysing documents which already exist or on textual representations such as transcripts of interviews or solicited written material such as autobiographies or self-characterization sketches. These fall into what might be deemed the traditional tools of research. These latter can be useful when the sequence of events is as important as a description of what happened.

Stimulated recall

In situations in which such experiences may be difficult for individuals to recall or when the interest is in how things were done, why did something happen and why at that time, then it is frequently helpful to use a family of techniques described as 'stimulated recall' (Bloom, 1953; Woods, 1985; Pope, 1981; Dolk et al., 1999). Some forms of this require some advance preparation. An activity, practice session etc. may be audio or video recorded, or still photographs may be taken at intervals during the activity. These are then used, as the name suggests, to stimulate recall by the examination of exemplar sections or scenes accompanied by questions perhaps about what was happening, why it was, what had led up to it, what followed and why, how could it have been different and so on. Just like Marcel Proust's (1922) madeleines, a taste, smell or recreated experience can bring back memories thought long vanished and these are not just scenes and events but physical sensations and moods as well. Sometimes a small snippet from a tape or a photograph is sufficient to trigger a flood of recollections about what one was thinking and feeling at the time. These artefacts can also be used by an interviewee who took part in the activity to exemplify or illustrate what they meant by answers to interview questions of this nature. Using the control button on the video player need not be the prerogative of the interviewer!

Nor need the stimulus materials be actual records of an experience. Sometimes evocative material can be obtained from sources such as advertising material, archived photographs or general pictures of a professional activity. Similarly they can be manufactured, perhaps by collecting photographs of similar situations or by drawing or making diagrams to represent a scene. One research student (Sexton and Denicolo, 1997) used photographs which illustrated a broad spectrum of the situations a practitioner in a particular profession might meet in everyday life. Each was capable of being interpreted in a variety of ways and participants were invited to examine the photographs and relate any recent events in their professional experience which were brought to mind by the photographic image. This is an example of retrospective examination of a real incident through a representation of it. The selection and review of critical incidents within work or education settings is valued as both a staff development and a research activity since it illuminates aspects of actual practice, allowing details about meaning and effectiveness etc. to be unpicked. Cormack (1996), addressing the setting of research into nursing, particularly notes the versatility of such techniques. The next sections deal with other examples of the genre.

Illuminative incident analysis

This technique was developed by Cortazzi and Roote (1975) as a means of investigating the thoughts and feelings of members of teams working together in the health and social services. It is based upon the notion that team development can be encouraged by frank interchange of ideas and feelings about incidents which have happened while the team have been working together. Cortazzi and Roote use as their starting point the illustrations of incidents drawn by team members. They point out that, since there is often a great deal of emotion connected with certain incidents which often blocks verbal discourse, the drawings help clarify the position of each team member. They suggest that words can hide reality whereas feelings, as every art therapist knows, are more accurately portrayed in drawings. The drawings encourage each team member to confront his/her own feelings about the incident and allow, by comparisons between drawings, each one to come to an understanding of the others' perspectives. Thus the drawings are a conduit from the non-verbal to the verbal. Revans (1975), in his foreword to Cortazzi and Roote's book, agrees that such a method allows individuals to convey to others what we sincerely feel and what we honestly fear. He also emphasizes its value in helping each of us to understand why we say and do the things we do, helping us to interpret what we mean by them. We include here an example (Figure 5.2) of an Illuminative Incident drawing produced within an educational context. The drawing was produced by a postgraduate student and could be entitled 'The Postgraduate's Dilemma'.

The postgraduate, dressed in a Sex Pistols tee shirt, was attempting to portray a problem which he encountered when joining an educational

Figure 5.2 An illuminative incident example.

research institute. Having been outside a formal educational system for many years he felt that his vocabulary was not adequate to communicate fully with other members. The 'sophisticated' members of the institute (the wine-drinking French man and woman) spoke in a language which, to him, was 'foreign'. Words like 'epistemology', 'phenomenology', 'heuristic', 'paradigm' and 'ethnomethodology', to name but a few, to him posed a problem of translation. This drawing was originally produced as an overhead transparency with which he introduced a student seminar. During the course of the seminar with its consequent discussion, the student was relieved to find that he was not the only student with this particular problem. This was the seed from which grew our own introductions to research methods courses, in which we combine glossaries of terms with opportunities for students to express and listen to each other's concerns. It also acts as a reminder to us as tutors that we must not leap to conclusions about the meanings that others attribute to experience. Analysis of such drawings requires the combined efforts of the listener and the producer of the drawing to interpret the nuances encapsulated in the lines and to tease out their full significance. In other words, the drawing in its production provides the first step in expressing ideas and feelings and then acts as a catalyst to the verbal commentary.

The use of drawings is particularly useful in this respect with children. Ravenette (1997) provided many examples of the power of this method for shedding light on the worlds of children, especially children who had had difficulty in articulating their fears and worries. Both Ravenette and Dalton and Dunnett (1992) advocate drawings as a relief from intensive verbal explorations, which can push children back into their protective silence, and also as a method for opening up levels of personal knowledge that were not previously available at higher levels of awareness. One form that all these authors have used is to encourage the drawing of scenes which record happy (positive) times and those which capture sad (contrast) occasions. By exploring what it is that makes the difference between these in the drawings, a route is provided to the identification of what 'makes the difference' in real life.

For adults who are more self-conscious about demonstrating their artistic prowess than most children, it is worth emphasizing that it is the simple, unrefined nature of the line drawing which allows it to capture the essence of meaning. It is this very simplicity which underpins the valuable contribution that the following technique also affords to understanding how others interpret the world.

Interview about instances

Osborne and Gilbert (1980) used this technique to explore students' views of the world in relation to scientific concepts. They generated a series of cards on which there are drawings representing situations in which some aspects of areas of science are depicted. Normally the cards included situations which contain an instance of the concept under investigation (say, force or energy) and others show situations that do not contain an instance of the concept. The cards were used as an initial stimulus to generate a conversation about the concept and these conversations were audio-recorded, then transcripts were prepared. From analysis of these the alternative, but coherent, understandings that both children and adult students have about the concepts were demonstrated, and these frequently diverged from scientists' views. Awareness of such alternative frameworks by a teacher is an important step in helping the students move from the understandings they bring to the classroom towards understandings held by experts in the field. An example of an Interview about Instances card is provided here (Figure 5.3) with an extract from the transcript of a conversation between our colleague Mike Watts and a young teenage boy about the concept of force.

Boy: He's forcing it on the ground ... forcing the golfball for when he hits the ... golf club onto the ball ... um ... there's force on the ball and that sends the ball away.

Interviewer: Mmmm mm and so if you were just talking about forces on the ball at the moment?

Boy: Yes.

Figure 5.3 An interview about instances example.

Interviewer: What would you say was there?

Boy: Well it's still got force of the golf club and it's still going along ... hmm and you've also got force of gravity pulling back down to the ground again.

The scientist's view would be that there is no 'driving' force on the golfball in mid air. There is gravity and the friction of the air which combine to act against the ball. The 'driving' force of the club on the ball ends as soon as they lose contact, though the boy still thinks that the ball has 'got the force of the golf club' because it is still moving on. Clearly the boy's and the scientist's views are at odds and this would be a good point for the teacher to begin negotiation between the two viewpoints.

Such uncomplicated stick figure drawings encourage a focus on the action in which they are engaged and this method can be readily adapted for use in a variety of situations in which understandings about 'what is going on and why' could be explored. As the drawing here demonstrates, what is going on now has its roots in the past and the next technique uses a simple drawing technique to explore the influence of the past on the present.

Snakes, rivers and connecting threads

Contradictory as it may seem, the anticipatory power of constructs lies in the past. In order to come to an understanding of the present we need to compare and contrast it with experiences we have had previously and use these to predict the future. Merleau-Ponty (1962: 297) expresses it thus:

> Experiencing a perceived truth, I assume that the concordance so far experienced would hold for a more detailed observation; I place my confidence in the world. Perceiving is pinning one's faith, at a stroke, in a whole future of experiences, and doing so in a present that never strictly guarantees the future; it is placing one's belief in the world.

The success of our predictions will depend on our selecting appropriate and relevant constructs and being willing to contemplate adapting them to fit current circumstance or amending a network of constructs to meet new situations.

It is clear that biography has an important influence on the constructs we bring to bear on any situation we find ourselves in at present. The ones that predominate while engaged in a particular activity are likely to be ones that have served us well in what appear to have been similar circumstances in the past. Since much of life is hectic, encouraging us to act rather than reflect, we are often unaware of the constructs which are guiding that action and from whence, in our pasts, these are derived.

Unfortunately, though they served us well in the past, some constructs may now be redundant or even counterproductive but, unless they are explicitly noticed and challenged, they remain influential in orientating our being.

To illustrate this notion, one of us for most of her life perceived herself as 'no good at Maths'; relative to a brother who won prizes and gained a degree in the discipline, her struggle to gain a mere 'A' level in the subject stood out as indicating poor ability. For many years, although she successfully solved complex equations with and without the aid of a calculator, each confrontation with batches of numbers was accompanied by a sense of dread at expected imminent failure. Our career development work with mature health service professionals, who were successfully completing postgraduate degrees without having gained a first degree, alerted us once more to how long past school experience influenced the self-concept of adults. Many described themselves as 'non-academic', 'not likely to make much of themselves', 'a bit of a dumbo'. It sometimes took considerable unpicking with sensitive interviewing to discover why they saw themselves that way and to encourage them to challenge their current self-concept.

This experience, coinciding with reading others' reflections on similar phenomena, led us to what we then termed 'career snakes'. The essence of the rationale for these drew on our recognition that constructs evolve over time and are particularly influenced, consciously or unconsciously, by formative experiences. Only by understanding these constructs by reflecting on their origins can the opportunity be provided for contemplating alternatives and breaking free from biography.

In a search for a means to facilitate this process we were impressed by an observation by the philosopher Dilthey, writing at the turn of the century and quoted by Rickman (1976: 215):

> The person who seeks the connecting threads in the history of his life has already, from different points of view, created connections which he is now putting into words ...
>
> The units are formed by the conceptions of experience in which present and past events are held together by a common meaning. Among these experiences those which have a special dignity, both in themselves and for the passage of his life, have been preserved in memory and lifted out of the endless stream of forgotten events.

The metaphors of 'connecting threads' and 'streams of life' reminded us of a method used in social skills training called the 'snake' technique by Priestley et al. (1978). It also resonated with a description of an image or construct described by Connelly and Clandinin (1984: 47) as reaching 'into the past gathering up experiential threads meaningfully connected to the present. And it reaches intentionally into the future.' Our first efforts at designing a simple process for our students to engage in was described in Denicolo and Pope (1990). It involved participants in drawing up in private a representation of their lives in the form of a winding snake, each turn of its body depicting a personal experience which influenced the direction that their career took. These turns were annotated briefly and formed the bases for later discussion and elaboration, with us, about their significance as formative experiences both for career decisions and for their personal style as practitioners. One example is provided in Figure 5.4.

We were impressed by the process for it seemed to require little input from us other than interest as the participants went through a personal interrogation of themselves about the reasons for isolating a particular incident and why it was still influencing their practice and professional identity. They reported feeling empowered by the recognition of potential which had previously been untapped or constrained not because of circumstance as it now is but because of how it had come to be perceived or construed. Our intervention with the technique had provided what might be a form of disorientating dilemma which results in perspective transformation as described by Mezirow (1990: 13–14). He suggests that our meaning schemes may be transformed by reflection on anomalies, providing as an example the housewife attending an evening class and finding to her amazement that other women do not have to rush home to feed their husbands as she does. He concedes that such dilemmas may also be invoked by eye-opening discussions which challenge presuppositions and act as catalysts to critical reflection.

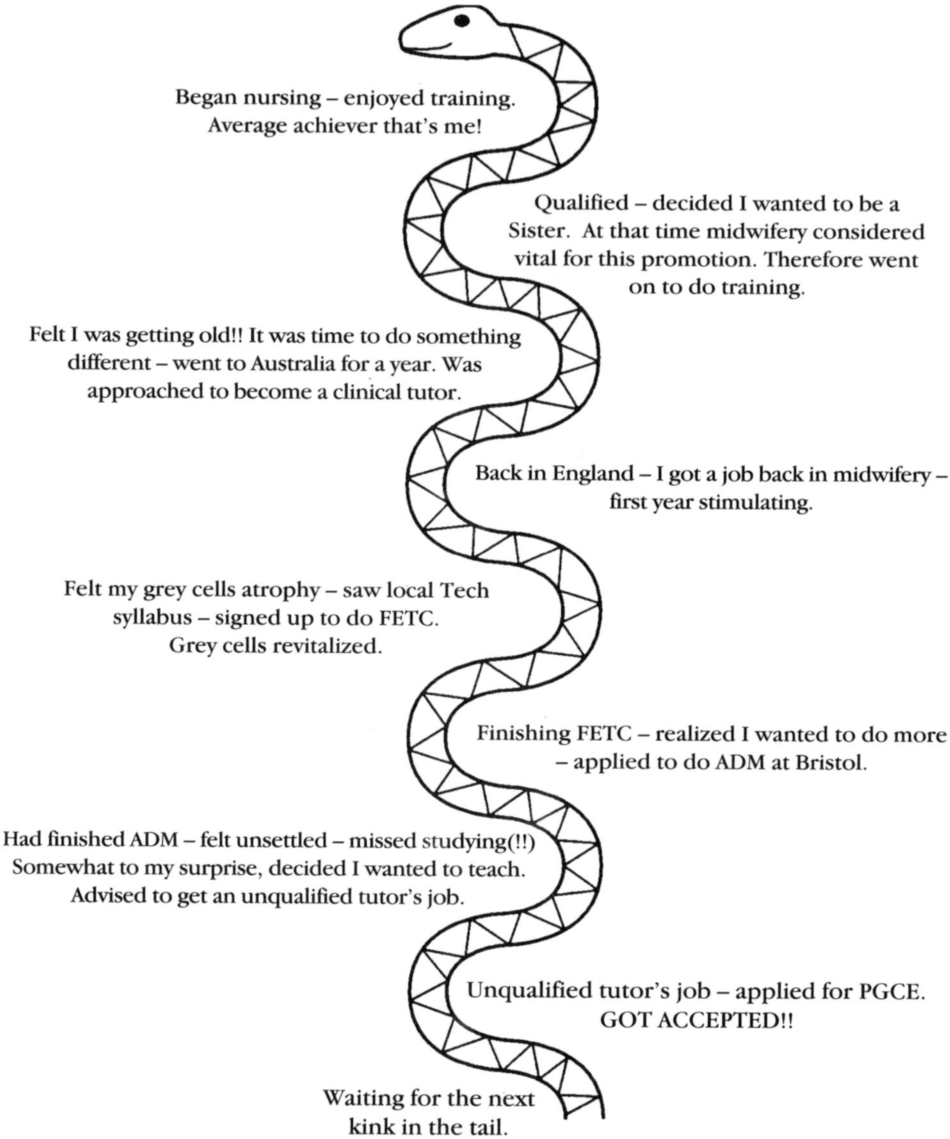

Figure 5.4 An example of a career snake (typed from the original).

In the last decade or so, we and our students (see Chapter 7) have used the technique in a variety of contexts and for a range of purposes, both to enhance professional development and to research practice. We have acceded to those who are sphiophobic (hate snakes) and used a river of life analogy, a useful one to explore for converging tributaries and undercurrents. At other times needlework metaphors have emerged with threads being composed of many strands which can link things together in an intricate patchwork – but still become knotted. Whichever form we use, we encourage the use of artful image making as substantiated by Diamond and Mullen (1999: 30):

> a vital experience stands out meaningfully in our minds because of contributions to an ending. The culmination and the path chosen to reach the ending make the experience meaningful. The quality that pervades the experience often emerges only after being represented in artful form.

As our lives flowed, wriggled on and became more tangled, we received feedback from former participants who had fruitfully continued to use the technique to illuminate their own lives and those of colleagues and students. The most affirming incident was one which occurred some twelve years after our first trials of the technique. One of the original participants who had been on one of our teacher training courses, having successfully developed her career, returned to undertake a doctoral degree. At that time we were interested in the impact that such study had on the lives of our students and several of them engaged in a range of techniques, including 'snakes', to share their experiences with us (Denicolo, 1996). The focus of the snake exercise was to identify critical incidents in their lives which led them eventually to embark on PhD studies. It was salutary that, though she could recall drawing and talking about her snake in relation to her deciding to become a teacher, she could not remember which incidents she had chosen. After she had completed the new version, a rake through old files in the attic unearthed the original. The incidents chosen to represent her life up to teacher training were almost identical in both versions. It is clear that the selection of incidents is more than serendipitous; as Dilthey suggested, they stood out of the endless stream of forgotten events.

Another technique which we used with our research students was the development of concept maps, which we describe further in the next section.

Concept maps

In 1984 Novak and Gowin introduced a technique, which they termed concept mapping, to help learners identify the links they made between concepts and what the nature of these links was. In a more recent paper, Novak (1995: 1) made more explicit link between his ideas and those of constructivism.

> Concepts are perceived regularities in events or objects ... designated by a label ... humans have the innate capacity to perceive regularities in objects and events ... and to use language labels to designate these regularities. Each person has a unique sequence of experiences and, hence, to some degree, each person's concept meaning will be idiosyncratic even though they use common labels to represent meanings ... Moreover, concept meanings derive primarily from the relationships that are perceived between concepts ... Because human beings are unique in their capacity for using symbols or language labels to represent concept and propositional meanings, I have called the process of knowledge acquisition human constructivism.

We need only substitute our technical labels, 'elements' for concepts and 'constructs' for relationships or propositions to identify common ground here, which is further exemplified as he goes on to say (p. 3):

> As learners mature in a discipline, their relevant knowledge becomes more and more complex, and therefore, meaningful learning involves seeking integration with a larger and larger framework of concepts and propositions. In turn, the meaning of prior concepts and propositions are altered somewhat by the incorporation of the new concepts and propositions.

Thus our use of concept maps has involved the identification by participants of relevant elements in a realm of discourse. These are then ordered on a page (or screen for those who are computer literate) in such a way as to demonstrate their relationships with each other. The linking lines between elements are annotated with labels which identify relationships. We present here (Figure 5.5) Novak's own concept map about concept maps to demonstrate their major characteristics.

These can be produced in a simplified form using thickness of lines and proximity to demonstrate relationships or can be very elaborate, using extended labels for lines/constructs. We have found them particularly valuable to help identify novice ideas on a topic at the beginning of a course, as a prelude to building on these. Another benefit can be drawn from encouraging learners at the end of a course to repeat the exercise so that they can make comparisons between previous and current understandings. This also serves as an evaluation for us of the success of our teaching activities.

The flexibility of concept mapping as a tool is demonstrated in the research with doctoral students mentioned in the previous section. The elements were significant roles in their lives, with the central one for this exercise being the research student role. Through this exercise we were able to share together how this latter role impinges on other roles or is influenced by them. This was by no means a trivial experience as regrets became apparent about how the significance of some roles had faded, how

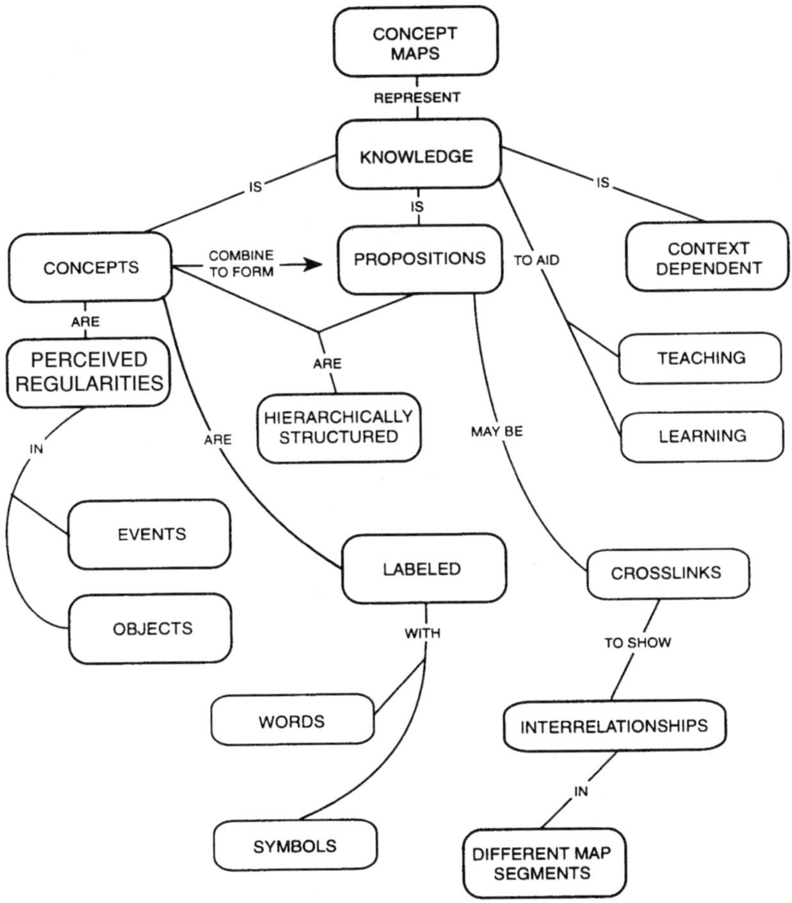

Figure 5.5 Novak's 1995 concept map about concept maps.

others appeared to require reviewing if their research role was to be successful, how yet others had crept up in importance to them as their lives changed. Nevertheless, though we gained in information about our research area, the participants reported that they too had profited in having an opportunity and means for re-assessing their priorities. An example of one of these concept maps (Figure 5.6) illustrates these points.

Lawless et al. (1998) provide a thorough review of concept mapping and related techniques (e.g. semantic networking – Stewart, 1980) in a paper which describes their application in business contexts as well as in education. They conclude with an observation that this family of techniques has potential for development and elaboration in many fields of endeavour where understanding the meaning systems of others is

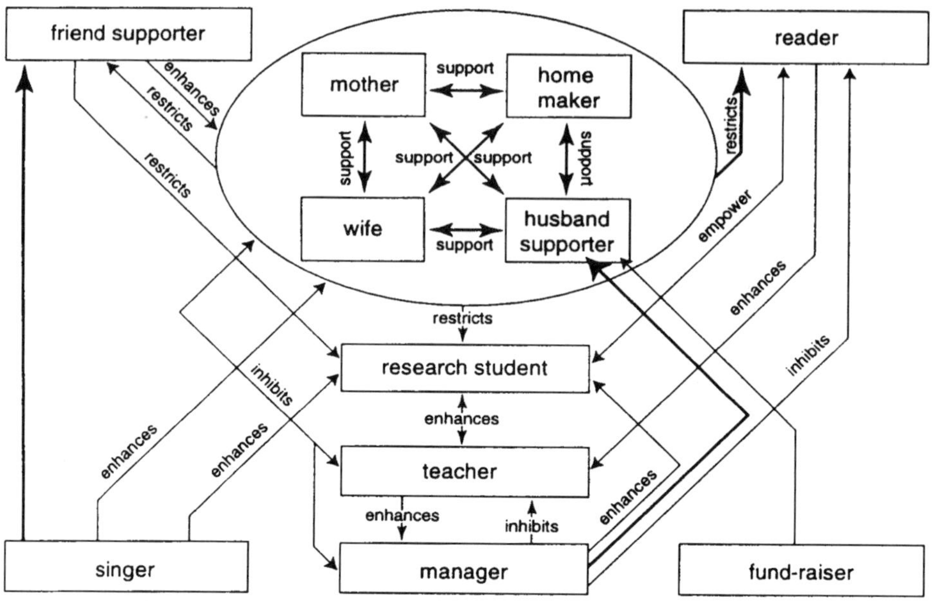

Figure 5.6 An example of a research student's concept map about life roles.

critical. We would endorse this evaluation for this and all the techniques described in this chapter but add that each provides a glimpse of only one facet of that meaning system. It may be useful to use more than one technique to gain a fuller understanding.

In the concluding section of this chapter we raise other caveats relevant to such explorations.

Interpreting others' perspectives – health warnings

Sometimes we are confronted with the cry – 'I tried that but it didn't work.' The problem often lies with the inappropriate choice or implementation of the technique or both! That is one of the reasons why we have been so assiduous in emphasizing the importance of purpose in our descriptions. It is important that a tool which is 'fit for the purpose' is chosen; one which seeks the answers to specific questions, for human beings are so wonderfully complex that we might learn much about them using one particular instrument, but not what we want to know. Just as important as the enquirer knowing the purpose and nature of their enquiry, is the requirement that the respondent is let into the secret too! This is not just an ethical consideration, as we discuss in Chapter 6, but is also a practical one. Kelly suggested that if we want to know something about a person then we should ask him/her but he did not suggest that if we want to know about some aspect then we should ask about another. Apart from common sense and ethical objections to such subterfuge, he recognizes the power of the respondents as 'personal scientists' who will form hypotheses about what is required, what questions are leading up to, what will fit the bill in a particular encounter, and will respond accordingly. (It is salutary to remind ourselves again at this point that participants and enquirers are following different agenda as was noted by Kompf in Figure 5.1.)

Similarly, we have emphasized that each tool provides an insight into a particular aspect of the person's complex construct system, so that if we wish to expand our outlook then we might want to combine information derived from an array of techniques – triangulating methods to add dimensions or to gain different perspectives to enrich what we learn. It is important to remember, too, that what we learn is very dependent on what the other wishes to teach us. This underlines the need to build rapport and a justified sense of safety and begs us to consider that our interpretations of another's constructs is dependent on our own. If we truly want to understand their interpretation of the world then it might be better if we checked our interpretations with them and would be best if we allow them to work with us in the process of interpretation.

Nor should we neglect to account for the effects of context (see Goodson referred to earlier) of both the enquiry environment and the one in which constructs are formed. Mud, which is construed practically and even joyfully when having a dig and delve in the garden, is viewed differently when attired in best bib and tucker on the way to a professional meeting. Equally, we have not all had the opportunity to acquire and elaborate our constructs freely; they may not be so much of our own choosing as they are the result of our not realizing that alternatives might exist. It is well worth considering the opportunities and constraints on elaboration that confine or limit others' constructs or how they express them. A simple example might suffice here. We cannot assume that people do not have emotions or complex ideas about something just because they do not have the vocabulary to express them. We will elaborate on this in the next chapter.

Interpreting others' perspectives might seem a time-consuming business; something we cannot nor would not deny. All of the techniques we have described do take time to implement. They also demand skill for successful use so practice is a significant factor in planning the process, and the most appropriate guinea pig to use at first is yourself. Like repertory grids, these are sharp instruments which can do much damage if not employed carefully so practice should not be conducted on the innocent or unwary. The examples we have given, or will provide in later chapters, demonstrate their power. Nevertheless, many might seem fun or illuminating for those who take part and they can be that too, but are more likely to be so when they are used with discretion and dexterity. It is wise not to assume that because participants are willing to work with you, and are likely to gain greater access to their own meaning systems as they do so, that they will find this a pain free process. Nor will you, if you try the tools on yourself. We recommend that in both instances you ensure that support systems are available and offered, either from your own resources or with the help of others.

In this chapter, although we have used short examples to explain methods, we have attempted to introduce the techniques in a relatively context free way so that the main tenets stand out. In Chapter 7 we will provide and elaborate on some applications of personal construct psychology techniques within professional practice, but first it is important to consider some of the practical points and ethical issues raised in this and the preceding chapter.

Chapter 6
Developing an appropriate climate

Cecily: When I see a spade I call it a spade.

Gwendolen: I am glad to say that I have never seen a spade. It is obvious that our social spheres have been widely different.

Oscar Wilde 1854–1900, *The Importance of Being Earnest*

In the preceding two chapters we have introduced techniques and their procedures which encourage others to explore their constructs and share them with you. The focus so far has been on asking the right questions in such a way that constructs are revealed but contaminated as little as possible by the form or style of the question. In this chapter we will address some further important issues. The first concerns reception rather than transmission problems, the latter being dealt with later in the chapter.

Listening: a fundamental skill which underpins all interactive techniques

In the normal course of a face-to-face interactive process the researcher, teacher or staff developer receives copious information, much of it through the auditory channel.

This is more than simply a process of hearing it. Hearing is concerned with the reception of auditory stimuli whereas listening involves the additional intellectual and emotional aspects which support meaning and understanding. Listening is, therefore, a more complex act that involves not only hearing but also selecting, attending to, and processing or interpreting what is heard.

> We hear with our ears, but we listen with our eyes and mind and heart and skin and guts as well. (Ekman, 1969: 295)

There are a range of things which act as blocks to listening, not least the strong motivation to talk. This can result in a preoccupation with one's own thoughts and the diversion of attention from what is being said to what might be contributed to the communication. One of the more difficult tasks within a construct elicitation process is that of keeping quiet. The dilemma is that participatory activities demand input from both parties to be maintained. The listener must encourage the flow of communication while not significantly contributing his/her views to it. Continual verbal interjection on the part of the listener serves to disrupt the flow of the process even though it may help to clarify particular parts of what is being said.

It is useful to practise non-verbal signals which convey encouragement, such as nods and smiles, while listening in non-critical situations and to have ready a series of neutral responses to interject if the flow ceases, such as 'tell me more about that', 'what does that mean to you?', 'can you give examples?'. It is important to allow for pauses for thought. A little silence often prefaces a further flow of ideas so it is worthwhile being patient to allow for thoughtful responses.

Skilled counsellors will be adept at these techniques but those with less experience need to get used to this form of elicitation before they use it for a special occasion such as data collection or a staff development workshop.

It is also a salutary experience to tape record an informal or trial interview for careful listening at a later time to check on:

- how much talking is done proportionally by the interviewer/interviewee;
- how frequently an interesting theme is curtailed by interruptions;
- whose ideas are being pursued in the interaction etc.

There is a tendency for all of us to hear what we want to hear or to focus on what is familiar to us, hence the 'cocktail party' effect when we suddenly pick up a mention of our own name among a hubbub of chatter around our own particular conversation. Care must be taken about not solely picking up and pursuing particular constructs that we are interested in or expect to be there to the detriment of unpredicted ones.

When there is a great deal of information available, listening can become a very selective process. Sometimes the taking of notes can aid listening, directing attention to what is being said, and aiding the possibility of going back to pick up points that were dropped as others came into focus. However, it is not easy to listen, interpret the message and write legibly at the same time, and the non-verbal signals of the interviewee may be missed while concentration is on the writing paper. The grid process can be helpful with this because the structure can allow and encourage agreed main points to be written down. Even during a grid elicitation and certainly during the less structured elicitations described in Chapter 5, it is very helpful to audio-record the session, if the interviewee gives permission, so that elaborations and asides that provide further clues to meaning can be extracted later.

A variety of things can interfere with a listener's ability to concentrate on what is being communicated. Such distractions, or 'noise', can have internal or external sources and may affect the sender as well as the receiver of communication. Concerns about the time, whether the session can be overheard, and anxiety about whether you are being taken seriously are examples of internal 'noise' whereas too warm a room or a distracting view as well as a busy environment can constitute external 'noise'. This means that the physical environment and the timing of the interaction need careful planning and consideration. However, even the best laid plans can go awry so it is wise to have contingency plans. If this is not possible or these fail, then later interpretations need to take account of these limits on the data.

Honest and meaningful communication can only be achieved in an environment of respect, trust and openness. This demands an ethical framework, an issue which will be considered after the next section which explores how misinterpretations can arise even when we have carefully listened to what is being said.

Common words, uncommon meanings – the problem of language

Robert Burns, the poet, assured us that by any other name a rose would smell as sweet while George Bernard Shaw reminded us that Britain and the USA are nations divided by a common language. Both writers recognized that language of any kind is merely a system of symbols, arbitrarily chosen and signifying different things to individual users. A mundane example follows.

A handbag to us is a life-support system, to our husbands it is a place to deposit keys and odds and ends when a jacket pocket is unavailable, to others it might be merely a decorative fashion accessory while to Oscar Wilde's Lady Bracknell it was a source of disdain. Thus the cry 'I have lost my handbag' has different import to different people.

Thus we must be careful when interpreting the meanings of things communicated in words. Descriptions of entities such as 'stressful' or 'fabulous' depend very much on an individual's experience of stress or astounding things as well as on popularity of usage. Twenty years ago few occupations would have been described as 'stressful', perhaps brain surgeons and air traffic controllers, whereas many people describe their work roles as stressful as the century turns. Without further exploration it would be precipitate to assume that the work itself has changed rather than the popularity of the term. In our very young years 'fabulous' was a term used to describe, say, Fabergé eggs. In our teens it became common parlance, was shortened to 'fab' and applied to pop groups, clothes and innumerable other artefacts.

The discriminating power of these words was lost, one might say, and other words for other generations are used to describe extremes. It is not sufficient and can be considered patronizing, though, to adjust interpretation of word use according to the perceived age and social context of the participant because individual idiosyncracies derived from abundant experience also have a part to play.

Some people have a rich and varied vocabulary with which to discriminate between things while others tend to use a restricted range of words. Some people have a tendency to use extremes of descriptions while others are more conservative and so on. If a person, object or event is seldom part of their experience, or is of little interest to them, then they are likely to have fewer constructs about it than one with which they are familiar or very interested in. One of us has few constructs for cars and a multitude for shoes, another has a wide range of vocabulary to describe ballet and a restricted range to describe a game of football. Such information tells us something about our construct systems, but more so if the focus is wider than just one universe of discourse. It might be important to explore in some circumstances whether a restricted range of constructs derives from a lack of interest, a lack of experience or a lack of vocabulary, or any combination of these.

Many of the techniques used in personal construct elicitations are specifically designed to help with this problem. We have emphasized earlier the importance of trying to elicit a description of the submerged pole of a construct. Finding that 'stressful' contrasts with 'restful' for one person and 'boring' for another gives us clues about how the term 'stressful' is defined. Exploring the links with other constructs helps us further – activities which are seen as stressful might also be seen as 'imposed' or 'stimulating', for instance. Laddering techniques also help us not to jump to conclusions about which is the preferred pole and why and so on.

Of course, it might be that individuals are 'lost for words' to describe something but it should not be assumed that they do not experience it deeply. It could be that their vocabulary is inadequate to the situation or it might be that they choose not to share it. The latter might be through natural reticence, because of distrust, or because they are unused to sharing such ideas or are unfamiliar with the techniques employed. Robert Browning, in 'Rabbi ben Ezra', xxv, clearly recognized the former problem:

> Thoughts hardly to be packed Into a narrow act, Fancies that broke through language and escaped.

The next section deals with issues related to the ethical procedures which may serve to allay distrust while methods for helping people to become familiar with the process and techniques are described in the last sections of this chapter.

Building an ethical framework

How we interpret our world, and how those interpretations are structured and organized is a personal and generally private thing. We may choose to give our opinions on some aspects of our world readily while others we only share with significant and 'safe' companions. Why we hold such opinions or construe the world as we do might not even by shared with close companions, indeed we may not always recognize in our daily lives from whence such constructs derive, or even that they exist at all to influence our being.

Thus, asking people to engage in processes which are intended to reveal, for us and for themselves, such intimate details of their thinking, whether it be for research or for developmental purposes, demands that a special duty of care is espoused and an ethical framework adopted.

The first aspect of this framework is the need to respect a participant's right not to participate at all or to restrict participation. An individual can only effectively make such a decision if they have had both the process of elicitation and how the data will be stored and used clearly explained to them. In medical contexts the equivalent notion would be that of 'informed consent'. This issue of voluntariness is an ethical stance on our part but is also related to the practical value of what can be obtained using personal construct procedures.

People will only share with others their version of the 'truth' if they feel that their views are respected and if they experience trust in the situation. This is why we advocate the negotiation and establishment of a contract with participants. Such a contract should involve:

- an honest declaration of the aims and intent of the research or developmental activity;
- an overview of procedures with a recognition that the instruments are powerful and incisive;

- a commitment to complete anonymity unless specific agreement has been reached about in what contexts identification of source is permitted (in group work, for instance);
- the confidential storage of data, so that identification codes are stored separately from the data;
- the planned and accessible provision of support should the process or what is revealed prove to be distressing in any way;
- an acknowledgement that any instrument/interaction can only be a partial record of a person's perspective.

The last point is emphasized by Kompf (1999: 6) in his paper 'There is more to me than my story':

> In spite of all cautions we can only see that which we can seek and perceive. What the participants see remains, for the most part, invisible to the researcher. We are allowed glimpses through self-report and disclosures made but only as edited prior to utterance by the informant.

It is clear that how partial that record is will be dependent on the level of trust developed between individuals as well as on the power of the instruments used. While we recommend the use of a variety of techniques, used in triangulation, to explore a particular aspect of the world and achieve rich data, it is also our experience that the use of such instruments spread over a period of time is also beneficial. This allows for an atmosphere of trust to be developed so that ideas and constructs are elaborated on in subsequent sessions.

A further caveat is worth raising in this respect. Unlike some means of enquiry, it is not assumed within this approach that participants will be left 'unchanged' by the intervention or that data collected on one occasion will necessarily be reliably replicated on another. Indeed, it is recognized that the act of exploring constructs encourages re-assessment and perhaps revision of them. The recommendation about support provision being part of the contract is in recognition that such re-assessment and revision may not be a pain free process. It is important that a concern for doing no harm is substituted within this paradigm of work for that of instigating no change within other paradigms.

Indeed, it may be that the investigation aims to monitor change by exploring constructs before and after a certain intervention. The techniques themselves cannot but be part of such an intervention, perhaps raising issues for conscious deliberation which were previously submerged or went unnoticed, and such an acknowledgement should be part of any interpretation made.

Similarly, any interpretation made by another of an individual's construct is, in the last analysis, informed by that other's constructs. We alluded earlier to the alternative interpretations that we impose, for instance, on specific words. Especially in the case of an in-depth study which aims to have a significant influence on practice, we would recommend that interpretations are taken back for checking to the original participants. Only they can confirm that a correct rendering of their meaning has been achieved though it is wise to be prepared that they might have developed or changed some ideas in the intervening period. The emphasis may need to be on an agreement that the meaning 'as it was meant at the time' has been accurately conveyed.

Not everyone is comfortable with the notion that their ideas or constructs might change, even if only at the peripheral level. Some people prefer to see themselves as stable and consistent in their views and would prefer not to be confronted with any paradox in their thinking. They may need a particularly supportive atmosphere and environment in which to engage in reflection. We will explore how that might be established in the next section while the following one extends that idea by discussing mechanisms for helping participants to focus on experience, especially suited for those, as mentioned in the previous section, who are unused to sharing verbally their experience with others.

Stimulating reflection

As we indicated when discussing the grid procedure, there is no magic formula, or swift means, for accessing the rich and significant meaning which people attribute to their experience. All the techniques which we explored for doing so in the previous chapter require for effective use a degree of trust between participants, a process which itself eats time, and a suspension of engagement with the hustle and bustle of work and other survival activities. The context in which they are implemented should be conducive to reflection – some physical comfort helps but relative safety and confidentiality are critical. It is a rare, and perhaps foolish, person who will voluntarily and frankly divulge their inner feelings, attitudes, beliefs and anticipations to a stranger in a busy venue with no guarantee of, or respect for, privacy. Nor yet will those meanings reach the surface of consciousness while discomfort or threat take the centre stage, or when other urgent tasks demand attention.

When we attempt to stimulate others to reflect, or to foster self-reflection, it is important to note the 'iceberg-like' properties of the process – far more is contained in the hidden portion than will be revealed on the surface.

Mezirow (1990: 13) contended that:

> By far the most significant learning experiences in adulthood involve self-reflection – reassessing the way we have posed problems and reassessing our own orientation to perceiving, knowing, believing, feeling, acting.

This cannot, therefore, be an objective (in the sense of unemotional or unpartisan) activity nor one that is undertaken without commitment. As we have argued earlier, this does not make it unscientific, but it does mean that a particular epistemological position is espoused. Both Kelly (1969) and Koestler (1976) in his article 'The Vision that Links the Poet, the Painter and the Scientist' demonstrate the similarities between the scientist and the artist in their desire to construct meaning from experience and subject these constructions to reconstruction. Further, McGee (1973:68) in discussing Popper's philosophy of science, noted that Popper suggested that there are not two distinct cultures:

> One scientific and the other aesthetic, or one rational and the other irrational – but one. The scientist and the artist, far from being engaged in opposed or incompatible activity, are both trying to extend our knowledge and experience by the use of creative imagination subjected to critical control.

McGee further emphasized that such an enterprise 'puts the greatest premium of all on boldness of the imagination'. We suggest that there are at least three enterprises in which people who adopt constructivist approaches must apply their imagination:

1. in allowing that their own world could be interpreted in a different way than the one they are used to;
2. in recognizing that others may see that world very differently;
3. in devising ways to access the alternative frameworks, or world views, of others.

In order to introduce this notion to our students and collaborators in exploring constructivist approaches, we have found it helpful to engage them in a thought experiment. This activity not only demonstrates the pervasiveness and commonness of alternative constructions of reality but also provides reassurance that holding different perspectives is derived from different prior experience and priorities and so is internally rational and can be useful. It stimulates for many people interest in what other possibilities for construing the world exist, and why. It also indicates to those whose constructs we hope to share that we are open to learning from them rather than seeking to judge their apparently 'strange' views. Readers might like to try the thought experiment for themselves and perhaps adapt it for use with others.

Activity

> Imagine yourself standing on a hilltop looking out over the countryside. Further, imagine that you are a farmer contemplating your land. What catches your attention? What is important for you in what you see? How do you interpret some of the specific things you see?
>
> Now, blink hard and look at the scene again, but this time as an artist planning a picture. Ask yourself those same questions again.
>
> And for good measure, blink hard once again and examine the landscape from the point of view of a property developer, again thinking through the questions.

When we and others have tried this we found the 'farmer' in us focusing on such things as the kinds of crops that were growing or the animals that were feeding off the land. We thought about the fertility and drainage of the soil and how we might improve it. We wondered if it was time to plant or harvest.

The 'artist', on the other hand, concentrated on appreciating light and shade, colour and texture, wondering how to capture form and structure, intensity and subtlety. Our 'property developer' had different interests and concerns. The accessibility of the land, how it could be subdivided into plots or reshaped to make room for more units predominated these thoughts.

From this simple, preliminary exercise we can recognize readily that different roles, motives and experience, among other things, lead us to deem some things more important than others even though the object of our attention remains the same. Indeed, some things may be ignored or not noticed at all, depending on where we are 'coming from'. Other things will be interpreted differently. Friable soil may be the farmer's joy and the property developer's problem. The action that such interpretations lead us to is, of course, equally diverse. We may seem to inhabit the same world, but each of us construes it differently.

> All experience is the product of both the features of the world and the biography of the individual ... influenced by our past as it interacts with our present. (Eisner, 1985: 26)

Focusing on experience

We have noted on several occasions that many constructs are not readily available for inspection. They may seem so obvious to the people who hold them that they refrain from articulating them – they convey how the world is, surely? Equally, they may seem irrelevant or trivial to them. They may, on the other hand, be difficult to articulate, for all sorts of reasons.

For some people formal interviews or very structured techniques are not appropriate. For instance, young children, people with learning disabilities or the many adults who are not used to expressing their ideas or even having other people interested in what they say, might find the traditional grid techniques constraining. This is one reason why we have been interested in exploring the alternative techniques described in the previous chapter.

Many of us are unused to airing personal opinions and ideals which have a strong emotive content and some cultures have a tradition of not talking about oneself or revealing the thoughts that guide action. Burr and Butt (1992: 80) refer to the technique called 'McFalls Mystical Monitor' which Don Bannister used to help people elaborate for themselves their reasons for doing things. This involves having a continuous conversation with oneself into a tape recorder for a fixed period of 1 hour 15 minutes, any periods of 'drying up' being explained on the record. The recording is then reviewed and the tape erased. The exercise is repeated for a further 30 minutes, with the tape again being reviewed and erased. The revealing thing about this exercise, which the authors emphasize, is that, despite the only audience for the conversation being oneself, it is still difficult to say certain things. It may be that only with practice using such freewheeling methods are some, perhaps preverbal, constructs accessible even to ourselves.

In the latter part of the last chapter we focused on methods which help people to express their ideas, values, perceptions of their worlds by using stimulus materials other than words. Since our objective in this book is to review PCP methods for use in education, training and professional practice, rather than in therapeutic settings, we concentrated first on those which enable the sharing of personal meaning with peers. Whatever the intended technique(s) within a peer learning environment, some preliminary steps might facilitate the process.

Initial exercises

In situations where people meet for a short period, say a day or two, for the purposes of sharing in an educational or professional development activity it is useful to have activities in which they get to know each other. In some contexts these are known as 'ice-breaking techniques'. When the session is underpinned by a PCP philosophy then it is important that the activity should involve some sharing of personal constructs in a relatively safe form, allowing participant control of what they choose to reveal.

However, we recognize that an invitation to 'say something about yourself' to an audience of strangers can be a paralysing experience. Or at least one which makes one deaf to others' contributions while one collects one's own thoughts. We have found it helpful to ask people in advance to bring with them a small object which demonstrates some aspects of themselves which they feel comfortable in sharing. This allows for advance preparation, is generally regarded as quite fun and is less threatening since the object of attention is, on the surface at least, the chosen artefact. People have brought a plant to describe their interest in gardening, their ability to change with the seasons, their sensitivity to environmental conditions such as blossoming in a conducive context etc.; others may choose a picture frame, a particular book or a ring that has a significance to them and says something about their taste and preferences.

In our higher degree research training classes, we have asked newcomers to introduce themselves by means of a simple drawing which conveys how they currently view their research activity. They are assured that artistic ability is not important and they are invited to describe what the choice of scene means in terms of their research. This metaphorical exercise has produced, for example, a ship setting out on a voyage of adventure, a map of an island with only a few known landmarks, a view of some foothills with mountains shrouded in mist beyond, a dense wood with creatures lurking behind trees and some sunny clearings.

We introduced this activity because we remember clearly our own experience of joining such a group, convinced that everyone else knew just what they were doing and where they were going. We have had reports from students who successfully completed their research projects long ago that this was a turning point for them in becoming members of a mutually supportive research group. Each year it is pleasant to see the serious, and sometimes tense, faces which enter the room, leaving it bearing smiles or at least more confident expressions. We contend that we would have less positive results if we had asked each person to summarize their research interests for the group before engaging in this exercise, though they are sometimes eager to do so afterwards having contacted the humanity in each other. Bridges have been built through the process.

In the chapter which follows we describe examples of the application of PCP approaches and techniques in different professional contexts and for different purposes. We hope that, now you are familiar with the basic tenets, these will act as planks in a bridge between your current experience and practice and what might be possible using a constructivist framework.

Chapter 7 Transformative applications

> Stories can provide powerful insights into the lived experiences of others in ways that can inform, awaken, and disturb readers by illustrating their involvement in social processes about which they may not consciously be aware. Once aware, individuals may find the consequences of their involvement unacceptable and seek to change the situation. In such circumstances, the potential for individual and collective restorying is enhanced. Sparkes (1994: 178)

So far in this book we have concentrated, in Chapters 1, 2 and 3, on the theory and philosophy of alternative perspectives on education and research and, in Chapters 4, 5 and 6, on the basic practicalities of espousing and putting into action a personal construct approach to professional practice. Brief examples from practice have been used to illustrate particular points in those chapters, but now we endeavour to provide a greater insight for the reader into the lived experience of those who have sought to transform professional practice using constructivist approaches.

In our work with colleagues and research students whose vocational base is different from ours we have been afforded privileged access, literally or 'virtually', to the complex worlds of other professions in the public and private sector. Similarly, through consultancy activities in the business and health sectors, we have looked through windows and learned about other organizations and their procedures. We will draw on that experience to demonstrate how constructivist approaches can inform, having awakened and disturbed, professional change and development. We hope that the examples provided will speak to the reader, providing inspiration for future practice. The intention, then, is not to provide answers per se, i.e. the particular results of others' initiatives, rather it is to note the diversity of issues that have been addressed in specific contexts using some of the tools and techniques described earlier in the book.

References are provided so that readers can explore the detail of results and procedures for themselves from the original authors' texts, where these exist. However, we are also concerned to describe work which is current at the time of writing so when detailed reports are not yet available for reference, readers are urged to contact the investigators in person through the Centre for PCP in Education, the University of Reading.

In making a selection from the potentially enormous range of research and development activities using PCP in the professional context, we have focused on those interventions with which we have had personal involvement of some kind – as supervisors, co-researchers etc. – though we will occasionally refer to some publications by colleagues known to us through the European Personal Construct Association and the international PCP network. We are particularly indebted to all those who provided us with summaries of their work for this purpose.

In gathering the pieces together for this chapter, we were at first struck by their diversity, though gradually overarching themes emerged as we sifted through the wealth of ideas submitted. Nevertheless, the themes finally presented here are only one way of categorizing them. We have chosen as headings the general focus of the work under which specific topics are explored using a range of techniques. The first of our foci concerns studies which derive from a current concern with collaborative working between professions.

Interprofessional education, training and work

All of the work summarized in this section has been inspired by a shift in emphasis from maintaining professional boundaries towards interprofessional, inter-disciplinary and inter-agency initiatives. Griffiths (1988), for instance, had highlighted within the UK context that professionals involved in providing health and social care services would need to alter their views of themselves and their work. A largely quantitative national survey by the Centre for the Advancement of Inter Professional Education (CAIPE, 1992) of training initiatives based on an interprofessional approach indicated the need for a more in-depth and rigorous evaluation of such education. Then Cowley (1994), while recognizing the importance of each specialism preserving a positive self-image, suggested that there was a need to identify underlying principles that may apply to a variety of roles through the development of common core programmes. Different aspects of the challenges drawn to our attention by this literature are taken up by the following investigations.

The diverse roles of medical health professionals working in a child psychiatric clinic formed the focus of work by Kirkcaldy, Pope and Siefen (1993) which explored the cognitive structures of the doctor and nurse using role repertory grid analysis. Insight was also offered about the configuration of the clinic organization, with detailed evaluation of occupational boundaries and interactions between roles, through SOCIOGRID analysis. (SOCIOGRID analysis involves comparison of a group of grids with a common core of elements. This identifies constructs which the grids have in common with each other and allows for a network diagram to be produced which shows the degree of similarity between grids.) This extended work done in the preceding year by Kirkcaldy and Pope (1992: 50) which 'demonstrated that repertory grid technology, when implemented as a heuristic device, could provide the basis for discovering the terms in which different actors in the network see their roles and negotiate their aims and objectives'.

Preparing health professionals for practice through education and training also involves professionals with different role remits. Mazhindu (1995) (see also Mazhindu and Pope, 1996) advanced the case for inter-professional education by examining the personal constructs employed by nurse lecturers, nurse practitioners and students in three discipline areas of nursing – Adult General, Mental Health and Learning Disability. Repertory grids explored what for them constituted an 'ideal' nursing student, using as elements particular examples of achieving students, from high to low, and the worst student in their experience as well as their notion of an 'ideal' student. Themes derived from the constructs included attitudes, abilities, personality, academic and behavioural factors. Similarities and differences in the frequency of use of themes as well as in particular constructs used by each group of participants were compared. The analysis of the data led to the devising of a Staff and Student Development Strategy.

The focus becomes even finer in the work of Ewens (1998) who sought to explore the impact of a newly integrated curriculum on the role perceptions of community nursing students. We have summarized her findings in the following case study:

Case study 7.1 (Ewens, 1988)

The students in this study were qualified nurses studying for an additional professional qualification in one of eight community nurse specialist branches. The integrated curriculum had been introduced to bring these traditionally isolated branches together on one course with the aim of promoting interprofessional collaboration.

The repertory grid technique was used in the research to explore the students' role perceptions. Repertory grids were elicited in taped one to one interviews at the start of their course, at the end of their course and after six months in their new professional role. The domain of the repertory grid was the contribution made by different health and social care professionals to client care. A common element set was used, 14 health and social care professional

> roles and a self element. Additionally, using the same element set, a group of experienced community practice teachers and university tutors had repertory grids elicited during a taped interview, again with the meanings behind constructs being explored.
>
> Utilizing the common element set the repertory grid data was then compared: individual students over time; the student group over time and students and teachers.
>
> PCP achieved an in-depth understanding of how students were developing on the integrated curriculum and most importantly helped to uncover some of the powerful process involved in professional education. For example the findings revealed that the integrated curriculum was successful in helping students gain a secure role identity for their new professional role. However, the aim of the integrated curriculum to promote interprofessional collaboration was not found to be supported. These findings were then explained by the powerful processes of professionalization within subsets of the profession. PCP proved to be invaluable in piecing together these different findings. It is also worth noting that, since the method provides opportunities and feedback directly to the participants, this encourages commitment to the research process. In the case of this research, a longitudinal design, the response rate was 100% over a period of 18 months.

During the course of her doctoral studies, Ewens also collaborated with two colleagues in her HE department in devising a methodology for measuring the effectiveness of interprofessional education. They too used repertory grids to measure the individual change over time of students' construing while sociogrid analysis allowed for comparisons between individuals and between professional groupings. A preliminary discussion of this work, with an emphasis on methodology, can be found in Howkins, Badger and Ewens (1995), while Howkins (1994) provided the background to the integrated curriculum under review.

The views of the above authors are echoed from a slightly different discipline base, Mental Health Services, in a different national context, Australia, by Tooth (1996) in her research on the impact of professional training on group construing. Her multi-professional participants completed 'working with clients' grids, the elements being identified by descriptions of different client types, in her study of the role played by extant values and training in their constructions of their work with clients. She concluded that each profession involved in mental health care has far more in common with the others than many are prepared to acknowledge; that the values that each individual brings to training are more important than the training itself; that professionalization works towards increasing the specialization of members of a profession in spite of pressure to break down professional barriers. She suggested that a healthier approach might be for professions to view the mental health system as their culture rather than each profession trying to foster its own.

From the same national context, Australia, Ellis (1994) outlined her attempts to develop a framework based on PCP which could be used in an educational role with health professionals. She saw the challenge as being to encourage them to identify their personal meanings or constructions of caring, and the implications of the behaviours/actions which are a result of these constructions, so that they can become self-aware of a caring identity. This would encourage, she proposed, an acknowledgement of what each profession's definition of caring is, where it comes from, what it means in clinical practice and where it could move to, if the carer so wished. She provided a detailed argument of how PCP can contribute to carers identifying alternative ways of construing caring so that they might produce for themselves constructs which would help them to manage creatively the situations that confront them in a caring environment.

Tensions between different professionals in the way they view the sharing of client confidences, another aspect of collaborative caring in professional practice, formed the focus of a paper by Allison and Ewens (1998). They pointed out that, just as any object or image can be viewed differently by different people, then so also can the limits of confidentiality be defined variously by different professionals depending on the priorities and values brought to the exchange. This is one of several ethical issues currently being studied in a nurse education context by Allison using a PCP approach.

Moral dilemmas presented to the constructivist were discussed by Jankowicz (1997) in a keynote paper 'Professions: Public Arbiters of Private Meanings' in which he argued that the professions, rather than the sciences, are the main social institution in which personal constructions become publicly shared. He contended that only the professions have the socially agreed power to compel a particular way of construing phenomena, through their power to determine the appropriateness of personal needs and purposes. One of the questions he explored was what happens when people disagree and, further, what might be a constructivist response to such a disagreement. He suggested four potential outcomes. Participants might:

- attempt to persuade each other of the value of their own way of construing;
- discuss and recognize any differences in their purposes;
- agree to differ and tolerate ambiguity to see what happens next;
- end the attempted collaboration and leave the encounter in a state of disarray.

This debate is apposite to the final study described in this section. We present Ashwell's own review of his current PhD research since he admirably sets out the value of a PCP approach in the context of interprofessional work, alerting novices to its strengths and demands. His description also includes much valuable practical advice derived from experience.

Case study 7.2 (Ashwell, 2000)

My area of research focused on how different organizations involved in community health issues, such as family planning or substance abuse, collaborated with each other. At the outset it appeared to be a straightforward task and one that could enhance current thinking about the creation of working partnerships in the delivery of services to the community. The answers were expected to provide some form of blueprint for others to use when they wished to consider collaborating with each other. However the major problem appeared to be, despite their every intention, that organizations and agencies appeared to be experiencing significant difficulties in collaborating with each other. Informal discussions indicated that this was mostly to do with structural issues and that this was where the research needed to focus.

It was clear that a methodology which was qualitative in nature was needed and it should also be inductive so that it could broaden an understanding of the process of collaboration by looking at it with increased precision.

What was not obvious at the time was that I had made a host of unexplored assumptions about the nature of the process of collaboration, so I was urged to make use of PCP. I approached, with the permission of their employers, the individual members of a collaborative project that had been created from a group of agencies. I adopted two approaches.

The first made use of the repertory grid. Using the names of each of the agencies as elements in a grid I began to elicit constructs using triads. The kind of question I used was:

'If you were to consider the ways in which these three agencies (who are members of this joint project) respond to collaboration, in what way are two similar to each other and yet different from the third?'

It was quite a mouthful but we got there in the end.

The second approach invited individual members of the joint project to describe in a narrative style what was happening and what it felt like to be part of a joint project in which the collaboration appeared to be working successfully.

However, the kinds of responses I began to collect suggested that I had not grasped the full intent of what the participants had to say and I found the answers to be contradictory. The problem was that the participants kept confusing me about whether they were referring to the agency or to the people whom they had encountered as representing that agency. The most common statement was that if you went to another person in the same agency the result would be different.

It took a little time for it to sink in but I began to realize that here was some valuable data that PCP had produced for me. People did not see organizations as structures but perhaps they saw them as people. This meant that I had to produce a new set of grids in which the elements could be drawn from a greater variety of conceptions about working together. To this end new grids were created in two ways. Where individuals were involved in only one collaborating project, the elements were assembled by drawing on the named people from that one project. On the other hand, as is usual with community-based enterprises, some individuals were members of a number of projects. For these people it was possible to invite them to select as elements the names of a number of projects in which agencies were collaborating. Thus the nature of collaboration within a particular project could be explored in depth while it was also possible to compare different projects in terms of their collaboration. Such a variety of approaches was expected to provide data that would expose any further assumptions that could be made about this process of collaboration.

It has been valuable to examine the theoretical aspects of creating the grids, but it has also been interesting to examine how I went about creating the grids in practice.

I started with a blank grid on a piece of A4 paper. It was carefully coded and I had used coloured paper to make it appear just that bit more special. I invited the participants to list the names of the organizations that were involved in the project and wrote them down as elements. I then wrote each of these elements onto a separate piece of card and used these cards to set up the triads. Unfortunately I have difficulties with poor handwriting and so the cards and the elements on the grid sheet were not always so easy to recognize. The design of the grid sheet meant that the names of the elements had to be written sideways. The added difficulty was in the wording of the constructs. Often, as participants were invited to find a more precise form of words for the 'converse' pole, they wanted to change the wording of the 'similar' pole. This produced a messy piece of paper, which was difficult to use as a working document, even if process had produced useful data in the form of a record of the discussion. A further problem lay with the creation of the FOCUS and PRINCIPAL COMPONENTS diagrams. When the grids were recorded in paper form it became necessary to produce the analysis diagrams once I had returned to the office, and a valuable opportunity was lost in seeking an immediate reaction to the analysis product.

I experimented with different paper designs and with how to gain a response from the printed diagrams, but eventually I made greater use of a portable computer (in this case an Apple PowerBook 140) in conjunction with a tape-recorder as the best way of collecting the data. I kept the carefully designed grid sheets handy in case I had to resort to using them, in the event of practical constraints or the preference of the participant.

My equipment appeared cumbersome so I felt the need to camouflage some items as much as possible from the person being interviewed in order to reduce distractions. The laptop computer was positioned in front of the participant but at an angle from which I could also see the screen. I had my own keyboard and mouse in front of me which meant that I could both position the pointer for the insertion of words and move on the programme to its next stages. It also ensured that the participant was free to type in their own version of words if they so wished. I ran a tape-recorder for the entire time in which the research was being discussed. It was easier to ensure that I had full permission from the participant (previously arranged) to switch it on and to just leave it on. It was the last item I dismantled before leaving. The use of C90 tapes meant that only one turn over of the tape was expected in any one interview and I found that clip-on microphones, the little ones, were the best to use. We had one each and, after the initial fuss about which part of the person's clothing was appropriate to use, they became unobtrusive because they were out of sight. I placed the tape recorder by my side, usually on the floor, so that it was accessible to me, was out of the sight of the participant, and did not distract them. I had to remember to take with me an extension cable with sufficient outlet sockets for the tape-recorder, the computer and, where possible, the printer. I also learned to carry with me, in reserve in the car, an extra long extension lead after I had been obliged to run a cable from the next-door Art Department because the Youth Centre in which I was holding the interview was being re-wired.

The computer program allowed elements to be listed, one under the other, on the one screen page. It selected triads at random for discussion. This set-up enabled the participant to concentrate only on the three selected by the machine with the result that the constructs were elicited with greater ease and with reduced level of the anxiety that anyone experiences when being asked fairly personal questions about their work. It saved fumbling with the cards, having to worry about handwriting and the less-than-professional look of the cards. A further advantage lay with the greater detachment that the machine offered. The invitation to select three cards, in this case from a small bundle of about 8 to 10, inevitably gave rise to biased selections. As the cards became used crumpled corners, small tears and minor discolorations were quite sufficient to enable participants to become inappropriately selective when choosing triads thus running the risk of reducing the range of elicited constructs.

Where the use of the computer was at its best was when it was able to show the results immediately. The program could assemble the FOCUS and PRINCIPAL COMPONENTS diagrams on the screen, making it possible to review these to compare responses more speedily. In this way the interview could be extended so that participants were able to elaborate on or to disagree with what they had just created.

The outcome of this approach meant that different forms of data were made available from the one interview as follows. The outcomes of the repertory grid analysis could be stored on the machine or on a disk and the pictures of the results could be printed off easily and left with the participants. A tape-recorded version of the discussion was available and it could be transcribed for later analysis. The format allowed the results of the grid analysis to be discussed more rigorously and in greater depth, with a record of the discussion being compiled in the process. (Ashwell, 2000)

Intra-professional issues – the health and social services sector

While the preceding examples were concerned with interactions between different professional groups, there is a plethora of studies concerned with particular issues and problems within professional boundaries. This section includes a selection of those whose specific focus is a vocation in the public sector, though the questions they address might find parallels in many occupations.

One such topic is attitude to role and how this develops in novice practitioners. Dearmun (1997) explored the perceptions related to professional practice of a group of newly qualified paediatric nursing graduates during their first year of work, following successful completion of the first degree course with that specialism in the UK. The study aimed to gain an appreciation of their thoughts and feelings about their new role, in particular the aspects that were rewarding and demanding, the support they received and their future career decisions. The methodological approach was firmly based in the naturalistic paradigm, the nurses engaging in extensive interactive interviews and providing pictorial narratives of their experiences at three-monthly intervals, all of which revealed constructs which either remained or were changed throughout the process. Thus it was possible to chart initial reservations about fitness to practice held by the participants and their colleagues, how these were confronted and dealt with, and the gradual development of confidence and competence. It was interesting to note the profound influence, not always positive, that the milieu had on their job satisfaction and the extent to which each participant could capitalize on the skills acquired from the degree course. The findings made a useful contribution to knowledge for both purchasers and providers of education and for those offering professional support to novices.

A similar concern with role perceptions formed the basis of a comparative study of the experience of student nurses and probationary police officers during their first two years of encounters with the public. Sexton provides a description here of his research, though further detail of the methods and techniques used can be found in Sexton and Denicolo (1997).

Case study 7.3 (Sexton and Denicolo, 1997)

This research was based on six-monthly interviews with two cohorts over a period of two years, a total of five interviews per participant. Each cohort contained 15 participants, one of probationary police officers and the other of student nurses.

An important aspect of the research was to be able to make effective comparisons between time-frames. Its main objective was to determine not only what changes had occurred over each period but also what had happened to effect those changes. I therefore developed a unique method, which involved the use of stimulated recall, as the means by which elements for the repertory grid process were developed.

Participants were shown 12 photographs of different situations which a member of their profession might meet in the course of their everyday duties (the same 12 photographs were shown on each occasion). At the first interview (on entry to the training establishment) the photographs themselves were used as the elements for the elicitation process. However, in all subsequent interviews they were asked to examine each of the 12 photographs in turn and identify an event which had occurred in the previous six months, which was in some way related, however loosely, to the photograph and which had been significant for them in terms of their professional development. Sometimes the physical context of the scene would trigger a memory, sometimes it was the particular type of person portrayed, and at other times it might be the atmosphere evoked which would remind them of a recently experienced situation.

The participants were invited to discuss each of their experiences and it was interesting that during these disclosures there was often considerable discussion about their feelings and their own personal perspectives of what had occurred. It was equivalent to a 'narrative' construct elicitation process, which provided some validation for the grid but also acted both as an enrichment of the constructs captured within the grid and as a valuable source of additional constructs which did not appear within the grid diagram itself.

Once the 12 incidents had been derived, these were then used as the elements for the subsequent elicitation process and participants were asked to identify differences in the manner in which professionals had reacted in each instance. This produced constructs related to how people undertake their duties in a practical way and also revealed attitudes connected with those duties. The reason for concentrating specifically on incidents which occurred within the previous six months was related to my theory that recent significant events would have been instrumental in any adjustment of the construct system since the previous interview. To use those incidents as the elements for elicitation would therefore result in a more focused construction than might otherwise have occurred.

It was not possible to undertake a normal comparative analysis of the grids, such as sociogrid using computer software, as both the elements and the constructs on each occasion were different and consequently participants were not asked to rate them. However, a comparison was made of the differences between constructs over the time-frames by identifying those constructs which had not previously arisen as well as apparently common themes which became apparent within and between participants. The assumptions made from this evidence were then checked with the participants during a final interview. Participants also completed a critical incident 'snake' on each occasion about the critical incidents occurring in the preceding six months. This complemented the grid information and helped to inform the process.

The key issues which arose from the analysis were that police officers' attitudes appeared to be affected far more by external factors than by internal social enculturization. Public reaction to them as individuals by the general community and by different sections of the community seemed to have a much greater influence than the so-called 'canteen culture'. They also did not seem to develop role models to the same extent as nurses because of the intensity of feeling which public reaction invokes.

In relation to nurses it was evident that the system of six-weekly placements in different specialist environments meant they were unable to establish themselves within the social system of each specialism they visited. This allowed them to take a more detached view, to be critical of the methods used by different professionals and to identify good and bad practice. In this way they were able to establish an image of how they wished to operate once they

> were qualified. They therefore identified role models and were less influenced by the reactions of their clients than they were by fellow professionals. Reinforcement of good professional practice occurred through discussions at college between placements and this enabled a form of inoculation against bad practice.

Sexton also provided us with reflections on the use of PCP in his research, thus:

> I am confident that the use of PCP was instrumental in achieving the final results for two reasons. First it enabled me to question participants sympathetically, while reaching deeper into their values systems than a simple interview would achieve. Secondly it meant that I was able to make very effective comparisons between time-frames by identifying matches and contrasts amongst the constructs elicited from the various interviews. To have attempted this through a more conventional interview method would have been more difficult and, to my mind, less convincing. It enabled the further opportunity to question participants and to check out theories and assumptions by reference to the constructs the participants themselves had identified in the grid completion exercise and the additional constructs which had been identified from the interview material and the critical incident snake charts.
>
> The process I used is to my knowledge original. The drawbacks have been in terms of the complexity of the process, especially in the context of a longitudinal study and the consequent difficulty in maintaining the interest and commitment of some of the participants. However, as well as being willing to contribute to research about their profession, many enjoyed the experience and valued the opportunity to reflect on incidents and situations in which they had been involved and how they had been affected by them.
>
> There were two significant reactions from the participants which signalled the relevance of the outcomes, and consequently the relevance of PCP as the chosen methodology. First each participant was asked at the end of each session to look through the list of constructs we had developed to determine whether it was a genuine reflection of how they viewed their role at that time. On every occasion they agreed, although on a few occasions a participant did add other important constructs which were not reflected within the grid (although in most instances they had been discussed during the interview). On a significant number of occasions participants actually commented that the resultant grid was 'quite scary' or 'amazingly accurate'. Additionally the final analysis of the grids was also said to be very accurate and participants reflected again on key incidents which explained the reasons for changes that had been identified.

While the last two examples focused on professionals' perceptions of their encounters with others, colleagues and the public, two further studies explored the practitioners' views of their clients and their problems. The first, presented by Quinn, grew from a concern to facilitate reflective learning by what she terms 'reluctant learners'. She explains it in the following case study.

Case study 7.4 (Quinn, 1999)

Reflective learning requires active, motivated learners, and stimulating reflective learning when the student is uninterested in the subject is problematic. In the case of social work students an example of such disinterest is their negative attitude towards work with older people. (Many studies have shown a hierarchy of students' client group preferences with children and families at the top and older and disabled people at the bottom.) In Britain, older people are the major group of users of social services. There is a mismatch between users' (and agencies') needs and social work students' client group preferences. Students' negative attitudes about work with older people also conflict with the social work professions' ethical base.

I introduced a repertory grid technique to enable students to articulate and reflect on their views about work with older people. I used:

1. triadic elicitation in small groups, with a list of different social work posts (covering work with older people and work with children, in a range of settings);
2. feedback of constructs to the full group, and development of a list of constructs;
3. individual grids completed by students, and submitted anonymously. The elements of the grid were the posts used in (1), plus 'my ideal social work post'; the constructs were ten that students selected from the list developed in (2);
4. feedback to the whole group of the results from the individual grids, in terms of

- constructs selected, and frequency;
- a list of those posts seen as most like the ideal social work post;
- a list of those posts seen as least like the ideal social work post.

The use of the repertory grid technique gave a structure which supported students' reflection on their attitudes to work with different client groups and in different settings, with the focus on attitudes towards work with older people. The initial elicitation of constructs helped students compare attitudes to different social work posts within the members of their small groups, and encouraged reflection about the basis for these attitudes. There was the benefit of personal reflection alongside an anonymous sharing of group responses. In these ways, a dialogue about work with older people was started. Enabling students to critically reflect on their own attitudes towards work with older people is a necessary first step in eliminating barriers to their learning in this area.

I had earlier used a PCP based instrument developed by Vacc – the Gerontological Counseling Grid. This is described in Quinn (1999).

She also provided a reflection on the value of using PCP in this circumstance that readers might like to consider if they encounter similar situations in which there exist blocks to, or problems with, learning:

I think PCP techniques are of considerable use in facilitating reflective learning. Even in the absence of specific barriers to learning, not everyone starts with the necessary skills for reflection. The technique of triadic elicitation, exploring similarities and differences, provides a structure within which reflection can be developed in dialogue with others, and completion of a grid can enable individual and private reflection.

When there are barriers, and students are reluctant to engage with the topic at all, PCP techniques can encourage them to explore aspects of that viewpoint, and have the advantage of starting where the students are – that is, disinterested in work with older people. By discovering similarities as well as differences between social work posts with younger and older people, negative judgements can begin to be questioned; the basis for judgements is also scrutinized. The approach is non-threatening – it engages students in examining their attitudes, but without labelling such attitudes unacceptable. Students can discover that some views are inappropriate and discriminatory for themselves.

Anti-ageist strategies within social work education have predominantly been cognitive and impersonal, relying on information-giving. These are unsuccessful in promoting attitude change. PCP methods help students articulate and assess their attitudes, and I have found them successful in promoting students' readiness to learn about social work with older people – perhaps primarily because they can be used to demonstrate the diversity of views within the student group, and to challenge assumptions.

Another researcher concerned with professionals' views of clients was also exercised by the need to compare the constructs of both practitioners and clients. McElroy's study involved the development of the psychological nursing care of self-harming/suicidal patients in acute psychiatric wards. This complex research is currently being written up for a PhD but he shares with us these reflections:

Case study 7.5 (McElroy, in progress)

The success of psychotherapy is defined as being dependent on the quality of the relationships developed between the nurses and their patients. The findings at this point indicate that episodes of self-harm were often related to the individualized meanings that patients gave to interpersonal events which took place between themselves and their nurses. Perceived rejection, disappointment and unmet expectations, which often went unnoticed by the staff, could assume catastrophic proportions in the minds of the patients. Failure to deal with (i.e. acknowledge and work through) these perceptions undermined the therapeutic relationship and potentially exacerbated the patients' difficulties. To enhance psychological care it was therefore essential to assess the quality of these relationships from the patients' perspective. A group of four patients agreed to participate in a programme that would help to develop nursing care in this field.

The repertory grid technique was used to provide some understanding of the cognitive subsystems used by the patients to give meaning to the things they saw and heard on the ward. As relationships with carers was the area of construing being investigated, the elements were (anonymized) people who had cared for them. The constructs differentiated interactions which the patient found 'therapeutic' and those which made them feel more distressed. Being alerted to these constructs, and reflecting on how their own constructs had been revealed by their behaviour in practice, the nurses were enabled to gain understanding of how they contributed positively and negatively towards the likelihood of further self-harm.

Another study currently in progress also explores the differing perceptions of client and nurse in the realm of perception of risk of falls in the elderly. Snowling, in the course of developing for community nurses a more effective protocol of assessment of this risk, employs grids to elicit the nurses' views of risk factors and, so that comparisons can be made and the nurses' views on appropriate care elaborated, older people in their care engage in a more discursive 'river of life' (or snake) discussion in which they illuminate their constructs in relation to 'risky' and 'safe' events and episodes. This will enable nurses to consider how their advice and recommendations are received and interpreted by their clients.

The concept of risk, but more specifically the fear engendered when risk is perceived and experienced by practitioners in social work settings, forms the focus of a current doctoral study by Smith at the University of Reading. Although the study is based on psychodynamic theory, Smith has found the philosophy and techniques of PCP to be complementary. He has used grids to explore with participants what they consider the opposite of fear to be, using triadic elicitation techniques to elicit core constructs related to the fears of social workers and counsellors. The river of life technique also provided illumination of the experiences of counsellors. This revealed that what constitutes fearful events differs between individuals, that fear itself is differently construed by them and that their reactions and attitudes to fear take different forms.

In another demanding setting, that of a High Security Hospital, McAdams explored the impact of critical incidents on staff in the course of a developmental evaluation of the support system introduced into the hospital. More detail on the method and results can be found in McAdams (1999) but here she provides us with these thoughts on her research:

Case study 7.6 (McAdams, 1999)

Because experience had shown that not everyone reacts and responds to the same incident in a similar way, I wanted to explore in depth how a group of nursing staff viewed the stressful and dangerous incidents that formed part of their professional practice.

In order to do this, repertory grids were used with the nurses on one ward as the basis for interviews repeated over time, in order to provide snapshots in time and indications of change in relation to the kind of education and support offered. A wide mix of incidents was used for exploration, provided through a common list of general descriptions of incidents which had been derived from previous interviews with the staff themselves. This common list of 12 elements couched in their own professional jargon (e.g. an incident I dealt with well, an incident which could not have been avoided, the worst incident I have had to deal with) at a higher order level enabled them to identify and provide examples of particular incidents from their own experience.

Each participant's examples were individual to them, and were used to elicit further constructs about them. Thus there was a varying set of incidents to satisfy each element in the aggregated data and these demonstrated at a general level that an incident in common to participants was not always categorized under the same heading. Two general constructs were provided at the end of the grid interview for rating alongside the elicited constructs. These were 'felt/did not feel supported' and 'beige/fire-engine red', the latter being a construct which seemed salient to participants that was derived from the original interviews. These enabled me to look for clusters of constructs which related to the provided poles for individuals and for the whole the group. This provided a baseline on which to explore consensus and divergence, and gave a useful focus for identifying related constructs. In spite of diverse individual reaction to incidents which some had experienced together, a sense of helplessness pervaded discussions relating to the 'worst incident'. This was always a significant feature and was reinforced by the constructs used.

The second grid and interview revealed that there had been some alteration in the perception of incidents over time; a shift was noted in the recorded awareness of their own reactions by participants and their ability to deal with them.

These grids provided detailed descriptions of types of incident and a range of constructs related to them. This information was used to compile 'real' vignettes, with a range of provided constructs to respond to using a rating scale. These formed the basis for the design of a questionnaire which was used as part of a Supplementary Study and sent to every member of ward-based nursing staff. Thus each one of the larger group of participants was given an opportunity to respond in depth about their level of agreement or not with constructs about particular types of incident derived from a similar professional group. This added a quantifiable dimension to an otherwise idiographic study.

The use of the PCP approach permitted, and reinforced, the consideration that individuals will view each incident in the light of their personal experiences, knowledge and understanding. Repertory grids provided an essential framework for the interviews, giving to the participants a sense of control when they were talking about incidents which they had found difficult or distressing. Participants reported being comfortable with the process, though it wasn't always emotionally barren. They said that they liked the way it recognized their individuality and allowed them to contemplate and review their own reactions. However, since revisiting some of the incidents was frequently psychologically demanding, it did mean that care had to be taken to allow sufficient breaks and to provide counselling support beyond the interviews.

Finally in this section, lest the impression be emerging that PCP approaches are at their best with the articulate, we will report on the work in progress at Reading of Apraiz in the realm of counselling people with learning disabilities. With her permission we quote from a summary of her paper to be presented at a forthcoming conference (Apraiz, 2000):

Case study 7.7 (Apraiz, 2000)

> It is known that facilitative interactions, such as counselling or psychotherapy, can contribute to the creation of a context where the health of human beings can be promoted, maintained or restored. There is evidence to suggest that people with learning disabilities may have greater needs to help them to overcome abuse or loss. However, the therapeutic help available for them is still, often, confined to pharmacological or behaviour modification techniques. Furthermore, a review of the literature suggests that there is a lack of available, adequate psychological therapies for this group of people.
>
> Some of the barriers to progress may be related to a belief among some health professionals that people with moderate or severe learning disabilities might have difficulty in using the specific communication skills that might be regarded as necessary in order to benefit from the 'talking therapies'. Nevertheless, health professionals have an obligation to develop their own personal communication skills with clients. Consequently, the aim of my project is to devise, through the medium of visual art, a method of communication which might help a client/patient to communicate in order to promote personal growth and to facilitate choice.
>
> The paper describes a constructivist approach in which six adults with learning disabilities selected from a range of pictures (reproductions of famous works of art) some that they liked and some that they didn't care for. These were used during in-depth interviews to explore meanings attributed to the world. The results demonstrate that these pictures acted as strong enablers in facilitating communication, for instance the most evident theme from the combined data is that of loneliness – participants identified its presence and absence in the pictures they chose. As an example of the power of the technique, one participant, following a series of such interactions, requested, for the first time since his mother's death several years before, to be allowed to visit his mother's grave and he was able to mourn for her openly. He seems calmer and happier in spite of this and has exhibited, in the three months following this intervention, none of the challenging behaviour that he was accustomed to present. He has started mixing colours and has requested a visit to an Art Gallery.
>
> Doing research with lonely or vulnerable people brings with it a number of ethical issues which are highlighted in the paper but the findings of the study may prove useful to anyone wishing to increase their understanding of some of the personal constructions of those living with learning disabilities.

It may be of interest here to note that pictures, either as elements in a grid or as stimulants to producing constructs in a more fluid dialogue, have been used in many contexts, e.g. O'Hare and Gordon (1976), used slide transparencies of a variety of works of art to explore aesthetic preference while Daniel (1996) used cartoons as part of a multi-method approach to identify, through repeating emergent themes, perceived need for counselling across a range of individuals. In the section after next we will present another use of pictures, this time photographs, montage and mural, in the realm of Careers Guidance and Counselling, while the first example in the next section also employed pictures.

Health and social education

Before leaving the field of the health and social services entirely, three studies are described here, all related to explorations which seek understanding of what might be categorized as anti-social behaviour:

Case study 7.8 (Lynch, 1996)

Lynch's (1996) study was concerned with adolescent smoking and health education practice. A variety of techniques were used with a group of 16–17-year-old smokers and non-smokers, including repertory grids which used pictures (drawings and photographs) of smoking situations as elements and 'critical incident pathways' or snakes. A PCP approach was used because it takes a holistic view of the person. It does not isolate smoking from other personal experiences but attempts to explain smoking from an individual perspective and in relation to other aspects of life. By using sociogrids which include smokers and non-smokers, the study demonstrated many facets of the young smokers that contradicted conventional wisdom – they, for instance, tended to have idiosyncratic thoughts about smoking unlike non-smokers who tended to concur in their views. Young people who smoked also knew as much, and sometimes more, about the health hazards of smoking than their non-smoking peers. Smoking was strongly associated with exerting a sense of self-identity, perhaps an important part of their maturation process and, though they tended to associate together, this had as much to do with being with 'like-minded others' as it did with copying the behaviour of others. There was no evidence to suggest that smokers and non-smokers were different personality types – socializing or fun-loving, for instance – since they had these and many other constructs in common with each other.

The implications of this research for Personal, Social and Health Education (PSHE) are that much more emphasis needs to be placed on the psychological maturation process of adolescents and far less on simple information provision. The goal of PSHE should be to increase self-awareness and the development of a positive self-identity. Lynch contended that too much school-based health education time is spent in telling pupils what they already know, or what does not really matter, and insufficient time is spent in helping them to explore and understand what personal meaning this information has for them. He advocated the use of PCP techniques for eliciting and confronting that meaning.

Case study 7.9 (Mallick, in progress)

The aim of the second study in this group was to explore the perspectives and meaning systems of teenagers and their parents about drugs and the communication they experience with each other on the topic, so as to improve that communication. Mallick's research, a PhD study now drawing to a conclusion at Surrey University, Roehampton, consisted of a review, and further development, of the drug education programme 'drugsbridge: enabling understanding between parents and youth'. Using a case study design and two small groups, one each of teenagers and parents of teenagers, the main PCP technique used was the self-characterization sketch. For this each participant wrote about themselves in the third person as the main character in a film, in which the context was drugs. They were encouraged to write it both intimately and sympathetically as if from a best friend who knew them better than anyone.

The sketches provided, first, a baseline measure of the perspective and understanding of the participant and secondly characters for role-plays, using composite types to ensure anonymity. These role-plays involved 'family groups' of a parent with two children, the young people playing character roles which contrasted with their presented selves while the parent character was a composite, used to produce a rather extreme character compared to the 'typical' parent involved in the programme. The role-plays were based on a Rogerian listening exercise. Further opportunities to listen and interact were provided later by asking the participants to write a self-characterization sketch of the other person, parent or teenager, and again engaging in a 'listening' role-play based on the composite products.

These techniques were valuable in allowing each to have access to the other's perspective and to see themselves from a position 'outside' themselves. The role-plays allowed for the temporary subsuming of another perspective and increased sociality, in an atmosphere which was safe and maintained confidentiality. Mallick, in recognizing that recent research had demonstrated that much drug education is ineffective because it frequently fails to be meaningful and personally relevant for young people, found that this method enabled her to work with the participants' personal and individual perspectives in a spirit of open communication, so overcoming some of the difficulties which parents and teenagers face in discussing an emotionally laden and socially sensitive topic.

Case study 7.10 (Power, 1997)

The final study in this section investigated the changes in behaviour and attitudes that occurred in women attending a day-centre programme as part of their probationary orders as persistent offenders. The techniques planned for use consisted of a self-characterization sketch and a grid, elicited on entry to the programme and at its conclusion. The grid consisted of three self elements (as I am now, as I will be in three years and ideal self), two elements of power (someone who makes me feel threatened/who makes me feel safe), two elements of influence (someone who influences me in a good/bad way), two elements of control (someone in control/not in control of their lives), and one element relating to how women perceive criminals (someone convicted of a crime).

Rather than focus on the Centre's programme, though the tool did successfully evaluate the strengths and weaknesses of it, this example is provided here in illustration of the power of repertory grids in enabling women from difficult backgrounds in a demanding and stressful context to evaluate and re-evaluate themselves in much depth. It also provided indications of factors in life which seem to be linked to re-offending, for example low self-esteem, lack of a supportive environment and low social competence, so that the programme could be improved in terms of meeting needs. The self-characterization sketches were less successful and eventually abandoned, the researcher positing that they were too revelatory of a negative self image for the women to bear in that circumstance (Power, 1997). This provides a reinforcement of the caveat that it is important to be sensitive to the needs and concerns of participants by ensuring that the design of an intervention is flexible enough to encompass change if necessary. The collection of data should always be subordinate to the well-being of participants while techniques used should certainly not detract from their ability and potential to deal effectively with their worlds.

Helping people to deal more effectively with the world of work forms the central issue in the next group of examples.

Career decision-making, guidance and counselling

This section forms a bridge between the public and private sectors by examining examples of work related to careers, which has relevance to both. Individuals may need to consider both sectors when embarking on a career or in making career changes.

Having reached this point in the book, readers will already be alerted to the potential of constructivist techniques, perhaps particularly grids, for helping with many forms of decision-making. Although we must reiterate here the warning that grids cannot supply answers to questions such as 'which of these alternatives should I choose?', it is equally clear that they can provide a structured way to clarify the strengths and limitations of a variety of options, from a personal perspective. We have used them ourselves in workshops with students about career choices. One particular memory of that work stands out, which is that not only do grids provide an opportunity for people to rate the various options on various dimensions salient to them about a job, but they also alert them to information that they may not have about particular jobs. For instance, they may know that one job demands, say, a lot of travelling, but it is only when they try to rate other jobs that they discover that they do not know how much travelling might be involved in them. Thus the grid again performs as a catalyst to the finding out of other things.

Case study 7.11 (Chi-yi Wu, 1997)

Our first example derived from a concern with the problem of career 'undecidedness' exhibited by many undergraduates undertaking general rather than profession specific degrees. The context of the study was Taiwan but the problem can be recognized in many national contexts – the students have already evaded making a decision about career choice during the course of secondary school and early degree studies and their next steps may well still remain unclear to them. The most specific reason frequently articulated by students for being dissatisfied by conventional techniques employed in career assessment is that they find some items in standardized career inventories irrelevant to their own experience. By working intensively with 33 senior undergraduates, eliciting grids on potential career choices and using laddering techniques extensively to explore the reasons why jobs were seen in a particular light and what that implied for the student in practice, Chi-yi Wu (1997) identified that the students' pervasive concerns for professionalism were somewhat more peripheral than self concerns which were at the heart of their construing. Failure of control over an entire career construct system appeared to be responsible for indecision but through the grid process, with their awareness sharpened, career deciders were able to exercise more decision-making control.

Case study 7.12 (Fournier and Payne, 1994)

A similar conclusion was drawn by Fournier and Payne (1994) in their grid-based study about the effects of individual development paths and personal role meaningfulness on graduate self construction during the transition between university and employment. The authors demonstrated that for these neophyte professionals, having made a career decision, the early period of employment provides the first grounds for experimentation from which graduates can validate, invalidate or revise their self construction in relation to work. Constructivist support with these reflections can help them to adjust their orientation productively.

Case study 7.13 (Mantle in Pope and Denicolo, 1997)

The next example begins with a concern about those for whom an initial career choice seems to have been ineffective.

To set the scene, Mantle's study (for more detail, see Pope and Denicolo, 1997) was concerned with attrition early in the career of nursing, which was recorded in 1996 at a steady 30 per cent in the UK and, according to news reports and in spite of recent changes to education and training, has not improved since. In summary, she aimed to determine the kinds of constructs held about the profession by candidates on entry to nurse training, by experienced nurses who had committed to the profession and those extant in the recruitment literature and purveyed by the media. In doing so, she was able to demonstrate several important factors, among them that:

- students held stereotypical views about their chosen profession;
- these views are a reflection of both the recruitment literature and the image conveyed by the media;

- these views of nursing are in many ways at variance with current nursing philosophies and practice;
- the high attrition rate is linked to conflicts of expectation and experience;
- some constructs, present on entering nursing and, admittedly, elaborated by experience, are still salient to experienced nurses;
- these constructs influenced career pathways and selection of clinical specialism.

The data to date suggests that the attrition rate of the past might have been higher had not circumstances, many of them adverse, prevented a move to another occupation. In effect the experienced nurses sought out and found specialisms in which their interest and values constructs were best met. These findings, therefore, firstly suggest that more attention needs to be paid to the recruitment literature and an analysis of that literature is ongoing but so far demonstrates how misleading it can be. Secondly, it is proposed that it would be of value to new recruits to a profession, and the organizations training and employing them, to explore early on constructs held about the profession and what it entails so that inappropriate expectations are challenged, more appropriate ones are assessed for pertinence to personal values and so that career pathways might be determined in a less ad hoc, time-consuming and risky fashion.

It is Mantle's contention that the methods she used (grids and narratives) to explore with participants their views about their profession would also form the basis of tools to do just that, since her participants were enabled in the process of the research to reflect on and review their own career choice and development stories.

During the course of elicitation of constructs, or after the grid was completed if that was more appropriate, the source of each construct was explored, as were the reasons for choosing nursing and when decisions were made. By and large, these questions either flowed naturally in the course of the grid elicitation process or were unnecessary because participants elaborated on their construct descriptions, saying for example 'my aunt is a district nurse and she is always moaning about that aspect' or 'I can't wait to be in the thick of it like they are in *Casualty*' (the TV series).

The experienced nurses (ten in all) obviously told more elaborate stories than did the novices about what nursing meant to them in the course of completing their grids, each of which had between 16 and 24 constructs. The elicitation procedure also included an encouragement to reflect back on their early days to discover how they perceived their constructs to have changed or remained the same. The process of laddering was used with them to explore which pole of a construct was most important to them, whether it had always been so, why it was important, or not, at different stages in their careers and how it was operationalized in practice. At appropriate points in the interview their reasons for entering nursing were sought and they were encouraged to articulate how and why they chose their current specialist roles.

The descriptions of what they used to think, and why, were frequently so well illuminated by anecdotes that it was clear that some aspects were well embedded in memory. Thus the completed grid forms, although providing illumination of how different genres of the nursing profession were seen to group, especially in relation to the clustering of constructs, the richness of the process is demonstrated in the narratives that accompanied the elicitation of constructs and the rating of them.

This research demonstrates that members of the family and the media are by far the most influential sources of information – a view reinforced by Muncy's (2000) investigation of the relative importance of previous socialization and current education for nurses. When formal careers guidance is sparse or superficial it does little to counteract deep seated prejudices and stereotypes, mainly because these are not uncovered, even in the selection process, far less challenged.

It is informative to consider also the reactions of all the participants to the process of data collection. They concurred that for them the grid interviews and narrative elicitation had been a period of reflection and they expressed appreciation for the opportunity to re-examine their personal motives for entering nursing and to re-assess their personal values. Thus, it is our and Mantle's contention that the tools used in the research could productively be reoriented towards addressing this urgent need for exploration of vocational constructs in order to identify, challenge and revise them where appropriate and to act as means of guiding people more effectively into the branch of the profession which suits them best.

The final example in this section embellishes the foregoing, demonstrating that early work with young people, using innovative techniques which appeal to their culture and encourage reflection, rather than merely bombarding them with information, produces results which are illuminative for researchers, careers guidance personnel and the young people alike. Mignot first provides a rationale for his chosen approach and then goes on to explain the innovative techniques used in his exploration.

Case study 7.14 (Mignot, 2000)

A constructive and critical approach to researching 'career' is one that acknowledges that guidance practitioners need a means of working satisfactorily with both individuals and social structures. The positioning of 'career' at the interface between the citizen and the state, and of the individual and society, means that guidance is inevitably a political activity (Watts, 1996). Thus, guidance practitioners are presented with the recurrent dilemma of not only reconciling client-centred values with socio-economic interests, but also of finding ways of resisting oppression through anti-discriminatory practice (Cross et al., 1990; EOC, 1999; Thompson, 1993). Given this context, constructive and critical research is concerned with two things. First, it seeks to understand how contemporary 'careers' are constructed by individuals. Secondly, it is concerned with gaining a critical appreciation of how these individual constructions relate to social systems and structures.

So, how might metaphor function as a paradigm for constructive and critical research into 'career'? This is first and foremost an epistemological question because constructive and critical research seeks to embrace both personal constructivist and social constructionist perspectives. A brief outline on metaphor will now be given to explain how it can help research participants to address both the construction of self-narrative and the deconstruction of social discourse.

There are three predominant views on metaphor: the substitution view, the comparison view, and the interactive view. Constructive and critical research is founded upon the interactive view of metaphor, the crux of which is the notion of the 'duality of representation' – that metaphor can serve to represent and re-present meaning. As such, metaphor is both representational and transformative. Furthermore, the reflexive quality of metaphor to both represent and transform experience can be defined as a hermeneutic process (Weinsheimer, 1985). Hermeneutics, which has been defined as a 'critical theory of interpretation' (Rundell, 1991: 10), is particularly concerned with the reflexive relationship between the individual elements of a 'text' and its entire structure (Okrent, 1988), a differentiation otherwise described as 'text' and 'context' (Weinsheimer, ibid., p. 239). It is important to emphasize that historical and social context provides hermeneutics with its primary source of understanding (Crotty, 1998). Furthermore, it should be noted that a 'text' in hermeneutic terms, includes not only the written word, but also 'behaviour, artefacts, and social structures.' (Bulhof, 1980: 3).

Giddens, in developing his social theory of structuration, has drawn explicitly from hermeneutics as a means of bringing together questions of human agency and social structure. By placing human action (text) in a reflexive relationship with social systems (context), Giddens developed the notion of 'practical consciousness' – a consciousness through which the individual both constructs and is constrained by social structures. Constructive and critical research utilizes Giddens' structuration theory by regarding metaphor as being entirely consistent with the notion of 'practical consciousness'. The following set of proposals summarize this view on metaphor:

1. Conscious experience of the world is represented through metaphor. Given that metaphor amalgamates 'text' (human action) with context (social systems) then the immediate corollary of this is that our construction of meaning is always contextualized.
2. Given that metaphor and literal sense cannot be distinguished, then the contextualization of meaning through metaphor becomes sedimented within cultural practices over time. It is in this way that metaphor acts as a medium for human action within social systems. As such, metaphor has a constraining function in that it establishes the unacknowledged conditions of human action.
3. Conscious experience of the world is transformed through metaphor. This acknowledges the generative power of metaphor to create new and unanticipated ways of knowing. Here metaphor, as an outcome of human action within social systems, produces unintended consequences; as such metaphor has a transformative function which is central to an understanding of human agency.

4. Social structure is represented and transformed through the hermeneutic and reflexive process of metaphorical perception which constitutes the practical consciousness of individuals.

On the basis of these proposals, metaphor provides a paradigm for constructive and critical research founded upon the following tenets:

(a) an understanding of the practical use of metaphor by human agents provides a means of making manifest the nature of social structure;
(b) human agents have the capacity to construct alternative metaphors through a process of symbolic interaction (i.e. self-narrative is achieved through a symbolic and reflexive process of metaphorical expression and construal);
(c) given these considerations, constructive and critical research is necessarily a hermeneutic and reflexive process founded upon a sensitivity towards intrapersonal perceptions, interpersonal interactions, and social context.

It follows then that constructive and critical research can proceed by first eliciting the tacit metaphors that constitute the practical consciousness of participants. This relies in part on engaging with naturally occurring discourse and interaction, the focus being the day-to-day taken for granted social practices of individuals and groups. This ethnomethodological orientation is necessarily complemented by a hermeneutic concern with 'text' (image, behaviour, object, social structure) from which metaphors can be identified and extrapolated.

A practical example will now be given of how metaphor can guide constructive and critical research into 'career'. Metaphor, as a paradigm for practice-based research, suggests that 'career' is manifested in a variety of 'textual' forms. These texts include not only the written word but also the visual (drawings, photographs, video etc.), and the kinaesthetic (all forms of physical action). The following example is of the use of visual methods as a means of researching 'career' constructively and critically with individuals and groups.

This example draws on the hermeneutic method of 'freezing' a 'text', or 'text analogue', for the purposes of interpretation. Here photographs are used as text analogues in the following ways:

(a) participants are invited to construct a 'photograph album' of aspects of their lives that are significant to them in 'career' terms. By taking photographs of people, places, events, objects etc., participants have the opportunity to construct a personal map of any number of images. In so doing participants are 'sifting' images – their choices in terms of what, where and when to photograph will be guided by, and will in turn demonstrate, the way in which they make comparisons and apply concepts. This will also be influenced by the briefing given to participants at the start of the activity. In this case participants were invited to construct a photographic record of 'ideal' and 'less than ideal' career scenarios – here contrast was an in-built feature of the activity. The photographs provide the basis for a hermeneutic approach to interpreting 'career'. This interpretation is undertaken by identifying the metaphors that are embedded within the participants' self-narratives. This is achieved by inviting the participants to describe and manipulate their photographic 'texts' in ways that are meaningful to them. In so doing, participants are encouraged to iterate between the whole and the parts of the text. This iterative process includes the following procedures:

(i) as a general principle, the participant is asked to provide a descriptive account of each photograph; this descriptive act reveals the context of the 'text' which in turn guides the emerging narrative – for example a building in a photograph might be described as 'modern and colourful' – in so doing description is displaced by interpretation which is then elaborated in the form of narrative.
(ii) more specifically, the participant is asked to relate each photograph to the context of 'career' this can be achieved through 'laddering' type questions, e.g. 'given that we're discussing how you see your future, why did you decide to take a photograph of this building?'. It is here that the photograph functions as a metaphor in that it fuses the context of 'career' with the emerging text, in this case 'modern and colourful'. The photograph also functions as a metonym in that it contains innumerable parts each of which might be 'read' differently.

These alternative readings can be facilitated through 'pyramiding' style questions, e.g. 'In what way might a career be 'modern' and 'colourful'? This procedure is based on the acknowledgement that the photographs both disguise and reveal meaning. By iterating between the whole and parts of the photographic 'text' (i.e. between the metaphoric and metonymic) other parts of the photograph achieve foreground significance leading to further interpretations. As such this procedure relies on the viewers to engage in both 'relational' and 'distancing' acts of interpretation. This iterative process is designed to develop among the viewers an empathic understanding not of the photograph, but of the meanings that they construct and reconstruct as they interpret the photographic text in context.

(b) Text construction and reconstruction is facilitated yet further through the use of 'Montage'. The 'Montage' technique involves encouraging participants to manipulate their photographs in ways that are significant to them: turning some face down, placing some in linear sequence to denote the passage of time or the pursuit of goals, placing some in a group to indicate a relationship, placing some apart to express difference or contrast, etc. More specifically, a 'montage' is constructed by presenting a physical and visual relationship between two or more photographs in reference to a guiding metaphor/metonym, e.g. 'my future', 'success', etc. Thus, the symbolic and referential functions of metaphor combine in 'montage' to provide narrative space for the participant. The montage can subsequently be reconstructed in various ways; the following are examples:

(i) moving, removing, or adding photographs in reference to an alternative context, e.g. 'if this represented your future rather than your past, would you change the montage in any way?'; 'if we took this picture out of the montage would it tell a different story?'

(ii) asking the participant to consider missing photographs, e.g. 'if this montage became 'your future' what other pictures would you need?'; 'there are no pictures of people here – why do you think that is?'

(c) Text construction and reconstruction can be continued through the use of 'Mural'. The 'Mural' technique involves creating a wall mural from participants' photographs – this might include the use of collage, painting and drawing. The construction of the mural draws from the processes of 'montage' – new relationships, sequences etc. emerge as participants make decisions about their composition. 'Mural' is a group activity, designed to make public the private constructions of individual participants.

Each of the methods described above ('photograph album', 'montage', and 'mural') are hermeneutic in design and generate rich data. The methods are also designed to expand and extend the context of the research, i.e. the methods begin with individuals and progressively engage with groups and communities. This progressive movement provides the means to deploy these methods critically in the following terms:

1. At an individual level career aspirations can be regarded as metaphors which both enable and constrain human agency. For to construct one's self as a lawyer, builder, or child care worker etc., both expands and limits the possibilities for action.
2. At a cultural and collective level, career aspirations can reveal systemic patterns; these patterns can also be regarded as metaphors which guide social action. For example, collective metaphors may have gendered, racialized, or social class connotations, which in turn provide the rules of day-to-day practical conduct.
3. At a structural level, the concern is with how social structures are produced and reproduced over time through the practices of daily life; as indicated, these practices are guided by the generative metaphors that are present within cultural-collective discourse.

Collective discourse provides the theme for the next group of exploratory endeavours which have as their aim the transformation of practice at the group as well as at the individual level.

Team building

Case study 7.15 (Leyin, 1992; Ranade, 1985)

Like the previous topic, the need for building teams applies to all the sectors of work. Leyin (1992) provided a succinct discussion of his explorations of using grid techniques in the context of building teams in the Community Mental Handicap service. He argued that, though too much introspection at the expense of not getting the work done is obviously unacceptable, so too is having a demotivated, demoralized team. He described the grid method he used in helping a team to begin to function at its optimal level by identifying areas that need to be tackled. He found that the method could also be adapted to assist monitoring the outcomes of interventions and the process of change. Both he and another author who had used a similar technique, Ranade (1985), recognized that teams need criteria by which to assess the effectiveness of individual and group performance. For Ranade the lack of agreed criteria of evaluation formed the crux of the concern of a District Health Authority. She reported that the disciplined thinking involved in the grid technique prevented the rationalizations which would have occurred if 'effectiveness' had been discussed amongst the group of participants as a generalized abstraction. For her, the main value of the approach lay in the clarification of bases for judgements, with differing perceptions and expectations being brought into the open.

To illustrate further the potential of constructivist methods for developing teams in pressurized contexts, we paraphrase here a chapter by Denicolo published in Kalekin-Fishman and Walker (1996) which describes a novel implementation of a grid technique for sharing grid information.

Case study 7.16 (Denicolo, 1996)

The chapter in Kalekin-Fishman and Walker (1996) describes in detail how two doctoral students (Baker, 1992 and Tjok-a-Tam, 1993) used the technique of 'overlay grids' in different professional contexts to develop the work of staff groups, each member of which, through the exigencies of external pressures, had to move from relatively autonomous professional activity to group working modes. Each workshop began with a discussion emphasizing that individual differences in construing are inevitable, given that they are derived from diverse experiences and differential opportunities to test the validity of constructs. This was then illustrated by the use of a non-threatening and entertaining grid exercise, the overt purpose of which was to identify a suitable range of biscuits to provide for the group's coffee break. Of course, participants also recognized that this would provide them with an introduction to the process of a technique to be used later in the session. However, it also had the advantage of demonstrating that, even in relatively simple parts of our world, alternative but valid perspectives exist and that these can either produce conflict or be used creatively as resources for problem solving.

One lesson provided was that in the elicitation of the potential biscuit elements to be selected from for the universe of discourse, not all were familiar to all the participants – so alerting them all to a wider range than they would consider individually. Further, when constructs were elicited and rated individually and then shared with the group, some constructs were not salient to some individuals, e.g. the degree of 'dunkability' of a biscuit, was only relevant to a few, while others produced different perceptions about particular biscuit types (how could anyone conceive of shortbread as crunchy?). The subsequent discussion noted the practical benefit of including some types of coffee-break biscuits that only some people liked (more for those who do) and the sharing of knowledge achieved in the process (some are allergic to chocolate and others knew the calorific value of each type!)

After this orientation the grids which were the real focus of the work (for one group, the detailed aims of a course to be taught by the team and for the other, the learning methods that today's managers might use) were elicited in a similar way by negotiation of an agreed element set, and then negotiation of an agreed construct set. The elements were then individually rated as better fitting one pole or the other of each construct. The participants drew up their grids on transparent sheets on which each element/construct cell was divided by a diagonal line, producing two triangular segments. The rating was denoted by shading in either the bottom left triangle of the cell (to indicate agreement with the elicited pole) or the top right triangle of the cell (agreement with the emergent pole).

By overlaying the transparent grids in pairs and in groups, note could be taken of where blocked segments coincided (only the same triangle shaded in each) and where a totally shaded square indicated contrasting views. In addition, it is possible to note which elements are viewed very differently (several blocked in squares in a column) and which constructs convey different meanings in their wording to individuals (several squares blocked in across a line).

For each group, the stage of negotiating elements proved illuminating. Sometimes the same words were used to denote different things, sometimes they discovered that they used different words to mean very similar things. For instance, the activity of listening to speakers meant to only a few participants that advance preparation was required, the rest seeing it as an entirely passive activity, while people used the terms 'systematic reflection' and 'evaluating past experiences' to describe similar activities but the person using the latter description viewed the former as impenetrable academic jargon. When individuals shared potential constructs for the grid, it revealed that some were important to all while others were idiosyncratic, important but unique to an individual. For instance a common shared construct for one group concerned the degree to which the group were committed to achieve a particular aim, while in the same group only the part-time workers were concerned with being enabled or restricted in contributing towards an aim.

The overlaid grids produced yet more thought-provoking results. People found reassurance when they demonstrated that colleagues had similar concerns and views; as an example there was a sense of relief that everyone was equally short of resources. In contrast, the benefit of sharing a preliminary debate about biscuits became apparent as conflicting opinions emerged about more important work issues. A team felt more ready to explore, without attributing fault, the tensions raised when it became apparent that the team leader felt that responsibility should be shared while the rest of the group felt that responsibility resided only with a chosen few.

A particular product for both groups of this process was the realization that speaking the same language was not necessarily synonymous with communicating, that being in the same place at the same time did not always result in the same experience. Others were: the identification of specific common ground on which further work could be built, the recognition of the range of experience and knowledge that could be drawn on in the team, and the revealing but bounding of areas that needed further discussion to avert future communication problems. Such problems are common in business as the examples in the following section demonstrate.

Constructivist approaches applied in business and industry

It is not our remit in this chapter to review all the potential business applications of constructivist methods; rather it is to demonstrate the variety of purposes to which they might be applied and to describe some specific examples of techniques used. However, we would like to alert readers to two specific texts which provide further exemplars of the use of repertory grid techniques in this field.

Case study 7.17 (Jankowicz, 1990; Fonda, 1981)

Jankowicz (1990) focused on human resource management and included sections on job analysis, employee selection, induction and training, task analysis and employee effectiveness, training evaluation and performance appraisal. He provided an extensive resource of references as well as a clear, cogent review of the strengths and limitations of the processes in current use in these areas of endeavour. Fonda, in Stewart and Stewart (1981) has a more specific focus on the evaluation of training and she showed by rich examples how the diagnosis of training needs, and the measurement of change due to training, are made more sensitive using grid techniques. The illustrations also demonstrated how training might be more effectively marketed within an organization using these processes.

For our own illustrations we draw on our consultancy experience with industry. Although detailed confidential reports were made to the funding organizations, we obviously cannot reference them here but we will endeavour to provide a flavour of the work in anonymized form.

Case study 7.18 (Denicolo and Pope)

Difficulty in communicating implicit knowledge which forms the basis of a skilled job was one problem that we addressed on behalf of a manufacturer. The management's concern was that the skilled workforce currently employed would soon be retiring but there were no family members in apprenticeship, as there had been in the past, and no written detailed descriptions existed of how to do the task, a quality control activity.

Standing next to a fast moving conveyor belt, the operatives viewed the articles on the way to the packing station, selecting some for immediate discarding, others for more detailed inspection and apparently 'passing as fit' the remainder. These workers had performed the task for many years, and there were seldom complaints from the customers, yet they had difficulty in articulating any process guidelines for others to follow. A form of grid was used to explore their constructs of 'fit/not fit' but instead of using verbal labels for elements, a selection of the articles themselves were used, some from the discard pile, some from the 'test' pile and some from the good quality remainder. By using the triadic method, the workers were able to distinguish how one article was different from two others in general and to provide then a more detailed description, often through the process of laddering, to identify observable features, and the process of pyramiding to say why it was relevant to the perceived quality of the article. Perhaps it would not give too many secrets away to say that the articles were underwear garments. A discarded item might be described as having 'too tight stitching', indicated by puckering of the material, which would prevent the article being stretched over the appropriate body part, especially during activity. Such descriptions proved to be a great improvement on the 'just won't do' previously (accurately) given for rejection. Similarly, indicators of the need to test – for stretchability, minor size differences etc., were also identified by comparing good, not so good and poor examples and exploring why they had been 'instinctively' selected as such.

Case study 7.19 (Denicolo and Pope)

Our second example also concerns an industry in which custom and practice had resulted in an area of work developing with no clear job description being devised. This only became a difficulty when the small firm expanded its turnover without being able to allocate greater space for storage. It seemed that a 'just in time' policy would solve this dilemma, parts only coming at the point of need and the finished item being shipped as the customer required it. The warehouse personnel held the key to some aspects of this as they provided the parts to the operatives and got to know customer patterns of requirements. The ordering and despatch log books provided some information but could not tell us why certain parts were ordered, seemingly in advance of operative need. The warehouse people clearly had an idea of when parts would be required beyond the 'stocks are running low' imperative.

The Interview about Instances (IAI) method was employed fruitfully in the course of interviews with log books providing the instances when parts were ordered in particular numbers at different points in the calendar. This provided the stimulus for recollection of why that order was made at that point and not at another (a slack period during the holiday season being followed by a seasonal demand, for instance). It also provided information about volume of orders in other respects, such as some parts only being sold by the manufacturers in certain quantities while others had a limited shelf life. A spin off of this exploration was that the personnel concerned were able to suggest ways of responding to the current situation from the background of their accumulated wisdom and so, since they were involved in the decision making process and could see the rationale behind decisions, they more readily adapted to changes in working practice.

Case study 7.20 (Denicolo and Pope)

A company of a very different scale was the context of the third example. This multinational conglomerate, hereafter known as the Company, employed graduates in a wide variety of roles and the executive was alert to the perpetual flux which was the nature of its business. If the Company was to maintain its world-leader image, then its staff, whether executives, accountants, engineers or its many staff dealing with the public, would need to adapt continuously to developments in knowledge, technology and service requirements. Yet, in spite of having a comprehensive training division and a recruitment policy of selecting the 'best' graduates, some departments had difficulty in articulating their recruitment needs while some apparently well-qualified staff were struggling to adapt to new demands, with all the personal dissatisfaction and general professional frustration that such a situation entails.

A review of the person specification for the jobs involved and the recruitment profiles demonstrated little significant difference in the qualifications and attributes of those who were adapting successfully and those who were not. In spite of its size, the espoused culture of the Company was that of a 'safe employer that cares for its staff', so there was a strong reluctance to dismiss staff or make them redundant. Clearly for recruitment purposes attributes required needed to be defined in more detail, especially in relation to changing needs. Equally, it was important to identify skills and attributes in current employees so that these could be matched with another job or their profile developed to better match their current one.

The first stage in the process included short interviews with the senior managers, personnel/training managers, and representatives of all levels in the organization who had some links with the graduate employees, including their internal clients, and those employees themselves. These served to establish a positive image for the project, and to familiarize us with the culture, language register and jargon of the organization – a key factor for the second stage of the project. This latter involved in-depth grid elicitations with small groups from each level of the Company, as described for the first round, but included whole teams of graduate employees, including their immediate supervisors. Of interest in this context is the process of group elicitation of individual grids.

As part of the continued establishment of rapport and to facilitate the elicitation of the project grids, a short 'fun' grid was demonstrated, much as described earlier in the Team Building section, though in this case the elements were a range of cars. For the project grids the participants were supplied with grid forms with printed generalized elements which were a range of short descriptions of employees derived from the first round interviews. These included: 'a real expert', 'a walking disaster', 'one steeped in tradition', and 'new era mover and shaker'. Each participant was asked to identify an individual in their work environment who fitted the general description, using a code to remind them on the grid.

Having been alerted to the purpose of the grid – to consider the people in terms of how they were as employees in the section – they were then guided through the grid process, recording and rating for each element bipolar constructs elicited through the triadic process. During the process they were asked laddering and pyramiding questions and encouraged to write these elaborations on to the grid as appropriate. Towards the end of the interview they were encouraged, having become familiar with the process, to add constructs using the full context method, particularly ensuring that they had considered what skills, attitudes and attributes were present and how these were manifest in practice. A final exercise included the participants in annotating on the grid form the three most important positive poles of constructs and two negative poles which would give them grave concern if displayed by a candidate or colleague.

Practical details that may be of interest are that each group interview took about two hours, with the most manageable number in the group being between six and ten, though a caveat is that the interviewers were experienced 'gridders' who interspersed general process instructions with individual help and guidance to those who requested it. This took a lot of concentration and skill so that the pace did not become boring for some while no-one was left 'stuck'.

Dealing with the resulting data was also demanding though we appreciated the help of Shaw's (1993) Repgrid 2 Analysis programme. Each individual was supplied with their own analysed grid with a short commentary of interpretation. The grids were also analysed in groups to allow comparisons between groups, for example the graduate teams were compared with each other, with the views of their managers, their internal clients and the personnel team. Finally, the constructs from all the grids were aggregated so that, using the clustering method, constructs could be reviewed to produce a comprehensive list of superordinate attributes (each with detailed descriptions of how they are manifest) of an 'ideal' employee, a 'good' employee, and one in need of specific development. This also allowed for the compilation of attributes which were negative indicators.

Obviously, this project met its main aim of providing detailed person specifications for graduate employees and information on which specific training programmes would benefit current employees. It also had additional benefits, one of which was that, in the course of construing in a structured way the attributes of colleagues known to them, managers and supervisors were able to recognize greater value in some they had almost written off. For instance, they reported that they had sometimes been misled by noticing one negative characteristic, which might be addressed by training or extended experience, to the neglect of other more positive ones which provided a useful contribution to the team. They also recognized more fully the need for variety in team members. They had begun by seeking paragons who could meet all the criteria and now realized that it was productive to have some 'creative dissonance' in some teams.

Equally, they were sometimes astonished to find that the few 'square pegs' that they had identified would be ideal fits for some previously unconsidered square holes in the Company. It was instructive to them also to see how different, occasionally opposite, attributes were required by, for example, team colleagues and their internal clients. A simple example is that the two groups have different ideas about the approach to be taken to exploring a presented problem – colleagues prefer a swift decision maker while clients want someone who will take the time to really understand their needs. Finally, the data made it clear that sometimes a new recruit should be sought who had the potential to develop through working in the Company and being trained by it, rather than always seeking people exhibiting the attributes in fully fledged form.

This last point has relevance for the next section which addresses the topic of professional or staff development and training.

Personal development and professional training

The final section which follows will make more explicit our perspective on the topic which forms the title of this section, but here we continue to follow our intention of providing exemplars of implementations in practice.

Earlier we mentioned the work of Tjok-a-Tam. In her thesis (1994), she explored the variety of pressures impinging on colleges of Further and Higher Education which demanded a review of their provision of management education. She then employed an action research approach, using personal construct approaches including Personal Development Journals, critical incident snakes and grids, to illuminate the perspectives of the managers on programmes of study and their teachers about their experiences and needs. In her thesis, she argued that, to enable transformative learning by manager-learners through a process of emancipatory education, a complementary, parallel process of critical, active reflection must be established for the teaching staff-as-learners within innovative educational programmes.

Case study 7.21 (Harwood and Denicolo, 1994)

In a contemporaneous study (Harwood and Denicolo, 1994), Denicolo worked with novice teachers from the same education sector, again using an action research approach, to help them reflect on their own learning development as they engaged in their first year of probation. This study incorporated professional self-characterization sketches, completed every three months and used to review the recent months and then the year as a whole. The following is a compilation of some excerpts from one teacher, whom we have called Naomie.

In the beginning ...
Naomie started with her new classes feeling very motivated and enthusiastic, but also very worried about whether she could remember all the things she would need to tell her classes. She is very approachable and enjoys the interaction with the students but has a niggling concern about her credibility to them ...

Later in the year ...
Naomie is still enjoying the practical experience and remains enthusiastic but the lesson preparation takes a long time. She must keep up with her reading as well as the marking and she is very nervous about experimenting with new teaching methods. She has discovered that she is a better time manager than she thought she would be but she does not always remember to project her voice clearly in larger classes. This is not a problem with small groups but does lead to repetition and embarrassment in larger ones ...

Near the end of the year ...
A visit by her mentor has boosted her confidence; her teaching voice is coming more naturally now and she had the opportunity to teach a very large group in

a lecture theatre. Although it was scary, everyone seemed to be able to hear her, looked interested and asked good questions at the end. Has tried a few new methods which worked well and the lecture session has encouraged her to let the students ask more questions and take a more active part in lessons. Still a lot to learn though ... letting go is hard when she is not yet confident of being in total control of the situation.

Naomie produced each sketch for a discussion about her progress and about what aspects of her role and how she could develop further. These she left behind and they were only reviewed in toto at the end of the year. Since she usually declared that she could not remember what she had written the last time, she was surprised at the threads and themes which re-occurred but delighted at the progress that was demonstrated in her thinking about her practice as well as in the practice itself. She had become used to standing back in a critical stance from the rush and tumble of her professional life, unearthing and confronting her 'niggling concerns', and devising steps to address them. Naomie planned to implement the process of 'reflective sketching' as she proceeds with her career and declared herself as transforming into her own mentor.

Harwood and Denicolo (1994) were also concerned to listen to people's voices, and to encourage them to listen to their own, in the realm of personal and professional development. Their method was the, by now, traditional grid technique but the topic and results are significant here. The participants were a group of people from a variety of professional backgrounds working within one large organization; the purpose was to learn from their experience of participating in any activities which might conceivably contribute to their learning and development as professionals. The elements of the grid were derived from a group elicitation of those activities viewed as developmental. These were then negotiated into a manageable set to include a range of activities, from individual and informal to group and formal. The first point of interest is that, though they were given the opportunity to complete separate grids for personal and for professional development, the majority chose to combine the two, indicating that they saw them as interconnected. All the detail of the analysis cannot be provided here but some points are worthy of note in this context.

More than two-thirds of the participants rated as very similar in-house activities provided by a presenter from the same organization or provided by a specialist from outside. From a purely practical aspect this might be interpreted as representing support for the use of expertise within an organization for staff development activities although a more detailed analysis demonstrated that several caveats are relevant. Proper time away from the temptation or pressing needs of daily activities needs to be guarded and a trusting, confidential atmosphere is needed. Staff development activities should 'widen horizons', 'improve performance' and be 'demonstrably relevant', to name but a few of the positive constructs, while they should not leave a participant feeling 'de-skilled and inadequate' or 'highly isolated' and instructors should 'take individuals seriously'.

It has been claimed (Moses, 1985, for example) that people participating in staff development and training activities want practical advice, prescriptive guidelines, dos and don'ts. This study did not support that view. Taken together, the constructs tell a story of the desire by staff for a developmental environment which offers the provocation of, and opportunities for, stretching and extending the individual in dimensions in which he/she is interested while providing the means by which there is time to reflect on what is being achieved. In common with Moses' participants, those in this study did indeed want a supportive climate, but they particularly valued a challenging, interactive learning situation in which views could be shared and discussed in a co-operative manner. They seemed to agree with Pope (1990: 5) that:

> Staff development strategies which do not invite challenge of a person's implicit theories may be seen as comfortable but will not lead to any reappraisal of current theory and practice.

Having been given insights, if only brief ones, into the diversity of contexts in which other professionals have found particular methods illuminative, we hope that readers will by now see the potential relevance for personal construct approaches and methods for their own personal and professional development – a topic we will pursue in the next, and final, chapter.

Chapter 8
Conclusions: answers none but choice aplenty

> New things are made familiar, and familiar things are made new. (Samuel Johnson on Alexander Pope, *The Lives of English Poets*, 1757).

> The only end of writing is to enable the readers better to enjoy life or better to endure it. (Samuel Johnson, 'On optimism', 1781)

Engaging with change

We began this book by noting that the world in which we live is rapidly changing. Developments in knowledge, technology and modes of delivery of professional services in response to client demand have produced consequent pressures on professionals for continuous learning beyond that which was previously assumed in more stable eras, i.e. the accretion of knowledge and the honing of skills derived from additional experience. Fullan (1991: xiii) raised a salutary question in the preface to his book about educational change, and this was how to get good at change – that is, how to increase the capacity of individuals and organizations to know when to reject certain change possibilities, to know when and how to pursue and implement others, and to know how to cope with policies and programs that are imposed on them.

Each of these possible responses to change, that is to resist, engage in or accommodate it, are improved if they are based on an evaluative stance. Such evaluation requires as a precursor that current purposes and values are rendered explicit to allow for adequate comparisons to be made with proposed modifications and developments. This provides a cognitive framework of justification for responses rather than allowing them to be simple, automatic reactions to perceived threat.

Fullan went on to suggest that even well-intentioned change can cause havoc unless individuals develop a healthy respect for change and ways of adapting to it. Bailey (1990: 68) had earlier declared that the times demand an adaptable and flexible workforce and that this is a matter of attitude. She proceeded to suggest: Individuals must be able to handle the process of change: to understand change and their reactions to it and to work positively with change rather than to oppose it.

Both of these authors eschew a passive response to change and appear to advocate transformative practice for professionals. Their views have some commonality at least with the way in which we described transformatory practice in our prologue, i.e. the development of alternative ways of looking at professional practice which can result in productive change. The essence of these ideas is optimism – the notion derived from Kelly's work that we need not find ourselves painted into a corner – well laced with a commitment to finding ways of actively getting out of the corner. In this final chapter we draw together for the reader some of the innovative ideas that we have proposed in the book, hoping that by now they feel more familiar. We also suggest that the new ways of perceiving the familiar, advocated in the book, present possible ways of finding solutions to Fullan's conundrum and Bailey's challenge of producing dynamic evolution of the professions.

Reviewing implications and imprecations

In analysing, in Chapter 1, the philosophical approaches which underpin education (compulsory, qualifying and continuing professional), we drew attention to a constellation of theories which had particular applicability to adult learning. Knowles (1978) had noted that adult learning was qualitatively different to learning engaged in during the early years of life. In his andragogical model he proposed six factors which, in dynamic conjunction with each other, made for this difference: the need to know; a self concept of being responsible for decisions; having experience; the presence of a readiness to learn; a life, task or problem orientation and internally driven motivation. Other educationists, for instance Schon (1987) and Mezirow (1990), emphasized reflection on and in action as critical processes, with Mezirow citing Habermas's (1971) emancipatory cognitive interest as distinctive in the adult domain. We argued that this kind of learning has little in common with the traditional view of learning as the simple reception of knowledge nor does it fit the technical rational model which deems that professional activity is solely the application of theoretical knowledge, derived from the clean world of the research laboratory, to the dirty and untidy world of real adult life. We suggested that education as defined within Personal Construct Psychology approaches to education, described in detail in Chapter 2, had more to offer in that it encourages the engagement of the individual with their own

learning in contexts which make that learning not only relevant but necessary and sometimes urgent.
These approaches, we proposed, involved activities that:

- encouraged the examining of ideas afresh, both those derived from received wisdom and those composed of personal theories and assumptions;
- involved self-consciously assessing personal and professional relevance;
- stimulated the re-interpretation of knowledge instead of the taking for granted of that which is presented;
- demanded engagement with life as it is lived rather than with a sterilized form.

This seems to us an appropriate and transformative way for professionals in the workplace to engage in learning. Most professionals that we have encountered in the course of our work recognize this description in the sense that it aligns with their espoused theories about how their own development should proceed. On the other hand, they have reported and continue to report that they frequently find difficulty in changing habitual methods and 'theories in use' in work contexts fraught with work overload and staff shortages. They also reported that the constraining effects of theories imposed from without, from other professions or from government policy, sometimes left a feeling of powerlessness. Other authors have noted the erosion of professional autonomy at a general level and the diminishing of a personal sense of efficacy at the individual level. For instance, Handy (1985), in his report of working within organizations which were in danger of fading away because they were unable to change, described staff as 'beavering away' at what they did best, working harder and more efficiently at diminishing tasks. They may, of course, be preserving current values but this analogy conveys an unreasoned response to imposed pressure.

A picturesque example of a similar notion was provided by Cuthbert (1988) discussing the implications for staff of the incorporation of educational institutions. He saw the staff symbolically as captive GERBILS (an acronym for the Great Education Reform Bill), condemned to run endlessly on a treadmill, dissipating energy, perhaps becoming leaner and fitter, but without making any progress in the sense of conserving what is good and making use of opportunity for productive change. There is further evidence of the human cost to staff of failure to recognize the implication of imposed change. Castling (1983) spoke of the intolerable levels of stress experienced by individuals during times of rapid change within their organizations while Dalin (1978) recognized that change can be energy draining, time-consuming and thus costly. Not all the costs are readily observable or financial. In addition to those for productivity, personal costs include the feelings of insecurity when expertise seems threatened, the associated loss of self-esteem, the fear of failure and demotivation. These can be profound and far reaching.

In such circumstances it is important that tools are found which empower people by allowing them to own changes to be made to their practice. Such ownership derives from change chosen as having *personal* relevance that results from research and explorations that are salient to the context and to fellow, respected professionals. Thus their behaviour can be deemed *professional* in the proper sense of the word since it incorporates the autonomy and informed, balanced judgement that society expects of its professionals. Consideration of what kinds of research might appropriately inform such judgements was given in Chapter 3, in which we noted the limitations of research:

- which neglects the importance of understanding the view of the world held by the actors in any situation;
- which misguidedly assumes objectivity;
- and which adheres to well-practised processes with traditional tools which barely skim the surface of an interaction.

We described a contrasting, more imaginative and, we argued, more scientific approach which encourages the exploration of alternative perspectives and understandings. In the three chapters which follow we then presented a range of tools, starting with the well-known repertory grid in Chapter 4 but then expanding, in Chapter 5, the principles which underpin that structured technique to a plethora of mechanisms which provide a framework for in-depth exploration of human construing. In the next chapter we amplified on ways to successfully implement these techniques, providing in Chapter 7 examples of their application in professional contexts and practice.

Drawing on recent and current work of our own, our colleagues and our research students, we gave a flavour of possibilities inherent in a range of diverse professional contexts.

We described explorations undertaken within the Health Service which addressed issues of concern to doctors, nurses (hospital and community), tutors and student health practitioners. Similarly, people engaged in youth and community work, social work and health and social education provided us with reports of PCP interventions with colleagues, with novice practitioners and with clients. Examples were chosen from the fields of careers guidance and counselling, management education and training and human resource management to illustrate how issues relevant to most professions might be addressed while responses to some specific problems within business and industry demonstrated further applications of the approach. Finally, acknowledging the link between formal education and professional practice, we provided examples of staff development from the further and higher education sector.

The range of problems exemplified as benefiting from a Personal Construct Psychology approach included:

- inter-professional issues such as role boundaries and interactions, implementing an integrated curriculum, ethical and moral dilemmas;
- the consequences for novices of interaction with clients and more senior colleagues;
- the selection of specialisms within a field of professional practice;
- the negotiation of understandings between client and professional;
- alternative perceptions of risk and fear;
- the impact of critical incidents in high stress occupations;
- the development of communication for and with the Learning Disabled;
- the exploration of diverse perspectives with regard to anti-social behaviour;
- team building;
- compiling detailed person specifications for jobs;
- job analysis;
- selection and training in business and industrial contexts;
- personal and professional development in turbulent times.

This was not intended to be a comprehensive list but we trust that it serves to highlight the potential of a range of techniques that promote understanding and transformation through the sharing of individual and group perspectives.

Implementing a dialogue

In the course of these chapters we have emphasized the value of liberating the mind from past habits by rigorous examination of current thinking. Although we have acknowledged that we cannot entirely escape our perspectives derived from previous experience, and that our current ways of knowing and ways of being may have many forms of value, we have challenged the notion that we are hostage to past involvements. In effect, we recognize the worth of role models etc. but urge that they do not become role corsets! We suggested dialogue as the starting point, but we reiterate here that the first dialogue should be with one's own self, recognizing that current hypotheses are open to gradual challenge or dramatic invalidation and that learning is a personal, creative act. Only then can we effectively engage with others in their personal journeys of learning. In that activity the process of stimulating the articulation of ideas and perspectives is paramount for, unless and until they are articulated, they cannot be challenged, nor can we, our colleagues and our students in negotiation with participants, be experimental in devising strategies to put them to the test. We have, in our examples, indicated that the techniques we and others have devised provide powerful means of clarifying thoughts and of promoting consideration of self-managed change.

This latter point serves to remind us that any intervention in professional lives should be a co-operative venture, though there may be an educative intent to transform the practice of others to help them to make it more effective. The dynamic evolution of a profession in response to the needs of the culture in which it is embedded is generally perceived as positive, not just expedient but desirable. However, although at the macroscopic level general movement may be identified as forward in direction, at the microscopic level, from the individual professional's perspective, it may seem more like apparently random motion. They may feel buffeted, like particles in the smoke rising from a chimney, by innumerable, and sometimes invisible, external pressures. It is proposed here that PCP, in providing processes which allow professionals to share their constructions of their roles and remits, to identify activities they feel impelled to engage in and the paths they choose to take and why, would both raise their consciousness about the direction of the propulsion and allow them to make an active, sentient contribution to it.

Throughout this book we have focused on the *individual* as he/she develops as a person and as a professional but recognize that construing includes a *social* dimension. Kelly recognized this himself and hence the commonality and sociality corollaries are important aspects of the theory. However, as psychologists we have an abiding concern with the individual and seek to redress the prevalent social emphasis on social determinism in much of the literature on education and training. Society through the processes of socialization certainly influences individuals in their development, personal or professional, but we take the view that these processes are mediated through the individual as they chose to be influenced by them, to a greater or lesser extent, or to choose which of competing discourses to heed or resist and which to validate themselves or their practice by.

Thus, we contend that PCP processes and techniques have an important contribution to make to the professions because they have the potential for promoting *real* development of staff rather than imposing 'pseudo-development' through the re-packaging of 'old and time-weary products' based on traditional education and training techniques (Gleeson and Mardle, 1980: 149). Developing staff, or rather instigating self development, is not about merely providing new tools but about helping people to choose their own and to learn the skills to use them and their own abilities to the full.

Interventions which will succeed in this aim will result from careful consideration of the paradigm in which they are based and its appropriateness for professional transformation. Their design demands careful planning, with methods chosen which fit comfortably with the aims of the project, the context in which it is embedded and the ability and needs of the participants. Attention needs to be paid to time factors in terms of manageability of the task, how much the participants are willing to commit and when it might be feasible to ask that commitment of them. Preparation time is also paramount. We have indicated throughout the sections dealing with techniques that some of them need a degree of practice for successful implementation, though they are extremely powerful when used well. Equally, time beyond that required for the implementation of some of these powerful techniques may be required so that participants can draw on support, having confronted previously submerged ideas or challenged strongly held ones.

A final demand is that for flexibility, a willingness to continuously monitor and review the process, on the part of the investigator or researcher. Although some adjustments might be relatively trivial, perhaps a subtle change of emphasis to incorporate additional needs identified during the process, others may be more swingeing. Some possibilities are that a change in technique might be required when the planned one proves less fruitful or it may be that a need for a follow-up becomes obvious as the exploration develops. Even the best laid plans ...!

A decision point: to join the dance or remain a spectator

In workshops which we run as part of the Centre for Personal Construct Psychology in Education to introduce the philosophy and approaches to novices we are similarly at pains, as we have been above, to provide caveats and warnings to potential users, yet each year new members join the group. Equally, each year we are able to provide reports not only of successful and innovative research and satisfied customers of our consultancy, but also of the enthusiastic reception of the ideas and techniques by those who participated in constructivist activities, interventions and research with us and our students. Sometimes colleagues jokingly accuse us of casting a spell over student participants in such workshops. Sadly this metaphor of weaving magic belies the hard work and dedication required of proponents and users of PCP, so we invite you now to reflect on what you have learnt during your reading of this book.

We recognize that within this wealth of ideas that we have presented there may be some which resonate with yours while others may be more provocative. If there is sufficient resonance then you may be tempted to adopt a PCP approach within your working practice. Our own experience suggests that this will be a challenging task to undertake. Our empathy with your plight is demonstrated from the following summary provided in a recent paper (Denicolo, 1996: 56).

> One of the frustrating things about espousing a personal construct philosophy, or indeed any of a range of phenomenological approaches to research, is that it behoves one to take into account an astonishing variety of possible interpretations or alternative constructions of reality. Holding to the tenets of these approaches does not compel one to agree with all the options or to rate them equally, but it does present an *embarras de choix* on which to base personal selection to inform decision making. How much easier it would be to return to a childlike belief that there is an answer to every problem as long as one conforms to a simple set of rules and obtains the relevant information from experts and books.
>
> Few of us are very old before we discover that the rules are not simple, nor is there only one set, and that experts frequently disagree and sometimes 'don't know'.

A declaration in that paper was that we increasingly find ourselves having to make decisions in a field of uncertainty and in the face of contradictory evidence, just as do other professionals. Since we cannot rely on conventional wisdom that implores us to look before we leap knowing that he/she who hesitates is lost, we take heart from Nussbaum (1985: 260) who declared;

> The experience of conflict can also be a time of learning and development ... a progress that comes from an increase in self knowledge and knowledge of the world.

Miller (1994) also provided consolation drawn from his work exploring the value of introducing the consideration of dilemmic situations into the school curriculum. This led him to suggest that by helping others to recognize the existence of dilemmas and by the encouragement of debate on their resolution, active learning can be assisted, which includes relativistic reasoning, dialectical thinking and reflective moral judgement. From another viewpoint, Goodlad (1984: 297) provided this additional salutary reminder:

> education for a profession is the product of several competing interests which act as checks and balances on one another. If any one agency comes to dominate at the expense of the others, then the rich, pluralistic (and therefore potentially democratic) texture of education will be diminished.

Remembering Ashwell's work, described in the preceding chapter, we might add that *not* exploring, trying to understand and take account of other's perspectives diminishes the fibre of any form of professional practice.

Nevertheless, such activities can be carried out to different degrees by individuals in the course of their work. We implore you to take advantage of a 'still point', having reached the end of this book, to consider the implications for your views of the world, and those of others with whom you might engage, if you decide to try out and experiment with the approach and techniques. We may have raised your awareness simply and sufficiently that you give pause occasionally to consider whether your constructs might be constraining you unnecessarily, or you may like to create opportunities for sharing views and perspectives with others, or you may decide to implement some of the techniques and ideas in the process of your work or even to engage in formal research about it. For our part, we will continue to stretch the notions embedded here to their limits, to experiment creatively with alternative techniques, yet adhering to the founding philosophy of the approach – to value and to try to understand and to learn from other ways of being. We would be delighted if, after due reflection, you joined us in the dance, sometimes following our footsteps, sometimes improvising your own.

References

Adams-Webber JR (1970) Elicitated versus provided constructs in Repertory Grid Technique: A Review. Br. J. Med. Psychol. 43: 349–53.

Adelman C, Walker R (1975) Developing pictures for other frames; action research and case study. In Chanan G and Delmont S (eds) Frontiers of Classroom Research. Slough: NFER.

Allison A, Ewens A (1998) Tensions in sharing client confidences while respecting autonomy: implications for interprofessional practice. Nursing Ethics 5: 441–50.

Allister D, Mair JMM (1968) The Evaluation of Personal Constructs. London: Academic Press.

Allport GW (1955) Becoming. New Haven: Yale University Press.

Apraiz E (2000) Visual art:a catalyst for communication with people who have learning disabilities? Paper to be presented at the 5th EPCA Conference, Challenging the Boundaries: PCP Perspectives for the Millennium, Malta, April.

Armitage A, Bryant B, Dunhill R, Hammersley M, Hayes D, Hudson A et al. (1999) Teaching and Training in Post-Compulsory Education. Buckingham: Open University Press.

Ashwell N (2000) Collaboration between Organisations in Community Settings. Ongoing PhD Research conducted at the University of Reading.

Bailey A (1990) Personal Transferable Skills for Employment: The Role of Higher Education. In Wright PWG (ed.) Industry and Higher Education. Buckingham: SRHE and Open University Press: 68–74.

Bakan D (1967) On Method: Towards a Reconstruction of Psychological Investigation. San Francisco: Jossey-Bass Inc.

Baker C (1992) A Model for Teamwork in Further Education: the Narrative of a Methodological Journey. Unpublished PhD thesis, University of Surrey.

Bannister D, Fransella F (1971) Inquiring Man. London: Penguin.

Bannister D, Mair JMM (1968) The Evaluation of Personal Constructs. London: Academic Press.

Bannister D, Salmon P (1975) A personal construct view of education. NY Univ. Educ Quart. 6, 4: 28–31.

Bateson G (1972) Steps to an Ecology of Mind: Collected Essays. Anthology; Psychiatry, Evolution and Epistemology. San Francisco: Chandler Pub. Co.

Beail N (ed.) (1985) Repertory Grid Techniques and Personal Constructs: Applications in Clinical and Educational Settings. Cambridge, Mass.: Brookline Books.

Beattie M (1995) Constructing Professional Knowledge in Teaching: A Narrative of Change and Development. Toronto: OISE Press.

Bell B, Gilbert J (1996) Teacher Development: A Model from Science Education. London: Falmer Press.

Ben-Peretz M (1984) Kelly's theory of personal constructs as a paradigm for investigating teacher thinking. In Halkes R, Olson JK (eds) Teacher Thinking: A New Perspective on Persisting Problems in Education. Lisse, Netherlands: Swets & Zeitlinger: 103–12.

Berger PL, Luckmann T (1967) The Social Construction of Reality. London: Allen Lane.

Berman LM, Roderick JA (1973) The relationship between curriculum development and research methodology. J. Res. Devel. Educ. 6(3): 3–13.

Biggs JB (1976) Educology! the theory of educational practice. Contemp. Educ Psychol. 1: 274–84.

Bloom BS (1953) Thought processes in lectures and discussions. Journal of General Education 7: 160–9.

Blumer H (1966) Psychological implications of the thought of George Herbert Mead. AM. J.Soc. 71: 535–48.

Blumer H (1978) Methodological principles of empirical science. In Denzin N (ed.) Sociological Methods: A Source Book. NY: McGraw-Hill.

Britton J (1976) Bread and water. J. Educ. Thought 10: 3–4.

Brook J (1979) A repertory grid analysis of perceptions of vocational counselling roles. J. Voc. Behaviour 15(1): 25–35.

Bruner JS (1966) Towards a Theory of Instruction. New York: Norton.

Bruner JS (1990) Acts of meaning. Cambridge, Mass.: Harvard Univ. Press.

Buber M (1965) Between Man and Man. New York and London: Macmillan.

Bulhof IN (1980) Wilhelm Dilthey: A Hermeneutic Approach to the Study of History and Culture. The Hague: Martinus Nijhoff.

Burr V, Butt T (1992) Invitation to Personal Construct Psychology. London: Whurr.

CAIPE (1992) A National Survey that Needs to be Repeated. Journal of Interprofessional Care 6(1).

Candy P (1990) Repertory grids: playing verbal chess. In Mezirow J, Associates Fostering Critical Reflection in Adulthood: A Guide to Transformative and Emancipatory Learning. San Francisco: Jossey-Bass.

Castling A (1983) Staff Development: A Case Study on Stress. In Squires (ed.) Innovation through Recession. SRHE Conference: Society for Research in Higher Education.

Carr W, Kemmis S (1986) Becoming Critical: Education, Knowledge and Action. London: Falmer Press.

Clandinin DJ (1986) Classroom Practice: Teacher Images in Action. London: Falmer Press.

Clark CM (1986) Ten years of conceptual development in research on teacher thinking. In Ben-Peretz M, Bromme R, Halkes R (eds) Advances in Research on Teacher Thinking. Lisse, Netherlands: Swets & Zeitlinger.

Clark CM (1995) Thoughtful Teaching. London: Cassell.

Cohen L, Manion L (1989) Research Methods in Education. London: Routledge.

Connelly FM, Clandinin DJ (1984) Personal knowledge at Bay St. School: Ritual, personal philosophy and image. In Halkes R, Olsen JK (Eds) Teacher Thinking: a new perspective on persisting problems in education. Lisse, Netherlands: Swets & Zeitlinger.

Connelly FM, Clandinin DJ (1990) C and C Stories of Experience and Narrative Inquiry in Educational Researcher 19(5): 2–14.

Cooley CH (1964) Human Nature and the Social Order. New York: Schoken.

Cormack DFS (1996) The Critical Incident Technique, in Cormack DFS (ed.) The Research Process in Nursing. 3rd edn. Oxford: Blackwell Sciences.

Cortazzi D, Roote S (1975) Illuminative Incident Analysis. London: McGraw Hill.

Cortazzi M (1993) Narrative Analysis. London: Falmer Press.

Cowley S (1994) Collaboration in health care: the education link. Health Visitor 67(1): 13–15.

Cox CB, Dyson AE (1969) The Fight for Education and the Crisis in Education. Black Papers 1 and 2, Critical Quarterly Society.

Cross M, Wrench J, Barnett S (1990) Ethnic minorities and the careers service: an investigation into the processes of assessment and placement. Department of Employment Research Paper No. 73. London: HSMO.

Crotty M (1998) The Foundations of Social Research: Meaning and perspective in the Research Process. London: Sage.

Cuthbert R (ed.) (1988) Going Corporate. Occasional Paper. Further Education Staff College: Blagdon.

Dalin P (1978) Limits to Educational Change. London: Macmillan Press.

Dalton P, Dunnett G (1992) A Psychology for Living. Chichester: Wiley & Sons.

Daniel GR (1996) World-view and Illusions: The Perceived Need for Counselling. Unpublished PhD thesis, University of Reading.

Dearmun A (1997) Paediatric Nursing Graduates' Perceptions of their First Year of Professional Practice. Unpublished PhD thesis, University of Reading.

Denicolo PM (1996) Productively confronting dilemmas in educational practice and research. In Kompf M, Bond R, Dworet D, Boak RT (eds) Changing Research and Practice: Teachers' Professionalism, Identities and Knowledge. London: Falmer Press: 56–66.

Denicolo PM (1996) Explorations of Constructivist Approaches in Continuing Professional Education: Staff Development for Changing Contexts. In Kalekin-Fishman D, Walker B (eds) The Construction of Group Realities. Malabar, Florida: Krieger: 267–82.

Denicolo PM, Entwistle N, Hounsell D (1992) What is Active Learning? Sheffield: CVCP/SDTU.

Denicolo PM, Pope ML (1990) Adults learning – teachers thinking. In Day C, Pope ML, Denicolo PM (eds) Insight into Teachers' Thinking and Practice. London: Falmer Press.

Denzin NK, Lincoln YS (Eds) (1984) Handbook of Qualitative Research. London: Sage.

Desforges C, McNamara D (1979) Theory and Practice: methodological procedures for the objectification of craft knowledge. British Journal of Teacher Education 2: 145–152.

Dewey J (1916) Democracy and Education; an Introduction to the Philosophy of Education. New York: Free Press.

Dewey J (1938) Experience and Education. New York: Macmillan.

Dewey J, Dewey E (1915) Schools of Tomorrow. New York: Dutton.

Dewey J, McLellan (1895) Early Works 1882–98, Vol. 5. Carbondale; S. Illinois: London: University Press; Schaffer and Simon (1972) New York.

Diamond CPT (1985) Fixed Role treatment: enacting alternative scenarios. Australian Journal of Education 29(2): 161–73.

Diamond CPT, Mullen CA (1999) Post Modern Educator: Arts-based Inquiries and Teacher Development. New York: Peter Lang.

Dilthey W (1976) W Dilthey – Selected Writings, ed. and transl. HP Rickman. Cambridge: Cambridge University Press.

Dolk M, Korthagen P, Wubbels T (1999) Instruments to investigate knowledge in teaching situations. Paper presented to ISATT Conference, Dublin, July 1999.

Douglas B, Moustakas C (1984) Heuristic Inquiry: the Internal Search to Know. Detroit: Center for Humanistic Studies.

Driver R (1982) Children's Learning in Science. Educational Analysis 4(2): 69–79.

Driver R (1988) Theory into practice II: a constructivist approach to curriculum development. In Frensham P (ed.) Development and Dilemmas in Science Education London: Falmer Press.

Driver R, Oldham B (1986) A constructionist approach to curriculum development in science. Studies in Science Education 13: 105–122.

Egan G (1975) The Skilled Helper. Wadsworth: California.

Eisner EW (1985) (ed.) Learning and Teaching the Ways of Knowing. Chicago: University of Chicago Press.

Eisner EW (1988) The Primary Experience and the Politics of Method. Educational Researcher 17(5): 15–20.

Eisner EW (1993) Forms of Understanding and the future of Educational Research. Educational Researcher 22(7): 5–11.

Ekman P (1969) Body position, facial expression, and verbal behaviour during interviews. Journal of Abnormal and Social Psychology 68: 295–301.

Elbaz F (1990) Knowledge and Discourse: the evolution of research on teacher thinking. In Day C, Pope ML, Denicolo PM (eds) Insights into Teachers' Thinking and Practice. London: Falmer Press.

Elliott J (1995) What is good action research? some criteria. Action Researcher. 2: 10–11.

Elliot J, Whitehead D (Eds) (1980) Action Research for Professional Development and Improvement in Schooling. Cambridge: CARN Publications.

Ellis J (1994) Challenging health professionals to care. In Scheer J, Catina A (eds) Empirical Constructivism in Europe. Giessen: Psychosozial-Verlag: 189–98.

Ely M, Vinz R, Downing M, Anzul M (1997) On Writing Qualitative Research – Living by Words. London: Falmer Press.

EOC (1999) Research Discussion Series: Gender Equality and the Careers Service. Manchester: Equal Opportunities Commission.

Eraut M (1992) Developing the knowledge base: a process perspective on professional education. In Barnett R (ed.) Learning to Effect. Buckingham: SRHE/OU Press.

Esland GM (1971) Teaching and learning as organisation of knowledge. In Young MFD (ed.) Knowledge and Control. London: Collier Macmillan.

Ewens A (1998) The Changing Role Perceptions of Students on Integrated Courses in Community Health Care Nursing. Unpublished PhD thesis, University of Reading.

Fals-Borda O, Rachman MA (1991) Action and knowledge: Breaking the Monopoly with Participatory Action Research. New York: Apex.

Fonda N (1981) Using the Grid to Evaluate Training. In Stewart V, Stewart A (eds) Business Applications of Repertory Grid. London: McGraw-Hill: 116-41.

Fournier V, Payne R (1994) Change in self construction during transition from univer-

sity to employment: a PCP approach. Journal of Occupational and Organizational Psychology 67: 297–314.
Fox D (1983) Personal theories of teaching. In Studies in Higher Education 8(2).
Fransella F (1983) What sort of scientist is the person-as-scientist. In Adams-Webber J, Mancuso JC (eds) Applications of Personal Construct Theory. Toronto: Academic Press.
Fransella F, Bannister D (1977) A Manual for Repertory Grid Technique. London: Academic Press.
Freire P (1973) By learning they can teach. Convergence 6(1).
Freud S (1913) The claims of psycho-analysis to the scientific interest - the educational interest. In Strachey J (ed.) (1953) The Complete Psychological Works of Sigmund Freud. Vol 13. London: Hogarth Press.
Fullan MG (1991) The New Meaning of Educational Change. London: Cassell Education Ltd.
Garfinkel H (1967) Studies in Ethnomethodology. New Jersey: Prentice Hall.
Giddens A (1979) Central Problems in Social Theory: Action, Structure, and Contradiction in Social Analysis. London: Macmillan.
Giddens A (1982) Profiles and Critiques in Social Theory. Berkeley: University of California Press.
Gilbert JK, Pope ML (1984) Making use of research into teaching and learning. Institute of Educational Development, Guildford: University of Surrey.
Gleeson D, Mardle G (1980) Further Education or Training; A Case in the Theory and Practice of Day-Release Education. London: Routledge & Kegan Paul.
Goodlad S (ed.) (1984) Education for the Professions, Quis custodiet? Guildford: SRHE and NFER-Nelson: 297–302.
Goodman N (1984) Of mind and Other Matters. Cambridge, Mass: Harvard University Press.
Goodman P (1972) Compulsory Miseducation. London: Penguin.
Goodson I (1996) Representing Teachers: Bringing teachers back in. In Kompf M et al. (eds) Changing Research and Practice. London: Falmer Press.
Greene M, Gibbons A (1991) Learning for Self-Development: Learning Logs. Training and Development 9(2): 30–2.
Griffiths R (1988) Community Care: Agenda for Action: A Report to the Secretary of State for the Social Services, London: HMSO.
Guba EG, Lincoln YS (1989) Fourth Generation Evaluation. Newby Park Ca: Sage.
Guba EG, Lincoln YS (1994) Competing paradigms in qualitative research. In Denzin NK, Lincoln YS (eds) Handbook of Qualitative Research. Thousand Oaks, Ca: Sage.
Habermas J (1971) Knowledge and Human Interest. Boston: Beacon Press.
Halkes R, Olson JK (eds) (1984) Teacher Thinking: A New Perspective on Persisting Problems in Education. Lisse, Netherlands: Swets & Zeitlinger.
Hamilton D, Delamont S (1974) Classroom research: a cautionary tale. Res. Educ. 11: 1–15.
Handy C (1985) Understanding Organisations. 3rd edn. Harmonsworth: Penguin.
Harwood AG, Denicolo PM (1994) Views on personal and professional development: listening to people's voices. In Scheer J, Catina A (eds) Empirical Constructivism in Europe Giessen: Psychosozial-Verlag: 220–28.
Holt J (1966) How Children Fail. London: Pitman.
Howard GS (1988) Kelly's thoughts at age 33: suggestions for conceptual methodolog-

ical refinements. International Journal of Personal Construct Psychology 1: 263–72.

Howkins E (1994) Designing an integrated curriculum with a common core for an inter-disciplinary course in community nursing. Nurse Education Today 14: 380–7.

Howkins E, Badger D, Ewens A (1995) A methodology for measuring the effectiveness of interprofessional education: a pilot study. A paper presented at the EMPE 9th General Meeting, Zaragoza, Spain, September.

Hudson L (1968) Frames of Mind. London: Methuen.

Hull C (1943) Principles of Behaviour. New York: Appleton Century Croft.

Hutchins RM (1936) The Higher Learning in America. New Haven, Conn: Yale University Press.

Illich I (1971) De-Schooling Society. New York: Harper & Row.

James, Lord (1972) (Chairman) Teaching Education and Training. London: HMSO.

Jankowicz AD (1990) Applications of Personal Construct Psychology in Business Practice. In Neimeyer GJ, Neimeyer RA (eds) Advances in Personal Construct Psychology, Vol. 1, Greenwich, Conn: JAI Press: 257–87.

Jankowicz AD (1997) Professions: Public Arbiters of Private Meanings, a keynote address given at the PCP Research Group one day conference. Constructing Meanings within the Professions, University of Reading, June.

Jones B (1989) In conversations with myself: becoming an action researcher. In Lomax P (ed.) The Management of Change. BERA Dialogue No. 1, Multilingual Matters Ltd.

Jordon DC (1973) ANISA: A new comprehensive early education model for developing human potential. J. Res. Dev. Educ. 6(3): 83–93.

Joyce B (1972) Curriculum and humanistic education. In Weinberg C (ed.) Humanistic Foundations of Education. New Jersey: Prentice Hall.

Kalekin-Fishman D, Walker B (1996) (eds) The Construction of Group Realities. Florida: Krieger.

Kelly GA (1955) The Psychology of Personal Constructs, Vols 1 and 2. New York: WW Norton. Republished (1991) London: Routledge.

Kelly GA (1966) Fixed role therapy. MS prepared as a chapter in Jurjuvich M (ed.) Handbook of Direct and Behaviour Therapies. Unpub.

Kelly GA (1969a) Ontological acceleration. In Maher B (ed.) The Collected Papers of George Kelly Clinical Psychology and Personality: New York: John Wiley.

Kelly GA (1969b) The strategy of psychological research. In Maher B (ed.) The Collected Papers of George Kelly Clinical Psychology and Personality. New York: John Wiley.

Kelly GA (1969c) The language of hypothesis: man's psychological instrument. In Maher B (ed.) Clinical Psychology and Personality: The Selected Papers of George Kelly. NY: Wiley: 47–162.

Kelly GA (1970a) A brief introduction to personal construct theory. In Bannister D (ed.) Perspectives on Personal Construct Theory. London: Academic Press.

Kelly GA (1970b) Behaviour as an experiment. In Bannister D (ed.) Perspectives on Personal Construct Theory. London: Academic Press.

Kemmis S, McTaggart R (1982) The Action Research Planner. Victoria: Deacon University Press.

Kirkcaldy BD, Pope ML (1992) A structural analysis of a psycho-oncology unit. In European Work and Organisational Psychologist: 33–51.

Kirkcaldy BD, Pope ML, Siefen G (1993) Sociogrid analysis of a child and adolescent psychiatric clinic. Social Psychiatry and Psychiatric Epidemiology 28: 296–303.

Knapper CK, Cropley AJ (1985) Lifelong Learning and Higher Education. Beckenham: Croom Helm.

Knowles M (1978) The Adult Learner – A Neglected Species. 2nd edn. Houston: Gulf Publishing Co.

Koestler A (1976) The vision that links the poet, the painter and the scientist. The Times, 25 Aug.

Kolb D, Fry F (1975) Towards an Applied Theory of Experiential Learning. London: Wiley.

Kompf M (1999) There is more to me than my story – examination of what narrative researchers leave behind. Paper presented at the 9th Biennial meeting of the International Study Association on Teachers and Teaching, St Patrick's College, Dublin. 25–31 July.

Kuhn TS (1970) Logic of discovery or psychology of research. In Lakatos I, Musgrave A (eds) Criticism and the Growth of Knowledge. Cambridge: Cambridge University Press.

Laing RD (1967) The Politics of Experience. London: Penguin.

Lakatos I (1970) Falsification and the methodology of scientific research programmes In Lakatos I, Musgrave A (eds) Criticism and the Growth of Knowledge. Cambridge: Cambridge University Press.

Lakoff G, Johnson M (1980) Metaphors We Live By. Chicago: University of Chicago Press.

Lawless C, Smee P, O'Shea T (1998) Using concept sorting and concept mapping in business and public administration, and in education: an overview. Educational Research 40(2): 219–35.

Leyin A (1992) Community mental handicap teams: team building and beyond. Mental Handicap, 20 March: 15–20.

Lincoln YS (1992) Sympathetic connections between qualitative methods and health research. Qualitative Health Research 2: 375–92.

Lincoln YS, Guba EG (1985) Naturalistic enquiry. Beverley Hills, Ca: Sage.

Lynch PA (1996) Alternative constructs of adolescent smoking – an enquiry into health education practice. Unpublished PhD thesis, University of Reading.

McAdams M (1999) Constructing professional lives in stressful conditions. In Fisher JM, Savage, DJ (eds) Beyond Experimentation into Meaning. Farnborough: EPCA Publications: 88–95.

McEwan H, Egan K (eds) (1995) Narrative in Teaching, Learning and Research. New York: Teachers College Press.

Magee B (1973) Popper. London: Fontana.

Mahoney M (1988) Constructive metatheory. International Journal of Personal Construct Psychology 1: 1–36.

Mair JMM (1970) Psychologists are human too. In Bannister D (ed.) Perspectives in Personal Construct Theory. London and New York: Academic Press.

Mair JMM (1977) The community of self. In Bannister D (ed.) New Perspectives in Personal Construct Theory. London: Academic Press.

Mair JMM (1998) Psychology as story-telling. International Journal of Personal Construct Psychology 1(1): 125–37.

Mair JMM (1989) Kelly, Bannister and story telling psychology. International J. of Personal Construct Psychology 2: 1–14.

Mantle F (1997) Ideas and realities in nursing: formative career constructs and professional developments. Unpublished PhD thesis, University of Reading.

Mason J (1996) Qualitative Researching. London: Sage.

Mazhindu G (1995) Professional Achievement in Nurse Education. Unpublished PhD thesis, University of Reading.

Mazhindu G, Pope ML (1996) Interprofessional education in nursing. In Scheer J, Catina A (eds) Empirical Constructivism in Europe. Giessen: Psychosozial-Verlag: 260–67.

Mead GH (1934) Mind, Self and Society. Chicago: University of Chicago Press.

Merleau-Ponty M (1962) Phenomenology of Perception, London: Routledge & Kegan Paul.

Mezirow J (1981) A critical theory of adult learning and education. Adult Education 32(1).

Mezirow J (1990) Fostering Critical Reflection in Adulthood: a Guide to Transformative and Emancipating Learning. San Francisco: Jossey-Bass.

Mignot PAT (2000) Metaphor: a paradigm for constructive and critical research into 'Career'. Unpublished PhD thesis, University of Reading.

Mignot PAT (2000) Metaphor: a paradigm for practice-based research into career. Unpublished paper.

Mignot PAT (in press) Using visual methods in careers education and guidance. Pastoral Care in Education.

Miller P (1994) Perspectives on the recognition and resolution of dilemma within an educational framework. Unpublished PhD thesis, University of Surrey.

Morris B (1972) Objectives and Perspectives in Education: Studies in Educational Theory 1955–70. London: Routledge & Kegan Paul.

Morrison A, MacIntyre D (1973) Teachers and Teaching. London: Penguin.

Moses I (1985) Academic development units and the improvement of teaching. Higher Education 14: 75–100.

Muncy T (2000) The good nurse: born or made? Unpublished PhD thesis, Cranfield University.

Neill AS (1964) Summerhill: A Radical Approach to Child-Rearing. New York: Holt, Rinehart & Winston.

Novak JD (1983) Personal construct theory and other perceptual pedagogies. In Adams-Webber J, Mancuso JC (eds) Applications of Personal Construct Theory. Academic Press: London.

Novak JD (1995) The use of metacognitive tools to facilitate meaningful learning and the construction of knowledge. Paper presented at the 11th International Conference on Personal Construct Psychology, Barcelona, July.

Novak JD (ed.) (1987) Proceedings of the 2nd International Seminar: Misconceptions and Educational Strategies in Science and Mathematics. Ithaca: NY: Cornell University Press.

Novak JD, Gowin DB (1984) Learning How to Learn. New York: Cambridge University Press.

Nussbaum M (1985) Aeschylus and practical conflict. Ethics 95: 233–67.

Nystedt L, Magnusson D (1982) Construction of experience. In Mancuso J, Adams Webber J (eds) The Construing Person. New York: Praeger.

O'Hare DPA, Gordon IE (1976) An Application of Repertory Grid Technique to Aesthetic Measurement. Perceptual and Motor Skills 42: 1183–92.

Okrent M (1988) Heidegger's Pragmatism: Understanding, Being, and the Critique of Metaphysics. Ithaca, NY: Cornell University Press.

Olson JK (1992) Understanding Teaching. Milton Keynes: Open University Press.

Osborne R, Gilbert J (1980) A technique for exploring students' views of the world. Physics Education 15(6): 376–9.

Patton MQ (1990) Qualitative Evaluation and Research Methods, 2nd edn. London: Sage.

Pedler M, Burgoyne J, Boydell T (1986) A Manager's Guide to Self-Development, 2nd edn. Maidenhead: McGraw-Hill.

Piaget J (1954) The Construction of Reality in Children, transl. M Cook. New York: Basic Books.

Polanyi M (1958) Personal Knowledge. Chicago: University of Chicago Press.

Pope ML (1981) In True Spirit: Constructive Alternativism in Educational Research. Paper presented at Fourth International Congress on Personal Construct Psychology, Brock University, St Catherine's, Canada.

Pope ML (1990) Academic staff development: a constructivist perspective and research-on-action. Address to the Finnish National Higher Education Symposium, Finland.

Pope ML, Denicolo PM (1986) Intuitive theories – a researcher's dilemma: some practical methodological implications. British Educational Research Journal 12: 153–65.

Pope ML, Denicolo PM (1991) Developing constructive action: personal construct psychology research and professional development. In Zuber-Skerritt O (ed.) Action Research for Change and Development. Aldershot: Avebury.

Pope ML, Denicolo PM (1993) The art and science of constructivist research in teacher thinking. Teacher and Teacher Education 9(5–6): 529–44.

Pope ML, Denicolo PM (1997) Student career decision making: a constructivist approach. Paper presented at British Education Association conference. September 1997, York.

Pope ML, Keen TR (1981) Personal Construct Psychology and Education. London: Academic Press.

Popper K (1963) Conjectures and Reputations: The Growth of Scientific Knowledge. London: Routledge and Kegan Paul.

Postman N, Weingartner L (1971) Teaching as a Subversive Activity. London: Penguin.

Power SS (1997) The use of repertory grid technique with persistent female offenders attending a day centre. Unpublished MSc in Research Methods in Psychology, University of Reading.

Priestley P, McQuire J, Flegg D, Hemsley V, Welham D (1978) Social Skills and Personal Problem Solving. London: Tavistock.

Pucheu R (1974) La formation permanente: Idée neuve? Idée fausse, in Esprit 10: 321–36.

Quinn A (1999) The use of experiential learning to help social work students assess their attitudes towards practice with older people. Social Work Education 18(2): 171–82.

Ranade W (1985) Assessing the effectiveness of members: the repertory grid. Technique, Hospital and Health Services Review, July, 168–71.

Ravenette AT (1997) Tom Ravenette: Selected Papers, PCP and the Practice of an Educational Psychologist. Farnborough: EPCA.

Read R (1985) In Hofstadter D (ed.) Metamagical Themes: Questing for the Essence of Mind and Pattern. Harmondsworth: Penguin.
Reason P, Rowan J (eds) (1981) Human Inquiry: A Source Book of New Paradigm Research. Chichester: John Wiley & Son.
Reidford P (1972) Educational Research. In Weinberg C (ed.) Humanistic Foundations of Education. New Jersey: Prentice Hall Inc.
Reimer E (1971) School Is Dead. London: Penguin.
Rickman HP (ed. and transl.) (1976) W. Dilthey – Selected Writings. Cambridge: Cambridge University Press.
Rogers C (1961) On Becoming a Person. London: Constable.
Rogers C (1965) Client-Centred Therapy. Boston: Houghton-Mifflin.
Rogers C (1969) Freedom to Learn: A View of What Education Might Become. Columbus, Ohio: Charles E. Merril.
Rogers C (1983) Freedom to Learn for the 80s. Columbus, Ohio: Charles E. Merril.
Rose P (1983) Parallel Lives. New York: Vintage Books.
Rundell J (1991) Jurgen Habermas. In Beilharz P (ed.) Social Theory: A Guide to Central Thinkers. St Leonards: Allen & Unwin: 133–40.
Salmon P, Bannister D (1974) Education in the Light of Personal Construct Theory. Education for Teaching 94: 25–38.
Sartre J-P (1947) Existentialism. New York: Philosophica Library.
Schon DA (1983) The Reflective Practitioner: How Professionals Think in Action. New York: Basic Books.
Schon DA (1987) Educating the Reflective Practitioner: Towards a New Design for Teaching and Learning in the Professions. San Francisco: Jossey-Bass.
Schutz A (1967) The Phenomenology of the Social World. Evanston: North Western University Press.
Schwandt TA (1994) Constructivist, Interpretavist Approaches to Human Inquiry. In Denzin N, Lincoln YS (eds) Handbook of Qualitative Research. London: Sage.
Sexton R, Denicolo PM (1997) Formative critical incidents in early professional life – a stimulated recall approach. In Denicolo PM, Pope ML (eds) Sharing Understanding and Practice, Farnborough: EPCA Publications: 133–43.
Shaw MLG (1980) On Becoming a Personal Scientist. London: Academic Press.
Shaw MLG (1993) RepGrid 2. Calgary: Centre for Personal Computer Studies.
Silberman CE (1971) Crisis in the Classroom: Remaking of American Education. New York: Vintage Press.
Skinner BF (1968) The Technology of Teaching. New York: Appleton-Century-Crofts.
Skinner BF (1971) Beyond Freedom and Dignity. London: Cape.
Slater P (ed.) (1977) The Measurement Of Intrapersonal Space by Grid Technique: Dimensions of Intrapersonal Space. Chichester: Wiley.
Snow RE (1974) Representative and quasi-representative designs for research on teaching. Rev. Educ. Res. 44: 265–91.
Sparkes AC (1994) Life histories and the use of voice: reflections on an emerging relationship. International Journal of Qualitative Studies in Education 7(2): 165–83.
Stenhouse L (1975) An Introduction to Curriculum Research. London: Heinemann Educational.
Stewart J (1980) Techniques for assessing representing information in cognitive structure. Science Education 63(3): 223–33.

Stewart V, Stewart A (1981) Business Applications of the Repertory Grid. London: McGraw-Hill.

Sullivan HS (1953) In Perry HS, Gawel ML (eds) The Interpersonal Theory of Psychiatry. New York: Norton.

Sutton C (1981) Making sense of new ideas. In Sutton C (ed.) Communication in Classroom. London: Hodder & Stoughton.

Sutton CR (1981) Metaphorical imagery: a means of coping with complex and unfamiliar information in science. Durham and Newcastle Research Review 9(46).

Taylor I (1997) Developing Learning in Professional Education, Buckingham: SRHE/OU Press.

Taylor SJ, Bogdan R (1998) An introduction to Qualitative Research Methods. New York: John Wiley & Sons Inc.

Thomas L (1995) The Medusa and the Snail: More Notes for Biology Watchers. Viking Penguin.

Thomas LF, Harri-Augstein S (1985) Self Organised Learning: Foundations of a Conversational Science of Psychology. London: Routledge & Kegan Paul.

Thompson N (1993) Anti-Discriminatory Practice. Basingstoke: Macmillan.

Tjok-a-Tam S (1994) Learning-in-action in management development: the facilitation of self-created learning opportunities. Unpublished PhD thesis, University of Surrey.

Tooth B (1996) Group construing: the impact of professional training. In Kalekin-Fishman D, Walker B (eds) The Construction of Group Realities. Malabar, Florida: Krieger Publishing Company: 243–65.

Usher R, Bryant I (1987) Re-examining the theory – practice relationship in continuing professional education. Studies in Higher Education 12: 201–12.

Von Glaserfeld E (1984) An introduction to radical constructivism. In Watzlawick P (ed.) The Invented Reality. New York: Norton: 18–40.

Watts AG (1996) Socio-political ideologies in guidance. In Watts AG, Law B, Killeen J, Kidd JM, Hawthorn R (eds) Rethinking Careers Education and Guidance: Theory, Policy and Practice. London: Routledge: 351–65.

Weinsheimer JC (1985) Gadamer's Hermeneutics: A Reading of Truth and Method. New Haven: Yale University Press.

Whyte WF (1991) Participatory Action Research. London: Sage.

Woods P (1985) Conversations with teachers: some aspects of life-history method. British Educational Research Journal 11: 13–25.

Wragg GC (1974) Teaching Teaching. Newton Abbott: David & Charles.

Wu Chi-yi (1997) A constructivist approach to the study of career decision-making: a sample of senior undergraduate students in Taiwan. Unpublished PhD thesis, University of Reading.

Index